BUSINESS LEADE … RAISE
STRA…

"Even more timely and effective today than when The Dow Chemical Company first adopted it in 1986."

—**Gary Hardy,** global leader of sales education and development, The Dow Chemical Company

"The idea of playing Win-Win has helped us considerably in the sales process and also in our interoffice dealings with one another. No other principle has impacted us as much."

—**Joe Dejohn,** vice president, direct sales division, Atlet, Inc.

"At Harris Corporation we have trained over 500 sales and marketing people worldwide on the original *Strategic Selling* concepts. Our old copies are worn out. The new and updated book is warmly welcomed. The old one helped us win many multimillion-dollar orders, and I'm sure this new one will win even more."

—**Carleton L. Smith,** vice president,
Asia sales and marketing, Harris Corporation

"A practical guide offering new insight into the way salesmen can successfully promote big-ticket items to large organizations."

—***Financial Post***

"A method that sales professionals can use effectively. The authors clearly and engagingly describe numerous 'workshops' in which readers can apply their own sales experiences. Professionally yet clearly presented."

—***ALA Booklist***

"We quickly went from just a few thousand a month in sales to over $100,000 a month. *Strategic Selling* gave us confidence in what we were doing. We pegged some accounts as low probability, and even on those we were able to penetrate deeper and put our action plans into effect. We've been able to get a portion of every account out there."

—**John Witkowski,** director,
Southeast business unit, Amersham Healthcare

more . . .

"The year after implementing Strategic Selling was our best sales year ever. This is the second full year we've been using the Miller Heiman processes, and we're going to come very close to doubling that."

—**Roger Ballmer,** manager, district marketing,
Owen Healthcare, Inc.

"The largest sale ever done at my previous position used Strategic Selling to win an extremely difficult and complex sale. The sale was over $5 million year one and it continues to gross over $2 million a year for the past three years. We couldn't have won it without the discipline and hard work of the team and certainly not without the Miller Heiman course."

—**Andrew Lee,** vice president, sales and marketing,
Microvision, Inc.

"The best books I have read on selling."

—**Scott DeGormo,** *Success* magazine, on *Strategic Selling* and *Conceptual Selling*

"Efficient, professional . . . the finest high-level training program I have seen . . . a mini-MBA in how to sell national accounts."

—**Henry J. Cockerill,** former senior vice president,
U.S.A. Fountain Sales, Coca-Cola Company

"Thousands of HP sales engineers worldwide have been trained in Strategic Selling, and its influences can be directly seen in the results they have attained . . . Its usefulness has spanned product disciplines and national boundaries."

—**John A. Young,** former president and
chief executive officer, Hewlett-Packard Company

"A totally professional planning process. If Willy Loman had taken the Miller Heiman program, he'd have been salesman of the year."

—**Walter H. Drew,** former senior vice president and
general sales manager, Consumer Products Division,
Kimberly-Clark Corporation

THE NEW STRATEGIC SELLING

The Unique Sales System Proven Successful by the World's Best Companies

Revised and Updated

STEPHEN E. HEIMAN AND
DIANE SANCHEZ

WITH TAD TULEJA

GRAND CENTRAL
PUBLISHING

NEW YORK BOSTON

Grand Central Publishing Edition

This Grand Central Publishing edition is published by arrangement with William Morrow and Company, 1350 Avenue of the Americas, New York, NY 10019

Grand Central Publishing
Hachette Book Group
1290 Avenue of the Americas
New York, NY 10104

www.HachetteBookGroup.com

Grand Central Publishing is a division of Hachette Book Group, Inc.
The Grand Central Publishing name and logo are trademarks of Hachette Book Group, Inc.

Printed in the United States of America
First Grand Central Publishing Edition: March 1986
Revised Edition: January 1998
Revised Edition with Preface: April 2005
30 29 28 27 26

Library of Congress Cataloging-in-Publication Data

Heiman, Stephen E.
The new strategic selling : the unique sales system proven successful by the world's best companies, revised and upload for the 21st century / Stephen E. Heiman, Diane Sanchez with Tad Tuleja. — Warner Books ed.
p. cm.
Rev. and updated ed. of : Strategic selling / Robert B. Miller and Stephen E. Heiman, with Tad Tuleja. 1st ed. 1985.
Includes index.
ISBN 0-446-67346-3
1. Selling. I. Sanchez, Diane. II. Tuleja, Tad, 1944– III. Miller, Robert B. (Robert Bruce), 1931– Strategic selling. IV. Title.
HF5438.25.M567 1998
658.8'1—dc21

97-29935
CIP

Book design and composition by L&G McRee

ISBN 978-0-446-69519-0 (Prefaced Edition)

CONTENTS

PREFACE

Every year I meet or hear from dozens of graduates of Strategic Selling, Conceptual Selling, and other Miller Heiman programs. I also meet a lot of these people face-to-face at places where I am speaking, giving a seminar, or on sales calls. Virtually all of them say the same thing to me. Invariably it is some version of, "Bob, thank you so much for all the money you have made me over the years! The greatest thing about Strategic Selling, and Conceptual Selling and LAMP is that they work!" Now I am as susceptible as the next guy to flattery like this, and indeed it is very gratifying to hear this over and over again from so many alumni. But I always respond in the same way, "We appreciate the great feedback, but you are the one who had the discipline to apply it." And therein lies the key. Countless seminars are filled with ideas, some good and sound, and many worthless nonsense. But no idea or concept is worth anything unless it can be applied to situational reality. This has always been a planned hallmark of Miller Heiman, Inc. programs. We can provide the knowledge and show our participants how to do something, but the individual must deliver the discipline.

Nor has it been just money that gives credit to Strategic Selling. Consider the stories of just a few of our alumni, of whom we are very proud:

- Mike Jackson, western region senior vice president and general manager for General Motors, was the Coca-Cola account manager for Jack in the Box when he first was exposed to Strategic Selling in 1981.
- Rick Justice, executive vice president of worldwide operations at Cisco was a twenty-two-year-old sales representative for Hewlett-Packard when he took Strategic Selling. He used the process on every one of his deals that year, became Sales Representative of the Year, and the rest is history.
- Mike Cronk was a young district sales manager at Saga Food Service (now part of Marriott Sodhexo) when he ran Strategic Selling for his district team. (Incidentally, it was the first seminar we ran for a *Fortune* 500 company.) He just retired from being president of Aramark International.

- Reed Hilliard recently retired from a general manager's position at Agilent Technologies. He was also a young newly appointed district sales manager at Hewlett-Packard when he introduced Strategic Selling to his team in 1976.

These are but a handful of people who thank Strategic Selling for helping their success over their careers. There are hundreds more.

Next year will be the thirtieth anniversary of the first Strategic Selling seminar. Of course, it wasn't called that thirty years ago, and the exercises were sort of a "work-in-progress," but you would recognize the same key principles: *Win-Win, Four Buying Influences, Four Modes, Win-Results, Red Flags, Ideal Customer.* These have all been concepts that distinguished Strategic Selling from the very beginning.

Many alumni comment that the principles in our programs have stood the test of time. "Everything you teach in each program is as valid today as it was in 1975, but more so. Why is that?" The fact that this is true is no accident. The reason they have stood the test of time is each of the key ideas taught in all Miller Heiman programs, and in all of our books, relate a fundamental *principle* of the selling *process*. Note the two words emphasized in the previous phrase, *principle* and *process*. That is the secret to what makes Miller Heiman programs so practical and useful. And that was done by design. We have always focused on teaching our participants the underlying principle instead of just the technique. If you learn only the technique without understanding why it works, you will soon forget it. If you understand the *principle*, you understand what its place is in the selling process and you will get more sales and better sales. For example, one technique taught in Strategic Selling is "Make sure you identify and cover the bases with the Economic Buyer." The *principle* underlying this is "There is one place and only one place wherein resides the final approval for each sale." In understanding that principle you now know *why* it is so important to identify and cover that Economic Buyer base.

Similarly, we focus on giving people *principles* that are part of a selling *process*. Selling used to be looked upon as a haphazard, trial-and-error, fits-and-starts, luck-related type of venture. One of the key contributions Strategic Selling has made is to prove to salespersons and their managers that, while selling is not a science, we can go about selling in a systematic way because there are repeatable *processes* involved in both buying and selling. It does not rest upon fickle luck. A *process* is simply a systematic set of actions we take to achieve desired results. Having repeatable *processes* is what takes the trial and error and guesswork out of life. Doctors have a very defined and systematic diagnostic procedure to determine the cause of illness. IT programmers have a systematic step-by-step method for developing software. The beauty of understanding and improving processes is that many, if not most, are universal, thus not dependent upon the specific knowledge and content of a particular situation.

Over the past thirty years I have been involved in coaching people in literally thousands of sales deals. I have helped Sikorsky Aircraft sell helicopters to the Thai government; I have coached Hewlett-Packard to sell huge complex computer systems; I have helped Coca-Cola national accounts sell marketing programs to Burger King; I have been involved in Cymer's sales of its excimer lasers to Nikon and Canon and in Kimberley-Clark's paper goods promotions to Kroger; and so on. Am I an expert in helicopter technology? In computer systems? In consumer beverages? In consumer paper goods? Or in excimer lasers? Absolutely not! I only have a layman's knowledge of each of these areas. I do have a systematic repeatable proven sales *process* in Conceptual Selling, Strategic Selling, LAMP, and our other process-based MHI programs. This *process* is applicable to all complex sales situations, so I focus upon the *process* since I am not knowledgeable in all these industries. Another thing about understanding processes is that they are slow to become outdated if they are effective processes. For example, the process for building a house is basically thousands of years old. Even though the technologies have changed, the first step is still to dig and lay a foundation, followed by framing of the outside walls and interior support structure, followed by the gables and the roof, and so on. Ditto for the making of wine, thousands of years old.

The third element is *practice*. Thirty years ago, the case study was the primary learning tool for business and industry. I always felt that the weakness in this approach when used in seminars was the transition from the case study to application in real life. So workshops to *practice* the *principles* and *processes* we espoused were built into all of our seminars from the very beginning. It is a methodology that has been much copied, but never matched in its effectiveness—learn the *principle* to understand *why* something works, learn the *process* step to understand *how* to do it, and finally take a real-life situation upon which to plan and *practice* how to implement this to reality.

Finally, now that I have talked about *why* it works, I want to talk about *how* it works. When talking to prospective clients, I practice what I preach with this Win-Win concept. I absolutely know that I 'win' when my customers get more and better sales by using our programs. I get satisfied customers, repeat business, and referrals. However, I also let them know, that we cannot deliver the results alone. I can provide and teach the *processes* and the *principles* to their salespeople and managers, and even provide the *practice*. But they have to provide the *discipline* that makes it work and gets the results. I urge client managers to take a disciplined approach, which says, "This is the way we sell in this company, and the expectation is that we will all do it this way. We will make deals that are Win-Win for our customers and ourselves. We do not play Win-Lose. We have a plan before going on a sales call. We seek out coaching, and don't close a deal until we have identified and covered bases with all buying influences. We ask questions, probing to understand the real issues; we talk no more than 20 percent of the time and listen 80 percent of the time. We try to find out what we don't know. We look for Basic Issues. We do all of this because we know that, if we do, we will have more sales and better sales and long-term customer relationships." Corporate mandate, with the expectation that the rigor used day in and day out, is what engrains the process into corporate culture. This is the *discipline* of successful selling organizations!

We know our *processes* and *principles* work. They have been proven in a crucible of reality for thirty years. You, our readers and clients, need to be prepared to provide the *discipline* to have your people use those *principles* and *processes*. It is our job to show you how, but we cannot do it for you. It is actually surprisingly simple: *processes*, *principles*, and *discipline*. We promise no magic. There are no silver bullets to selling success. We both need each other.

ROBERT B. MILLER
San Diego, California
September 2004

FOREWORD

Marriott International, Inc., has been fortunate to grow substantially over the years, to the point where today it operates in fifty countries around the world and employs over 200,000 people. Yet we remain in significant ways a family organization, still committed to the values that were honored by my parents seventy years ago when they started in business with a tiny root beer stand.

Among those values was a belief in the importance of relationships, both within and outside the company. Since 1927, we have said that if you commit yourself to taking care of your own people, you can be fairly confident that they will take care of your customers. In a service business like ours, that is essential to success. Marriott's global reputation for quality and value is the direct result of our honoring this principle. That same principle is the heart of *The New Strategic Selling*.

Throughout our history, we have found that our most productive business alliances have been forged with companies that share this orientation. One of the strongest of these has been with Miller Heiman, Inc., whose commitment to "Win-Win" relationships parallels our own. We have worked together since 1986, when our company introduced its first sales associates to Miller Heiman's *Strategic Selling* process. Since then, nearly a thousand Marriott people have been introduced to this process.

There is a practical reason for this. In the past decade, we have expanded dramatically, in both our lodging and our contract services group, so that today we can offer our customers a wide variety of choices. In managing the complexity that naturally accompanies such expansion, Miller Heiman has been an invaluable ally. *Strategic Selling* in particular has made important contributions to our position with business clients. In addition, Miller Heiman's systematic approach to managing change has helped to enhance our sales associates' flexibility as they keep pace with the rapid changes in our industry.

Aside from the practical benefits that *Strategic Selling* has brought us, I believe that our association with Miller Heiman is strong because of the natural fit between our companies. As we continue to expand toward our goal of operating 2,000 lodging properties by the year 2000, we remain committed to the "human side" of business. Miller Heiman understands and supports that commitment, and it's once again evident in *The New Strategic Selling*.

—J. W. Marriott, Jr.
Chairman and CEO,
Marriott International, Inc.

IF IT AIN'T BROKE: THE "WHY" BEHIND THE NEW STRATEGIC SELLING

Strategic Selling was first published in 1985. At that time, even though the process on which the book was based had been in place for only about eight years, it had already begun to reap significant benefits both for our company, Miller Heiman, Inc., and for the clients who attended our Strategic Selling workshops and programs. In 1985, many of corporate America's most successful selling organizations had already begun to see us as the "process experts," and we had earned the trust of such innovative market leaders as Hewlett-Packard, Marriott, General Electric, Hallmark, and Coca-Cola.

As we explained in the introduction to the original edition, we attributed much of our success with these and other forward-looking companies to our impassioned support of a non-manipulative selling philosophy that was the driving force of the Strategic Selling approach. That philosophy was based on the premise that getting an individual order is never enough: True selling success rests on such "beyond the order" achievements as repeat business, solid referrals, and long-term relationships. The key to securing them, we insisted, is to manage every sales objective as a joint venture—a mutually beneficial transaction where both buyer and seller "Win."

In 1985, the notion of selling as a "Win-Win" process—indeed, the notion of selling as a process at all—was still a novel approach to the profession. Even among companies who invested heavily in sales training, what was being taught was face-time skills and techniques—the traditional salesperson's grab-bag of hooks, lines, and clinchers. Manipulative tactics were still very much in vogue, and Miller Heiman was nearly unique among consultants in insisting that this time-worn approach—the old "Get the order any way you can" approach—was ultimately a way of shooting yourself in the foot. Twelve years ago, if you talked about "serving your customer's interests as well as your own," many salespeople still considered you unrealistic. Everybody paid lip service to customer need, but out in the trenches, according to the given wisdom of the 1980s, it was still numbers, and orders, and hardball, that brought you success. There was something anomalous—some even said revolutionary—in the customer-oriented process of Strategic Selling.

There was also something in it that was eminently practical—so practical that our clients, who were already sales leaders, realized that it was a way to make themselves even better. As "unrealistic" as traditionally trained salespeople might have considered our Win-Win approach, the incontrovertible fact was that it worked. The proof of that could be seen in our clients' financials, which regularly reported major revenue gains that could be traced directly to the implementation of our processes. It could be seen in the literally hundreds of success stories about how a "hopelessly confusing" account had begun to yield solid business once the sales team wrote a Miller Heiman–inspired action plan. As those stories poured in, and as our clients confirmed the contribution we were making, we were gratified to see that we had earned a reputation, in the words of one divisional manager, as "the people who brought process into selling."

It was process, to be sure, that lay at the heart of our success, and that was the case whatever in-house terminology our clients used. At Price Waterhouse, for example, our systematic approach is called a "methodology." At Coca-Cola, the preferred term is "technologies." Many of our other clients have adopted our language directly, speaking comfortably and naturally about Buying Influences and Win-Results. Whatever the terms, the point is the same. The systematic approach that we pioneered has fostered a quiet revolution among the nation's sales leaders.

We profited from that revolution as much as anyone. In a sense, by the time the first edition of this book went to press, we had already become our own best advertisement. By running our own business on Strategic Selling principles, we were increasing our revenues dramatically, year after year. Today, while countless companies are wrestling the downsizing dragon, Miller Heiman—like most of our clients—is still on a roll. Over the past five years, for example, we have increased our annual revenues by an average of 25 to 30 percent a year, tripled the staff in our corporate headquarters, and established offices from the United Kingdom and Brazil to Australia. Working with a sales force that has quadrupled in a decade—not to mention hundreds of valued client associates—we have introduced over 150,000 sales professionals to one or more Miller Heiman processes, and we continue to serve roughly 25,000 new ones every year.

All of this has occurred, moreover, during a period of tremendous international turmoil, of dramatic fluctuations in government policies, and of a bewildering "complexification" in selling itself. The world of sales has gone through a thousand major changes, but the processes we teach have been equal to the challenge. They're still relevant, they still work, and they're still improving the revenues of those who employ them. Books on selling "techniques" come and go. Strategic Selling, like the Energizer bunny, "just keeps on going."

Since so much of our success has been based on Strategic Selling—both the process and the book—you might question the rationale for this new edition. Why make adjustments to something that's already working so effectively? Or, to rephrase the old business adage, "If it ain't broke, why fix it?" It's a very reasonable question, and it has two answers.

The first is that our clients asked us to. Even though they found Strategic Selling to be just as effective, and the concepts just as relevant, as they had been in 1985, some of them felt that, after a dozen years, even the best of processes could use a face-lift. Some of the book's examples, they pointed out, seemed a little dated for the 1990s, and they might not be connecting as well as we wanted them to with sales forces who were increasingly geared toward the future.

When we described how rapid changes can generate "future shock," for example, we illustrated the point by referring to the Arab oil embargo of the 1970s. That pivotal event was still a vivid memory in 1985, but as the 1990s wane and the millennium looms, that's no longer true. "Many of the young lions who sell for us today," a district manager told us recently, "were still making mud pies when the oil crackdown happened. If you want to connect with them, you need fresh stories." Because we take such constructive criticism seriously, we've tried to give this new book a more contemporary feeling, so it could achieve an effective fusion of the timeless and the timely.

The second reason we revised *Strategic Selling* relates to a basic axiom of the process itself: "Whatever got you where you are today is no longer sufficient to keep you there." We had been telling our clients that since 1977, and last year—after considerable exhortation from both clients and colleagues—we finally decided to apply this axiom to ourselves, and to undertake a thorough rethinking of the program that had "got us there." In consultation with our expert field force, therefore, we went through *Strategic Selling* with a fine-tooth comb, sharpening and enhancing it line by line so that the resulting text would be even more real-world and useful than the original text had been for more than a decade.

Some of the changes we made were chiefly cosmetic—the illustrations, for example, have all been redrawn to give the book a more user-friendly appearance. But most of our changes were on a more substantive level. As we fiddled with this manuscript that wasn't really broken, we weren't content just to slap on some chrome and new paint. We wanted to improve the efficiency of the engine itself, to make the thousand and one minor adjustments that would ensure that the analytical tools we were offering our clients were just as sharp and powerful as they possibly could be.

The result was a thorough reworking of the original volume. In the entire text of *The New Strategic Selling*, you will not find a single page that has been left untouched. As good as the original was, it's now even better—more precise, more clearly expressed, and (most important of all) more useful. A few of its concepts, moreover, are completely new. In response, once again, to our clients' suggestions, we have added discussions of the following strategy concepts that were never a part of the original process or book, and that have only recently become a part of our corporate programs:

- **Degree of Influence.** The analytical foundation of any good strategy is the identification of what we call Buying Influences—the multiple players who can impact the outcome of any sale. Over the years, several clients have pointed out that, while covering all the Buying Influences is essential, it's also important to distinguish between degrees of influence, so that you can avoid the mistake of assuming that "all Buyers are alike." Our response to this observation appears in Chapter 5.
- **The Win-Results Statement.** One of the most useful, and yet trickiest, elements of *Strategic Selling* was the concept of determining your Buying Influence's "Win-Results." In Chapter 10, we clarify this concept with an analytical tool, the Win-Results Statement, that helps you to make a practical connection between a company's business Results and a key player's Wins.
- **Competition.** In response to clients who have asked us why we spend so little time talking about competition, we have added a entirely new chapter, Chapter 13, explaining our nontraditional approach to this critical issue. Here we provide a uniquely flexible definition of competition, explain why obsessing about your competitors can be just as debilitating as ignoring them, and show how to handle competitive pressures from a position of strength.
- **The "Refined" Sales Funnel.** In the original *Strategic Selling*, we introduced our time and territory management tool, the Sales Funnel, a couple of chapters ahead of our unique qualification tool, the Ideal Customer Profile. Because some clients found this sequence confusing, we reversed the order of these two elements, and also spelled

out their relationship more extensively. Their interaction is now described in Chapters 14 through 18.

We have also added, at the end of the book, a question-and-answer section in which we address some of the major selling challenges that our clients have posed to us, and provide some thoughts about process-centered solutions.

With these additions in place, and with the literally hundreds of smaller changes that we have made, we believe that *The New Strategic Selling* is a major "enhancement" to a process that has worked effectively for thousands since 1977, and whose very success has earned it the right to these refinements.

In its time, *Strategic Selling* pointed the way—both for our corporate clients and for a vast reading public—toward solid, incremental success in the Complex Sale. *Success* magazine's Scott DeGarmo spoke for many when he wrote, a couple of years after the book's appearance, that it and its companion volume, *Conceptual Selling*, were simply "the best books on selling I have ever read." Since then, both books have been continually in demand, and *Strategic Selling* alone has sold hundreds of thousands of copies.

Now, as Miller Heiman reaches its twentieth anniversary, and as American companies are challenged by ever fiercer global competition, the time is ripe for a "reengineered" version of our business classic. We offer it with confidence and enthusiasm to a new generation of readers, and also, with thanks, to the people who have made our company successful—the innovative professionals we are proud to call our clients.

To list every company with whom we have worked over the years would more than triple the length of this introduction. Therefore, as a representation of our work—and of our gratitude—we are happy to identify these currently active clients:

3 COM Corporation/U.S. Robotics
3M
Abbott Labs
ABB, Inc.
Ace Metal Crafts
ACI-US, Inc.
Adaptec
Adecco
Adia Personnel Services
ADIC
ADS Environment Services
ADT Security Systems
Advanced Control Systems
Advanced Technology Laboratories—ATL
AEI Music Network
Aerotek
Alliant
Allegiance Healthcare
Allen-Bradley Company
Allen Systems, Inc.
Allied Van Lines
AlliedSignal
Alternative Resources Corporation
Alvey
AM-RE Brokers
American Airlines
American Movie Classics
American Payment Systems
American Phoenix Corporation
American Printers
American Seating Group
American Technical Resources
American Teleconferencing Services
Amersham Corporation
AMP of Canada
Anderson & Anderson
Andrew Corporation
Angelica Uniform Group
Apple Computer USA
ARAMARK
ARK
Arkwright Mutual Insurance
ASAP Software
Ashland Chemical
Aspect Telecommunications
ATC Leasing Company
Atlet
Ato Findley Adhesives
ATOTECH USA, Inc.
AT&T Business Market Division
AT&T Global Business Communication
AT&T Wireless Services (McCaw Cellular Communication)
Aurora/Century
Automatic Data Processing—ADP
Avis, Inc.
AVL Medical Instruments
Bairnco
Baltimore Therapeutic Equipment

Balzers Pfeiffer N. A., Inc.
Bank Compensation
Bank of America
Bank of America, Seafirst
Baroid of Canada
BASF Mexicana
Battelle
Bay Creek Real Estate Company
Bay Engineered Castings
BBN International
Becher Carlson Risk Management
Beckett Publications
Beckman Instruments, Inc.
Becton Dickinson & Company
Beechwood Data Systems
Bell Helicopter Textron
Bell Packaging
Bell South
Bently Nevada Corporation
Berkshire Computer Products
Berlitz Translation Services
Bernhardt Furniture
Best Power
Better Baked Pizza, Inc.
BetzDearborn Paper Process Group
BetzDearborn Water Management Group
BF Goodrich
BI-TECH Software
Bio Whittaker
Biogen
BKM Total Office
Black & Decker
Blue Shield of California
Boehringer Mannheim Corporation
Bomarko/Hollymatic
Boston Scientific Corporation
BPS & M
Broadway & Seymour
Browning Ferris—BFI
Bryan, Pendleton, Swats & McAllister
Bunge Foods
Burlington Air Express
Burton Group
Buss (America), Inc.
Cable & Wireless Communication
CADD Edge
Cal-Surance Benefit Plans
Cal-Surance Companies
California Amplifiers
California Day Fresh Foods
California Eastern Laboratories—CEL
California Lottery
Cara Corporation
Cardinal Bergen Health
Caremark International
Cargill Processed Meat Product
Caribiner Communications
Carroll Company
Carvel Corporation

Cascade Communications
Century Circuits & Electronics
Ceridian Employer Services
CFM Technologies
Charles Schwab & Company
Checkfree Corporation
Checkmate Electronics
Checkpoint Systems
Chemical Leaman
Corporation
Chevron-Oronite
Cheyenne Software
Chiron Diagnostics
CIED
Ciena Corporation
Cigna Corporation
Cirqon Technologies
Clarify
Climatech Service Company
CMP Interactive Media
CMP Publications
CNA Insurance Companies
Cognex
Colad Group
Comdata
Comm Scope, Inc.
Commercial Insurance
Concepts, Inc.
Communispond, Inc.
Compass Group USA
Compucom Systems
Computech Systems
Computer Prep, Inc.
Computron
Computronix
Compuware
COMSAT International
COMSAT Turkey
COMSAT Venezuela
Comstream
ConAgra
Connoisseur Communications
Consolidated Printers
Consumers Power Company
Contel of California
Continental Sprayers
Coopers & Lybrand
Cornerstone Consulting
Cornhuskers Motor Lines
Corporate Travel Consultants
CPC Foodservice
Creative Labs, Inc.
Creative Office Interiors
Credence Systems
CSC Consulting
CSC Intelicom, Inc.
CSRG
Cuna Mutual Insurance
Group
C.R. Laurence Company, Inc.
Data Documents
Dataccount Corporation
DataFlo Corporation
Datex-Ohmeda
Dean Distributors
Decision One
Decision Technology
Defining Image
Dell Computer
Communications

Delmarva Power
Delphi Information Systems
Deluxe Corporation
DeNormandie Towel & Linen
Denron, Inc.
Development Dimensions International—DDI
DHL Airways, Inc.
Diagraph Corporation
Digital Sight & Sound
Dimensions Computer Automation
Diners Club Enroute
Disco Hi-Tec America
Dittler Brothers
Dornier Medical
Dow Chemical Company
Dow Corning
Dragon Systems
Ducks Unlimited
Dunsian Industries
Dupont Merck
Durkan Patterned Carpets, Inc.
Dyna-Trends International
Eastman Chemical
Eastman Kodak Company
ECC International
Edison Plastics
EDS—Sales Education
EISAI
Elkay Manufacturing Company
Emblem Enterprises, Inc.
EMC Global Technologies
Emmis Broadcasting/RDS
Employment Learning Innovation
Endeavor Information Systems
Engelhard Corporation
Engineered Data Products
EnviroMetrics Software
EPE Technology
Ermanco, Inc.
Ernst & Young LLP
Esterline Technologies
ETC
Etec, Inc.
Ethicon Endo-Surgery
Eyecare & Surgery Center
Fair Isaac & Company
Fanuc Robotics
Fidelity Investments
FileNet
Fina Oil Company
First Health Group
First Security Services
Fiserv
Fisher-Rosemount
Flometrics
FMC Corporation
Focus
Focused Marketing Associates
Foldcraft/Plymold Seating
Forrester Research
Forsythe Solutions Group
Fort James Corporation
Forth Shift
Four Gen Software
Friden Neopost
Frigidaire

FTP Software
Fujitsu Microelectronics
FurturLabs, Inc.
Future Now
Gates McDonald & Company
GEC Plessy Semiconductors
Geiger International
Gencorp
General Electric—Capital
Gensym Corporation
GN Nettest
Grace Specialty Polymers
Graphics Management
Great Western Chemical
Greenpages
Griffith Laboratories
GTE Supply
GTE Telops
H & W Computer Systems
HA Debari & Associates
Hackley Health
Haemonetics Corporation
Hallmark Building Supplies
Hallmark Cards, Inc.
Hallmark International
Handshaw & Associates
Hanson Group
Harbinger Corp.
Harris Computer Systems
Harris Corporation
Harris Semiconductor
Haworth Corporation
HBM, Inc.
HBO & Company
Health Net
Heppner Hardwoods
Herman Miller, Inc.
Herman Miller/Milcare
Hewlett-Packard Company
Hitachi Data Systems
Hobbs Group/Arkwright
Honeywell, Inc.
Houghton Chemical
Corporation
Hughes Network Systems
HUSCO International, Inc.
I-Stat Corporation
I Power KC Heartland
IBM Corporation
IBM Insurance
IDEXX Laboratories
IDF, Inc.
Intelligent Medical Imaging,
Inc.—IMI
In Focus Systems
Independent Health
Industrial & Commercial
Contracts
INET Corporation
Infographix, Inc.
Informatech, Inc.
Information Dimensions, Inc.
Information Mapping
Infotech
Initial Staffing
Insignia Systems, Inc.
Instromedix, Inc.
Insurance Auto Auctions
Integrated Furniture Solutions

Integrated Network Corporation
Integration Alliance
Intellicorp, Inc.
Intelligroup, Inc.
Interaction Associates
Interactive Business Systems
InterCall
Intercim Corporation
Intermate International, Inc.
International Billing Services
Interpath
Intertec Publishing
Iogen Corporation
IPRAX, Inc.
Irvin Automotive Products
ISI Systems, Inc.
Itac Systems
ITC
ITW/Signode
I.P.I.
J & H Marsh & McLellan, Inc.
Jabu Computer Services
Jamak Fabrication
Jet Line Communications
JLG Industries
Jobscope
John Wood Company
Johnson Controls
Johnson & Johnson Clinical Diagnostics, Inc.
Johnson & Johnson Latin America
J. P. Morgan Securities, Inc.
K & M Electronics
Keane, Inc.
Kelly Services
Keystone Group
KGA Engineering Company, Inc.
Kimball International
Kinetics Technology
Kipp Group
KLA Instruments
Kline & Company
Knoll Group, The
Korn/Ferry International
Korry Electronics
KPMG Nolan Norton
KR Services/ICAT Logistics
Krauthanner International
Krohne
Lam Research
Lambda Electronics
LAN Systems
Landis & Gyr Powers, Inc.
Lawson Margo Packaging
Le Febure Corporation
Lend Leaser Employer System
Lender's Credit/Info One
Libbey-Owens-Ford Co.
Life Technologies
Lifescan
Limitorque Corporation
Lipha Tech, Inc.
Little Charlie's Food Service
Lockheed Martin Telecommunications
LogiCare

Logicon
Logikos
Los Angeles Times
Lotsoff Capital Management
Lucent Technologies
M & M/Mars
Macdonald Dettweiler
Management Systems Associates
Manus
Marathon Special Products
Maritrans, Inc.
Marriott International, Inc.
Marshall Industrial Technology
Mason Laboratories
MassMutual
Master Chemical Corporation
Matlack, Inc.
Mayo Medical Laboratories
McCall Consulting Group
McDonald's Corporation
McGraw-Hill
McPeak Center For Eyecare
Medex
Medi USA
Medical Tracking Systems
Medicode, Inc.
Medicus Systems
Meditrol
MEDSTAT Group
Megasoft
Merck & Company, Inc.
Metrix
Metromedia Restaurant Group
Micro Motion, Inc.
Microage
Micrografx, Inc.
Micros Systems, Inc.
Microsoft Corporation
Midcon Cables Company
Millennia Vision
Mizar, Inc.
MMS International
MOAC
Modern Building Materials
Molecular Applications Group
Molecular Cooling Technology
Molecular Dynamics
Monsanto Chemical Co.
Moog Controls Inc.
Moore Products
Moosbrugger Marketing Research
Morrison Healthcare
Motorola
MTEL International
MTI Abraxys, Inc.
Murata Wiedemann, Inc.
M & I Data Services
National Car Rental
National Education Training Group
National Semiconductor
Natural Micro Systems Corporation
NAVCO
NCI Information Systems
NCS
Nellcor Puritan Bennett

Netcom Communications, Inc.
Neural Applications Corporation
New Age Electronics
New World Van Lines
Newsbank, Inc.
Nicholas Applegate
Noble Star Systems
Norstan Communications
North American Dräger
Northwest Bank
Nova Biomedical
Novell, Inc.
Now Software, Inc.
NutraSweet Company
O'Connor Burnham Productions
Oacis Healthcare
Object Time Limited
Octel
Office Pavilion
Office Specialists
Oliver Wight East, Inc.
Oliver Wight West, Inc.
Omega Performance
On Technology
One Wave, Inc.
Open Development Corporation
Open Group
Open Software Foundation
OpTel, Inc.
Optical Data Systems
Orange County Register
Orbcomm
ORC Electronic Products
Ormec
Ortho Diagnostics Systems, Inc.
Osborn Laboratories
OSI
Owen Healthcare
Owosso Corporation
PacifiCare
Padi
PADS, Inc.
Paradigm Group
Pathlore
Paychex
Payco American Corporation
PCS Health Systems
PDP, Inc.
Performance Software
Perrier
Phar Lap Software, Inc.
Pharmacia Biotech Inc.
Pharmacia Diagnostics
Pharmacia & Upjohn, Inc.
PHH Asset Management
Philips Medical Systems
Phillips Key Modules
Phoenix Technologies, LTD
Pick Systems
Picturetel Corporation
PID, Inc.
Pillsbury Company
Pilot Software
Pinkerton Security Services
Pioneer Electronics
Plastron
Platinum Technology

Poly Fibron Technologies
Potlatch Corporation
Powder River
Power One
Power Packing Corporation, Inc.
Powerserve
Powersoft Corporation
PR Taylor, Inc.
Prairie Development
Praxair Inc.
Precision Systems Concepts
Preferred Hotels & Resorts
Presentation Products
Pressure Vessel Service
Princeton Financial Systems
Princeton Softtech
Pro Business, Inc.
Progressive Networks
ProLight
PromtCare Company, Inc.
P.K. Taylor, Inc.
Qualix Group, Inc.
Quantra Corporation
Quantum Corporation
Racal Datacom
Radian Corporation
Radisson Hotels International
RCB Consulting
Red Brick Systems
Reed Travel Group
Reichhold
Reichold Chemical
Reliable Power Meters
Restat
Rex Packaging Inc.
Reynolds & Reynolds Computer Division
Richard A. Eisner & Company
Risk Management Group
Rittal Corporation
Riverside Paper Company
Rockwell Automotive
Rockwell Collins
Rockwell International Corporation
Rollins Hudig Hall
Rosemount Analytical
Royal Mahogany Products
RTMS
R. R. Donnelley & Sons Co.
Sabatasso Foods, Inc.
Sabre Travel Information
Sachs Group
SAP America
Sara Lee Bakery
SAS Institute, The
Scantron Corporation
Schenck Trebel
Schlumberger Industries
Scholastic
Schwab International
Scitex America Corporation
SDC Coatings, Inc.
Seagate Software SMG
Secured Funding Source
Seiko Instruments
Sensory Circuits, Inc.
Service Master
Servonex

Share Consulting Service
Shared Medical Systems
Shaw Industries, Inc.
Sheldahl, Inc.
Shine-Etsu
SHL
Siemens Energy & Automation
Siemens Medical Systems
Siemens Nixdorf Information Systems
Siemens Power Corporation
Sigma Aldrich Research
Sigma Diagnostics
Simtec HVAC
Situation Management Systems
Six Flags Over Georgia
SkyTel
SL Waber, Inc.
Smallworld Systems, Inc.
Smith-Blair, Inc.
Sofamor Danek USA
Software Artistry
Solectron
Sonoco Products Company
Southeastern Mill
Spectrum Management Group, Inc.
Sprint
SPSS
Square D Company
Standard Register
State Street Trust
Stellar Financial
Steri—OSS
Sterling Healthcare
Stralfors International, Inc.
Sun Data
SunGard Financial Systems, Inc.
Sungard Securities
SunRiver Data Systems
Supply Tech, Inc.
Sycom
Symbios Logic
Syncor International
Systems Research Labs
T Line Services
T & D Consultants
Talarian
Tally Systems Corporation
Tapemark Company
Tastemaker
Technology Service Solutions
Teklogix
Teknion Furniture
Teknowlogy
Tel Data Control
Telect
Telxon Corporation
Tencor Instruments, Inc.
Tesseract
Texas Instruments
Texonics
Textron Systems Corp.
Texwipe Company, Inc.
Time Resource Management
Time Warner Communications
Tivoli Systems
TMP Worldwide
Tony's Food Service

Tosoh SMD, Inc.
Transcat
Transition Systems, Inc.
Transwitch
Trend Circuits
Triple M Marketing
Tufts Health Plan
Tulin Technology
Tuscarora, Inc.
T.T.C.
ULTRADATA Corporation
Ultratech Stepper, Inc.
UMI, Inc.
UNC Business Development
UNEX Corporation
Unicco Services Co.
Union Bank
Union Gas Limited
Uniphase Corporation
United Visual, Inc.
Universal Flavors
Universal Forest Products
Universal Instruments
UNO-VEN Company
USA Roofing
U.S. Robotics Inc.
U.S. Tobacco
VALIC
Vangard Technology
Vanstar Corporation
Varian Associates
Verilink Corporation
Vertag
Verteq, Inc.
Vinta Business Systems
Visigenic Software
VLSI Technology
Voice Processing Corporation
Voice Technologies
VWR Scientific Products
Walker Interactive Systems
Walker Parking Consultants
Wall Street Investor Service
Watermark Software
Wausau Insurance
WEM Automation
Wendover Corporation
Wesley Software
West Coast Information
Westco
Western Atlas
Williams Tele-Communications
Wind River Systems
Wisconsin Power & Light
Wood Associates
Woodware Governor Company
Work Group Solutions
WorldCom
WOZZ/WFDF
Wyeth-Ayerst
W.L. Gore & Associates, Inc.
Xenejenex Health Videos
Xerox Canada
Xylum Corporation
Yaskawa Electric America, Inc.
York International
Yushin America
Zurn/Nepco

In compiling this list, we've been as thorough and up-to-date as we could. Given the pace of business change and the length of publishing production schedules, however, it could well be in need of revision by the date of publication. If we've inadvertently omitted any clients, we hope they will understand.

We must also offer our thanks to all the fine people at Miller Heiman, Inc., both at our Reno headquarters and in the field who have contributed so much to making our company a success.

PART 1

STRATEGIC SELLING

CHAPTER 1

SUCCESSFUL SELLING IN A WORLD OF CONSTANT CHANGE

An old Greek legend tells how the ruler of Crete, King Minos, has an underground maze, the Labyrinth, constructed near his palace to serve as an escape-proof prison for the infamous Minotaur—a ravenous monster who is half man and half bull. Anyone who enters the maze becomes hopelessly lost, and once that happens the Minotaur finds and devours him. This gruesome scenario repeats itself again and again until the young hero Theseus, with the assistance of the princess Ariadne, devises a strategy to kill the monster and get out.

Killing the monster is the easy part. Theseus is a hero, after all; killing is his business. The problem is finding a way out of the maze. Realizing this, Ariadne ties a long thread to his waist as he enters the Labyrinth, holding the other end tightly in her hand. It's a simple but effective solution. Deep in the cavern, Theseus dispatches the monster, and then retraces his circuitous route back up to daylight. He and Ariadne are married, and the people rejoice.

What in the name of Zeus, you are probably asking, does this ancient legend have to do with selling?

Quite a lot. If you will suspend your disbelief just long enough to imagine Theseus as a modern sales professional, we think you'll readily see the analogy we're developing. In selling today, especially at the corporate level, you have to contend every day with organizational labyrinths. A hundred years ago—even twenty or thirty years ago—it was possible, if not always easy, to close major business by calling on and satisfying a key decision-maker. Those days are gone. Today, in the era of what we call the Complex Sale, every major piece of business entails multiple decisions, and those decisions are virtually *never* made by the same person.

Not only do you have to contend with multiple decisions, but the people who make those decisions may not even work in the same place; to get a contract for delivery of a shipment to Milwaukee, you might easily need signatures from people in Chicago or Detroit—or Chicago *and* Detroit. To make things even more challenging, you can't be sure that the people who said Yes on one deal will have the same authority two weeks, or even two days, from now on a second deal to the same company.

In an era of downsizing, nonstop mergers, and executive musical chairs, selling has become so complicated, and so fraught with unknowns, that the labyrinth metaphor may even be a little too conservative. At least the original Labyrinth wasn't constructed on a fault line. In today's corporate labyrinths, it seems as if it's always earthquake season.

We admit that the type of bull you usually encounter in the business maze is not exactly the hungry Minotaur variety. No matter how confusing the organization chart, how tough your competitors, or how demanding your customers may be, you're never in danger of *literally* being eaten for lunch. But figuratively? It happens every day. And there's absolutely no way to prevent it *unless you have a strategy*. Just like Theseus, you need a plan of action, and you need a "safety line" to keep you properly oriented as you navigate through the maze of your sales opportunities.

You can think of this book as an Ariadne's thread, or as a floor plan of the shifting corporate labyrinth. Whichever metaphor you prefer, the point is the same. To survive in selling today, you need strategy. This book is a proven guide to helping you develop it.

To demonstrate the critical difference between having and not having a strategy, we'll relate a story about one of our corporate clients.

Not long ago, a major manufacturer of information systems—a company that does hundreds of millions of dollars' worth of business a year—was about to close the sale of a sophisticated computer system to a potentially huge new account. The sales representative who was handling the negotiations, a man we'll call Ray, seemed to have every reason to be confident. He had been talking to the client's top management for months, and as the deal moved closer to signing, he knew he was firmly entrenched. The department head who would use the new equipment, the purchasing agent who would sign for it, the data-processing people—all of them were delighted with his proposal. Ray even belonged to the same club as the company's CEO, and he knew that this executive too was behind the deal. With a five-figure commission practically in his pocket, Ray was already shopping for a new car.

Ray's company wasn't the only one with its eye on this account. A smaller firm had also approached the customer, and Ray was aware of the potential competition. Judging from the general receptivity to his proposal, though, he figured he had nothing to worry about. The smaller firm had half the market share of his own, and no matter how good its product might be, Ray was way ahead on reputation points alone. Rumor had it, he congratulated himself, that the salesman for the other side hadn't even met the CEO.

What Ray didn't know was that the rival firm had one major advantage. Many of its best salespeople, including an eager young lion named Greg, had recently attended one of our Strategic Selling programs. There Greg had acquired a whole new perspective on selling. He had learned how to identify the critical Buying Influences in a sale, how to minimize his uncertainties about a customer's receptivity, how to avoid internal sabotage, and how to leverage from his own strengths to maximize his competitive advantage. When he left the program, he took with him a detailed, pragmatic system that allowed him to analyze the components of the pending sale far more effectively than Ray could ever hope to. Armed with his understanding of these components, and of how they all fit together in the sale, he was about to steal a march on the market "leader."

It was true that Greg hadn't met the CEO. But thanks to the Strategic Selling program he had attended, he didn't have to. While Ray was congratulating himself for knowing the customer's senior management, Greg was quietly finding out who the real decision-makers were for this sale, and uncovering other information that could help him close the deal. Specifically, he wanted to know who would have to give final approval for the sale. He found what he was looking for in Jeff, an outside consultant whom Ray had entirely overlooked. Jeff was able to give Greg two invaluable pieces of information.

First, he explained that for this specific sale, it was the division general manager, not the CEO, who had to give final approval; Ray's connection to the CEO was thus ego-gratifying but irrelevant. Second, if Greg wanted to sell this critical decision-maker, he could do no better than to go through Jeff himself. Prior to becoming a consultant, he had been a valued senior member of the buying organization, and the division general manager had routinely relied on him for information about state-of-the-art technology.

What Greg did, therefore, was to show Jeff the match between the buying firm's needs and his computer solution—and then let Jeff demonstrate it to the general manager. Soon all the parties involved in the purchase decision were sold on his proposal. He was the one who got the new car, while Ray, who supposedly had had the sale tied up, was left wondering what had gone wrong.

When Ray's company realized its sure thing had fallen through, its sales management naturally wanted to know why. When they discovered that we had had a part in their misfortune, they contacted us to find out more about our programs. Today both Greg's and Ray's firms are our valued clients, and both report regular increases in account penetration and sales performance directly attributable to our principles and planning process.

Anybody who sells for a living can tell you similar stories about how a "locked in" deal fell through because the salesperson in charge had failed to cover all his bases, pitched his proposal to the wrong person at the wrong time, or overlooked a crucial signal that the sale was in trouble. No matter how expert or experienced you are, you have probably felt the pang of disappointment that comes when your competition unseats you from a totally "secure" position.

What you may not realize (and very few salespeople do realize it) is that there is always a specific, clearly identifiable reason that such a sale is lost, even though you may not know what it is. That reason never involves merely "luck" or "timing" or "hard work." When you lose a done deal at the last minute, it's always because you failed to bring to that sale what Greg brought to his computer deal: a clearly defined and reliable *process* for success that takes into account all the elements of the pending transaction, no matter how obscure or "trivial" they might appear.

This is true in any sales situation, but it's especially relevant in what we call the Complex Sale. That's what our sales development processes and this book are about. The goals of *The New Strategic Selling* are to help you understand why things have sometimes gone wrong in your Complex Sales, and to give you a tested, reliable system for setting them right from now on.

The Complex Sale: What It Is

Our processes are built on reality, not theory, and it would be unrealistic to suggest that everyone involved in selling could profit equally from them. That's why we need to start by defining the Complex Sale, so that you can determine whether or not, given the type of selling you do, you can benefit from the methodology we have developed. In our corporate programs and in this book, we use the following definition:

A Complex Sale is one in which a number of people must give their approval or input before the buying decision can be made.

That sounds simple enough, and it is simple, but the concept nonetheless has enormous implications. To flesh out this definition somewhat, we can say that in the typical Complex Sale, one or more of the following elements are in place:

- The buying organization has multiple options.
- The selling organization has multiple options.
- In both organizations, numerous levels of responsibility are involved.
- The buying organization's decision-making process is complex—meaning that it is seldom self-evident to an outsider.

The presence of these complicating factors makes selling in any Complex Sale arena complicated too. The variety of people involved in the Complex Sale, and the variety of often conflicting decisions that these people commonly have to make, mean that in Complex Sales the sales representative has to develop a selling method that's distinct from, and more analytical than, that of the traditional hand-pumping good old boy who made it on a shoeshine and a smile. As the story of Greg and Ray indicates, having this type of method can be the difference between failure and success. Our processes are in demand precisely because we demonstrate this difference to our clients.

If you've ever sold something to a couple as opposed to a husband or wife alone, you know how multiple approval can complicate a sale. If your selling takes place in a corporate or government environment, you know that the complications are even greater when approval has to come not just from individuals but from committees and boards of review. The bottom line here is that whenever two or more yes votes are needed for a sale to go through, you need a very special strategy to handle the situation.

This is true no matter how simple or complex the product being sold is, and no matter how much or how little it costs. The decisive factor in the Complex Sale is not product or price but *structure*.

Take basketballs—certainly a small-ticket product—as an

example. The salesperson who sells a dozen basketballs to old Pop Jones at the local sporting goods store is making a simple sale; he doesn't need our help. But if you're trying to place a hundred gross of that same product with Kmart, you definitely do need it, because making this sale will require so many approvals. People who sell in this kind of arena, at the business-to-business level, are confronted every day with structural complexity—and therefore with what we call the Complex Sale.

With this definition of the Complex Sale in mind, you should be able to determine how relevant this book will be to you. If you sell principally over a counter or door to door, you probably won't find it to be indispensable to your work, since you rarely need more than one yes to close your transactions. But if you're involved in any aspect of corporate selling—whether or not you've been stymied, like Ray, by corporate complexity—the Strategic Selling process can help you hone the skills you already have, develop new ones you may not have thought you needed, and fit them all together into a visible and repeatable strategy for sales success.

The people who have already learned this process, and who are now using its principles in their own sales operations, form a virtual Who's Who of American business: We deliver our programs mainly to the Fortune 1000 Industrials and the Fortune 50 Transportation, Financial, Insurance, and Commercial Banking firms. Many of these firms deal in obviously big-ticket items, such as airplanes (Lockheed) and computer systems (Hewlett-Packard, IBM). Others sell small-ticket products, such as Kleenex (Kimberly-Clark) and soft drinks (The Coca-Cola Company). All of them operate in the arena of the Complex Sale.

In that arena, the people who profit most directly and immediately from our processes are corporate field salespeople and their managers. In addition, we've brought significant success to inside salespeople, customer service people, product managers, and many senior executives whose work in one way or another involves sales performance. But you don't have to work for a *Fortune*-listed giant to profit from *The New Strategic Selling*. Whatever the size of your company, and whatever the product or service you deal in, if you're involved in the Complex Sale as we've defined it here, this book is for you.

To get the maximum benefit from reading it, however, you should understand its particular relevance to your current sales environment. That environment, as you already know, is characterized by virtually constant change. Because this change is often troubling to the sales representative, before we start laying out the Strategic Selling process, we want to describe the impact of this constant change on the Complex Sale.

THE ONLY CONSTANT IS CHANGE

A dozen years ago, when the first edition of *Strategic Selling* appeared, we used the then fashionable term "future shock" to describe the stress and disorientation produced by constant change. As relevant as the point was back then, it has become even more fiercely relevant today. In the early 1980s, "constant change" was probably felt most acutely in the computer, communications, and other high-tech markets. Today, it's safe to say that, whatever your business, betting on the stability of tomorrow is like building castles in the sand. Ask any of the thousands of corporate employees who, in the past decade, have lost their supposedly "lifetime" positions overnight. You may not know the exact height or direction of the next castle-threatening wave, but two things you can say with absolute confidence. One, there *will* be waves. Two, if you want to survive them, you have to *prepare*.

What are the "waves" that we are talking about? What are the changes that are threatening today's business stability?

When we ask that question in our corporate programs, we seldom get exactly the same answers twice. That's not surprising. In fact, that's our point. If we could predict exactly where the next change was coming from, the constancy of change wouldn't be problematic. It's precisely because you don't know what to expect that business inconstancy induces such uneasiness.

You may be experiencing change in your marketplace, your technology, your customer base, your product line, your competitive position, your marketing strategy and tactics, the structure of your organization—or in any number of these areas, in any combination. You may be experiencing change as a subtle, gradual erosion (such as the move of manufacturing sites offshore), as a sudden event (such as a precipitous drop in stock prices), or as continual growth (such as the computer and software industries are experiencing now). But whatever the scope or the rate of the changes that are affecting your environment, they can bring you head to head with the shock of the unknown.

This isn't necessarily cause for despair. It isn't change itself that produces disorientation, but the *uncertainty* that is often associated with it. No matter what changes are going on in your industry, you can still develop reliable selling strategies if you learn to sort out the opportunities from the threats, and if you continually develop the specific skills that are needed to establish stability where none now seems to exist.

This book is designed to give you those skills, whatever your business and whatever your product or service. You'll get maximum benefit from it if you first accept the reality that *change has become a constant*. To close the Complex Sale today, you need to know that yesterday's business as usual is today's outdated system and tomorrow's millstone around the neck. We believe this recognition is so important that we identify the acceptance of change as a prerequisite for understanding the Strategic Selling process. We even put this in the form of an axiom, or premise.

Premise 1 of Strategic Selling:
Whatever got you where you are today is no longer sufficient to keep you there.

This premise, we realize, goes against the grain of all those who have been doing things the same way for twenty years and are comfortable with their established patterns. Yet accepting this premise is essential to sales survival. Today, instability is the only thing you can count on. The person who refuses to alter his or her "time-tested" methods to adjust to this reality will soon be left behind because one fact is plain: Even if you've been selling for only a few years, the selling environment in which you learned to operate *no longer exists.*

The disorientation caused by rapid change isn't peculiar to the selling environment, but the specific changes associated with the Complex Sale are. A second premise is addressed to this fact. It's meant to identify one of the most important changes you will have to make if you intend to carry your success into the next century.

Premise 2 of Strategic Selling:
In the Complex Sale, a good tactical plan is only as good as the strategy that led up to it.

Tactics, as we use the term in our programs and in this book, refers to techniques you use when you're actually face-to-face with a prospect or customer in a sales call. It includes all the time-honored tools of the trade that you learned in Selling 101, such as questioning techniques, overcoming objections, presentation skills, trial closes, and so on. By strategy, on the other hand, we mean a series of less widely recognized, but equally identifiable, processes that you use to position yourself with the customer before the sales call even begins. You use tactics *during* your sales presentation; strategy must come *before* it.

In today's corporate selling environment, strategy is a prerequisite to tactical success. As Ray found out to his dismay, tactics will get you nowhere if you present them to the wrong person, or to the right person at the wrong time. Furthermore, good strategy, like good tactics, can be *learned.* In fact the entire focus of the process we'll be presenting in this book is on developing effective pre-call selling strategies.

Not that tactics are unimportant. We acknowledge the value of good presentation skills, and in fact our company's second oldest program, Conceptual Selling, focuses exclusively on face-to-face selling tactics—on what you have to do when you're in the call. But that's Act 2. Act 1 is getting you to the call in the first place.

The reason this matters to you is that, while sales professionals unanimously agree that tactics are important, they routinely, and disastrously, neglect strategic preparation. Strategy, in fact, is *the single most neglected element* in selling today, not only among sales representatives, but even among the very managers and sales trainers who are supposed to be teaching them to cope with the Complex Sale. In fact it was our frustration with training programs that led us to develop our strategic process in the first place.

Our third and final premise also addresses itself specifically to the sales environment, but is much broader in scope than Premise 2. If Premise 1 identified the reality of general social change and Premise 2 the reality of change in the Complex Sale, then Premise 3 points to the need for personal, internal change as a way of handling what's going on outside.

Premise 3 of Strategic Selling:
You can succeed in sales today only if you know what you're doing and why.

This may sound obvious, but it's not—at least judging from how infrequently today's sales representatives actually apply it in the field. We can demonstrate that to you by relating an experience we had frequently during the years we were sales executives in major corporations. As regional and national sales managers, we interviewed literally hundreds of prospective sales representatives. Most of them were already successful when they came to us, and so our task, in reviewing candidates for our own selling teams, was to sort out the very good from the excellent. To do this we devised a question to test not the candidates' individual performance (we already knew that was good) but their *perception* of that performance. We asked them, "*Why* are you so successful? What sets you apart from the other people in your branch or division whose sales figures consistently fall below yours?"

The answers were surprising. *Not one in a hundred* of our candidates was able to identify the real reason for his or her success. Usually, in trying to pin down the essential ingredients, they talked about luck, connections, or hard work. Only a tiny fraction understood that it was the way they went about their work—what we call their *methodology* or *process*—that was the real clue to why they did so well.

It was that fraction we sought to hire. Of course we knew

that working hard, building up contacts, and luck probably hadn't hurt these people's track records. But we also knew that these were trivial factors compared to their awareness of their own working methods, and their willingness to refine those methods to improve their success. What we found consistently was that the person with the best *understanding* of his or her own effective *way of doing things* was the one who would prove the most productive for us. Those were the people we hired, and with few exceptions their performance confirmed our expectations.

This was only logical. If you rely on luck or territory or connections, your work will always have a high degree of trial and error about it, and trial and error isn't a reliable tool in a world that's as riddled with change, and as competitive, as ours is. In addition, without an understanding of your own method, you're doomed to approach each sale as an entirely new experience. You'll never develop a *testing* procedure to see what works and what doesn't, and you'll therefore see each change in your business environment not as an opportunity that could be understood and developed, but as a danger signal saying "Go back. Do not pass Go."

Success today depends on your developing not this kind of catch-as-catch-can approach to your work, but a clearly defined, *professional* sales methodology. Knowing what you're doing and why is fundamental to the strategic professional's profile.

Profile of the Strategic Professional

Surprising as it may seem, many people who sell are reluctant to admit that their profession is a profession. The old, unfortunate image of the salesperson as a mere glad-hander, someone whose only skill is "knowing how to talk to folks," still commands a good deal of credence, even among sales professionals themselves. Think of the phrases that come to mind when you think of selling. "A good salesperson is born, not made." "Selling is 90 percent luck." "A real salesperson can sell ice to Eskimos." Underlying all these adages is the view that it's personality, not understanding; temperament, not training; magic, not skill, that make the top sales representatives what they are. For many people in the sales field, Horatio Alger's old "luck and pluck" is still the talisman to which we attribute our success.

Even if this view was accurate in former days (which is doubtful), it has no bearing on the world of constant change. Selling, no less than teaching or medicine or law, is a professional calling, and those who prosper in it are those with a handle on their own professional methods. They're the people who have developed a conscious, planned system of selling steps that are *visible*, *logical*, and *repeatable*. The person who makes our Strategic Selling process work never sees success in terms of magic or charisma or luck. No one who makes it big in the Complex Sales of the coming century will be able to rely on that old mythology. Tomorrow's sales leaders will succeed because they think like, act like, and—most importantly—consider themselves to be pros.

One of the things these pros will have in common is a special brand of persistence. We're not talking about the time-worn "Keep knocking on the door until it opens" kind of persistence. That's important, all right, as you can see from a recent survey done by a national association of sales executives: It concluded that 80 percent of the new sales in this country are made by 10 percent of the sales representatives—and that they close those sales only after making five or more calls on the client. But our research shows that another kind of persistence is equally important: the kind that top people show in working on their own selling *methods*.

In the follow-up surveys we do of our corporate program participants, we've observed one fact a hundred times. If you want to predict the next sales representative of the year, the next star regional manager, the next national account executive, find out which salespeople are analyzing their own methodology, which ones are constantly reassessing sales strategy and tactics, which ones are looking for reliable, repeatable methods to improve their competitive edge. An attention to inner process as well as to external change is fundamental to today's (and tomorrow's) sales leaders.

In addition to having a handle on their sales processes and understanding why process is important, all strategic professionals share one other profile characteristic: They're *never satisfied*. This fact helps to explain why the sales representatives and managers who are most excited by our programs, the ones who are most eager to introduce our strategies into their own companies' methodologies, are those who are *already* doing well. And it helps to explain why the firms that these commission leaders work for are also already leading their industries in sales volume.

As we've already mentioned, our clients are drawn primarily from among the most successful corporations in the country. Why do these firms, which are already leading the pack, have us work with their people? Why do many of them spend tens of thousands of dollars so that their salespeople can learn the principles of Strategic Selling? Why do they send their revenue leaders to our programs?

For the paradoxical but very good reason that it's the best who always want to do better. In any selling organization, it's that top 10 percent of individuals with persistence and dedication to their own selling skills who ultimately pay the biggest dividends to the company. So making it possible for that 10 percent to reassess and refine their already good work patterns just makes economic sense. As you go through this book, you'll see that disciplining yourself to follow these top companies' example makes the same kind of practical sense for you.

HOW STRATEGIC SELLING WORKS

What do these people learn in our workshops and programs, and how will you learn the Strategic Selling process from this book?

To begin with, at Miller Heiman we don't cook up any of our selling processes in a lab. Strategic Selling was not derived from a business professor's "optimizing purchasability" model but from our experiences as lifetime sales professionals in the field. In this we are very nearly unique. Sales training programs typically start with a squeaky-clean, highfalutin theory that they then attempt to impose on the facts. We don't do that. Our program is generalizable all right. As our clients can attest, it's been tested in the roughest arena possible, the global economy, during good times and bad, during recessions and booms—and it works. But it works because it's *practically*, not just theoretically, sound. The reason that so many national sales managers send their sales forces to our programs is that we help them fix the nuts and bolts of real situations.

The lessons of this book, therefore, aren't designed to illustrate some abstract "sales philosophy," to impress you with gimmicks, or to give you a briefcase full of five-dollar buzzwords that you can use in the place of Nytol at your next sales meeting. We'll keep the discussion simple and to the point, because the goal of the book is simple and to the point: It's to help you sort through the confusing data associated with every Complex Sale and to give you a reliable method for analyzing that data, for positioning yourself better with your accounts, and for closing business on even your most difficult sales. Among the specific skills that you'll learn from this book are:

1. How to position yourself with the real decision-makers and avoid those without approval power
2. How to spot the two key customer attitudes that can make a sale, and the two that usually break it
3. How to get not only the order but a satisfied customer, repeat sales, and enthusiastic referrals
4. How to increase sales penetration in your current accounts
5. How to minimize the uncertainties of a cold call
6. How to free up a stuck order
7. How to avoid selling business you don't want
8. How to identify and deal with the four different Buying Influences present in every sale
9. How to prevent sales from being sabotaged by an anti-sponsor
10. How to recognize signals that indicate when a sale is in jeopardy
11. How to avoid dry months by allocating time wisely to four critical selling tasks
12. How to track account progress and forecast future revenue

We want you to remember that this is only a sampling of the topics we're going to be covering, and to remember also two major distinctions between our approach and that of sales training programs you may have previously encountered.

First: Our focus is on success, not failure. In trying to avoid failure, many sales training programs actually guarantee it, by emphasizing long lists of things that can go wrong in a sales call, and by blaming the sales representative when they do. We don't want you to concentrate on your shortcomings, and for that reason we focus not on you but rather on your account or prospect: Our goal is to teach you how to understand that account so well that once you get into the sales call, you'll already have dealt with your own uncertainties and be free to devote your attention to making the presentation count.

Second: The work is on *your* accounts and prospects. Most training programs, in an attempt to link theory and practice, give you a series of canned case studies as illustrative material. By working on these hypothetical cases, you're supposed to develop the skills needed to work on your own accounts. When we were designing our programs, we realized that this was a roundabout and inefficient method of getting you to analyze your own situation, so we eliminated the case study approach and zeroed in on our clients' problems directly. This book, like our programs, takes a hands-on approach. Instead of hypothetical situations, you will get a series of Personal Workshops that are based on the workshops we use in our Strategic Selling programs. These will enable you to set strategies for your own accounts and prospects right now.

The people who have been through our programs tell us that this direct, real-case method is one of the most useful and lasting lessons of the experience. One regional manager put it well, months after his people had taken the Strategic Selling program, when he said, "I've been to a lot of different courses. This one my people are really using." Strategic Selling is *designed* to be used, and to be used at once. It's meant to help you deal with *your* stuck orders and trouble accounts, *your* inside saboteurs, *your* dry months and difficult renewals. And it's meant to help you do that right away.

By using the workshop method that we developed in our programs, you'll reap the benefits of your own hands-on experience, and turn those benefits to your advantage even before you finish the book. By the time you come to the last page, you'll be able to say, as so many of our client professionals are now able to say, "It's *the way I go about it* that makes me number one."

CHAPTER 2

STRATEGY AND TACTICS DEFINED

Imagine that you're the coach of the Washington Redskins, and that your team is anticipating an appointment with the Dallas Cowboys. The big game is one week away, and the films of the Dallas team's last couple of games have just come in. Your players are eager to see them so they can start working out game plans, but you've got a better idea. "No films this year, boys," you tell them. "We're going to spend this week working on the basics. Blocking, tackling, running, kicking, passing. We know the Cowboys are good, but by next week we're going to be better. Just concentrate on how hard you're going to hit them once you get onto the field. The rest will take care of itself."

How long would you last in the National Football League with an attitude like that? Maybe two weeks at the outside. In a league as competitive as the NFL, it would be suicide to ignore your pregame planning and devote yourself entirely to "basics." In the world of professional football, analyzing your opponents' moves in advance is as crucial as doing pass pattern drills, and the pro ball coach who neglected such planning would soon be shopping his résumé around on the high school circuit.

The same principle applies to professional selling. Yet, to judge from many sales representatives' reactions when we mention sales strategy, it would seem that "hitting the field with the basics" constitutes their entire sales approach. To many people, the only skills that count are those that emerge in the actual sales call: the tricks of the trade that help you deal effectively with the buyer once you're actually sitting in her office.

In other words, it's still *tactics* that are seen as essential. *Strategy*—by which we mean that process you use to lay out your moves in advance of the sales call—is still considered something of a gimmick: a newfangled, computer-age innovation that doesn't have much to do with how top people really perform in the field.

This limited (and limiting) view of strategy comes partly from the traditional picture of the salesperson as a professional shaker-of-hands, and partly from the influence of sales training programs that specialize in teaching sales call techniques. The old-time salesperson and the trainers who initiate most new sales representatives into their fool's paradise share the view of the salesperson as an "action" individual who would rather be on the road than at a desk any day, and who really comes alive only when the stakes are high and when she is going head to head with a difficult customer. Many of these gung ho counselors see strategy as a waste of time. "Get out there and sell!" is their advice. "Get out and get your hands dirty. You're not paid to sit in the office."

We have nothing against dirty hands and, as we've already said, this book promotes a definitely hands-on approach to selling. Nobody can afford to neglect the face-to-face fundamentals. But the tactical techniques you use in the direct encounter will pay off only if you develop a sound strategy beforehand.

WHY YOU NEED STRATEGY FIRST

Both "strategy" and "tactics" are derived from ancient Greek. To the Greeks, *taktikos* meant "fit for arranging or maneuvering," and it referred to the art of moving forces in battle. *Strategos* was the word for "general." Originally, therefore, strategy was the "art of the general," or the art of setting up forces *before* the battle. In military terms these definitions still apply; with them in mind, you can easily see why strategy must precede tactics in a military setting. Before you can fight at Gettysburg, you've got to get to Pennsylvania.

The same principle applies in the sales arena. The objective of a good sales strategy is to get yourself in the *right place* with the *right people* at the *right time* so that you can make the right tactical presentation. You can accomplish that only by doing your homework first, by logging the desk time that so many salespeople resent, so that once you get into the actual selling event, you're certain to have everything you need to make your presentation count. It was because he didn't have everything he needed that Ray lost the computer sale to Greg. If he had paid more attention to the uncertainties of the sale—in this case, the "hidden" outside consultant and the competition—he might have kept the "sure thing" in his own pocket.

When we ask our program participants what they like best about our program, many of them reply, "It helped me organize my data better." This isn't a surprising answer. Think of the bulk of information you have to deal with in any Complex

Sale. Think of the maze of offices, the overlapping managerial decisions, the games of receptionist roulette, the vice-presidential timetables, the sheer weight of paperwork that has to be attended to before you can close a deal and pocket a commission. If you plunge into the selling situation without having a reliable method of sorting, organizing, and analyzing this vast body of data, you're going to be in the same impossible position as the NFL coach who relies on a "wait until the game" approach to give him a victory.

The mistake that Ray made is a very common one in the Complex Sale. In Chapter 5 we'll look at that mistake in more detail, when we talk about how important it is to distinguish among the various Buying Influences, and to understand how the roles played by these Buying Influences can shift from sale to sale—even sometimes *within* the same sales cycle. Ray discovered how important that was a little too late to help him. So does every other sales representative who displays tactical wizardry at the wrong time or in the wrong place.

You've probably already run into this situation. You walk into Sam Wilson's office and give him a classic textbook presentation. He is suitably awed. "That was terrific!" he says. "I only wish I'd known ahead of time how well your product matches our needs. I would have had June Richards here to approve the sale. I'm sure she would have given the OK, but she's in Nigeria for a month."

Or take an even worse situation. You're in the middle of that brilliant pitch when you suddenly realize by yourself, without being told, that you're talking to the wrong person. And you realize that if you now try to go around him to get to the right person, he's going to cut you off at the knees. Realizing glumly that there's no way to rescue the sale, you walk out of the office mumbling, tactically flush but strategically unwound.

Situations like these are always the result of poor planning, of the salesperson's neglecting to get an important piece of information, and of going into the selling event with an overconfident or otherwise distorted view of reality. Only a strategic approach can provide you with a reliable method of *testing* your impressions of the pending sale at every step of the selling cycle, and therefore of being certain of your position before you begin the presentation. Without this strategic testing, you may act on the basis of what you *wish* were true rather than what *is* true, and find yourself in the ridiculous position of the fellow who lost a quarter in the park but decided to look for it downtown because the light there was better.

We're not saying that strategy is "better than" or "more important than" tactics. They're equally important elements of sales success—and they're inseparable. You can't use tactics effectively outside of a strategic Action Plan, and you can't set good strategies unless you're flexibly responsive to the new planning information that each new tactical encounter gives you. Once you've fully incorporated the principles of Strategic Selling into your work, you'll see that strategy and tactics must work together. We emphasize strategy because it's almost always neglected. And it's the place where every good sales process starts.

LONG-TERM STRATEGY: FOCUS ON THE ACCOUNT

The tendency of "tactics only" salespeople to ignore preparation is only one factor in their undoing. Another is a tendency to focus exclusively on the individual *sale* and to ignore the *account*. As we've already emphasized, it's the *selling event* that occupies the bulk of most representatives' attention.

There's nothing wrong with attending carefully to the selling event—whether it's a phone call, an introductory letter, or the sales call itself—but such attention can create real problems if it leads you to ignore the larger picture.

In a Complex Sale arena, you have short-term and long-term objectives. In the short term, you want to close as many individual pieces of business as you can. In the long term, you want to maintain healthy relations with the customers signing for these deals, so that they'll be willing to make further purchases from you in the months and years to come. It would be great if these two objectives always coincided, but you know that they don't. All of us who make a living in sales can point to business that we wish we hadn't sold—to sales that "seemed like a good idea at the time" but that turned out, down the line, to be liabilities.

You've probably seen this happen yourself in cases where somebody sells a product to a company that cannot really use it well—where the fit between the product and the company's needs simply isn't as exact as the salesperson would like it to be. What do you do in a situation like this? If you confined yourself to the short-term view, you might be inclined to gloss over the bad product fit and go for the instant payoff, your commission. But you wouldn't last very long with that account once the company discovered that it had been sold a bill of goods. You could forget about referrals and repeat business. And you would very soon discover that your tactical victory had turned out to be a strategic defeat.

One of the hardest decisions any sales professional has to make is the decision *not* to close a sale, even though it's possible to do so. One of our major clients faced this decision several years ago, just after completing production on a new computer assembly. The assembly was so sophisticated and difficult to operate that, if it had been put on the market (a market that was very eager to have it), our client would have been deluged in weeks with service calls and angry customers. The company's officers understood this, even though the potential customers did not, and so they made a painful but very savvy decision: They allowed a competing firm to be first in this hungry but inexperienced field. It was the competitor who ended up having to deal with frustrated customers, while our client reaped long-term profits from its caution and discretion.

This story highlights the importance of an account-centered approach. If you concentrate chiefly on tactics, you'll be likely to forget the account, and to go from selling event to selling event as if they were their own rewards. To revert to the military analogy, you'll tend to focus on winning individual battles while forgetting about the war of which these battles are only components. Our strategic approach offsets this self-defeating tendency.

One caveat, though. We do not mean to imply, by using the military terms "battle" and "war," that we see successful selling as a victory of the seller over the buyer. On the contrary. We use the military metaphor purely as a shorthand description. In contrast to what you might have learned earlier in sales training programs, in a successful Complex Sale you never beat the buyer or trick him into signing. That's another problem with the "tactics first" approach and with the "go get 'em" philosophy of many sales trainers. They set you up to keep score, to gauge your success by how many customers you've roped in.

We all know people who relish "sticking it to the customer," who are continually asking themselves, "How can I *con this buyer*?" The question we stress in Strategic Selling is very different. It's "How can I *manage this sale*?" Only by asking that question throughout the sales cycle can you avoid the adversarial view that so often turns tactical success into strategic defeat.

Setting the Account Strategy: Four Steps to Success

Now you're nearly ready to begin setting strategies for your accounts. Before you can do that effectively, though, there's one further principle we have to introduce. It's the principle of a step-by-step approach. We've found that many potentially excellent sales representatives ignore this principle. They "jump squares," thinking that the sooner they reach the end of their selling cycles, the sooner they'll pocket their commissions. This hurried approach almost always results in lost business.

In the following chapters, we'll be introducing what we call the Six Key Elements of effective account strategies. To understand and use them well, you have to keep the step-by-step principle in mind. Each time we introduce a new element, we'll ask you to examine its application to your accounts in a logical, step-by-step fashion. We know you may find this overly meticulous, but our experience shows us that it's necessary. Good strategic analysis reveals a logical sequence. The sequence that we have found effective has four steps:

1. Analyze your current position with regard to your account and with regard to your specific sales objective.
2. Think through possible Alternate Positions.
3. Determine which Alternate Position would best secure your objective and devise an Action Plan to achieve it.
4. Implement your Action Plan.

Since from now on you'll be constantly setting, testing, and revising your sales strategies, you should be referring frequently to these steps. We advise you to run through them in your mind every time we introduce a new Key Element of Strategy, and to use them as a benchmark every time you contemplate a change in the way you're approaching an account.

The four steps will be relevant to your thinking whenever you're trying to make something happen in an account that isn't happening right now. You could be preparing to sell a new product or promotion to an existing account, to qualify a new prospect, to penetrate other divisions of an existing account, or to get back in the door after losing out to a competitor. When we speak about setting account strategies, we're referring to all your selling situations and to all your prospects and accounts—past, present, and future. Strategic thinking is important to them all.

Notice two things about these four steps to success. First: Taken together, they illustrate the importance of constant review—or, to use a contemporary expression, of constant feedback. Review, feedback, reassessment: Whatever you call it, it's essential to good account planning. Second: Notice how frequently the word "position" appears in this four-step design. Understanding your position with regard to a given account is so central to setting good strategies that we often say "having a strategy" and "having a position" are two ways of expressing the same thing. *The whole key to strategy is position.* It tells you where you are now, and where you might have to move in the near or distant future to increase your chances of success with a given objective.

Because the concept of position is so fundamental, that is exactly where we begin the Strategic Selling process. The first thing you'll do in using this book to set a strategy is a Personal Workshop to determine your current position.

Chapter 3

YOUR STARTING POINT: POSITION

To the military strategist, position is a critical element in any campaign plan. The general who doesn't know where he is in relation to the enemy—whether in terms of geography, knowledge of forces, lines of supply, weather, or other factors—is simply setting his people up for the kill. On the battlefield, being in the wrong place at the wrong time can be a fatal error, because no matter how brilliantly an army may perform in a face-to-face encounter, it will never get a fair chance to do so if its leaders don't know where they are or if they're marching off in the wrong direction.

The same principle applies in selling. In account strategy, positioning is the name of the game. What "setting a strategy" really means is doing whatever you have to do to put yourself in the best position to accomplish a particular objective or set of objectives. Of course this can entail a great deal. It can involve all aspects of your selling situation—physical, psychological, economic—with regard to a given account or prospect and a given sales objective. Fully understanding your current position means knowing who all your key players are, how they feel about you, how they feel about your proposal, what questions they want to have answered, and how they see your proposal vis-à-vis their other options. It means in short having a reliable fix on all of your strong and weak points before each selling encounter even begins.

But even if you're foggy on some of these points, even if you're unclear about your position, you nonetheless *have* a strategic position. You *always* have a position, and for that reason you always have a strategy, whether or not you can articulate what it is. If you're not certain where you stand with regard to a given account, you are or soon will be lost—and *that* will be your position.

To avoid the perilous situation of being positioned in the Great Unknown, the first thing you need to do with each account is to make your current position *visible*. Just as a general would find a fix on a map, you have to fix yourself within your current sales situation, so that you will fully understand—as they used to say in the 1960s—"where you're coming from." You're going to do that now, with regard to a specific account and a specific sales objective.

First you need to pick the account or prospect. We don't want you to select one in which everything is going fine. That would defeat the purpose of the workshop and the process. We've designed this book, as we've designed our programs, to help you work through the difficulties of your current sales situations. Therefore, you should choose an account where something isn't quite right. It needn't be one in which everything is falling apart—although if that's the one you want to attack, fine. In the workshop environment clients usually discover that the best kind of account to work on is one in which, although things may look smooth on the surface, you still feel some twinge of uneasiness, uncertainty, or confusion.

You'll be working with this account or prospect throughout the rest of this book, so be sure the one you choose will repay the effort you put into it. Be sure it's one, in other words, where you're really eager to have reliable answers. Eventually, after you learn the principles of Strategic Selling so well that they become second nature, you'll be using them to set strategies for *all* your accounts. But for this first run-through, you'll be focusing on a single important piece of business. By the time you finish the book, you'll have analyzed all the elements of this one account and have devised an Action Plan for making your strategic position with it more visible and more effective than it is now.

Once you've decided on an account, you'll need the following tools: a spiral notebook (the side-bound school type rather than the top-bound stenographer's type), some pencils, and some highlighting devices. In our programs, we use small Red Flag and Strength stickers as highlighters; you can use similar gum-backed stickers or a Magic Marker. Find a place where you can work without distractions and give yourself about twenty or thirty minutes to think about your account position. Then work through the following Personal Workshop. It has been designed to identify the causes of your current uncertainty, to help you see how those causes affect your current sales objective, and to allow you to make your position with the account more visible.

Personal Workshop 1: Position

This workshop is divided into five steps. In the first step, you identify the particular changes in your sales environment that may affect your handling of the account.

STEP 1: IDENTIFY RELEVANT CHANGES.

Position would be a minor problem if you didn't have to deal with change, and more importantly with the uncertainty that change often makes us feel. In Chapter 1 we observed that it isn't change in itself that causes stress and disorientation, but the uncertainty of not knowing how to react to it. You probably can't do very much to stop the changes that you're now experiencing in your selling environment, but identifying those changes is a necessary first step in being able to deal with them more productively.

So take out your pencil and write the heading "Change" at the top of a left-hand page of your notebook. Then make a list, in no particular order, of all the changes that *you* feel are influencing the way you currently do business. Next to each one, as an extra check on your understanding of the change, note whether it is a sudden event, a longer process of subtle erosion, or an example of continuous growth. Don't worry about being exhaustive or "correct" in your choices. You're not taking a test. You're writing down what you observe to be happening. The best standard by which to measure the impact of changes in your business environment isn't necessarily the *Wall Street Journal*'s latest front-page story, but the way you are *feeling*, day to day, about your work.

Since the national economy affects the way all of us do our jobs, some of the changes you list will no doubt be the stuff of nightly news reports. Others will be specific to your industry, your market, your geographical base. Whatever *you* consider a significant change should go on this list. If you spend about five minutes on this step, you shouldn't have any trouble coming up with eight or ten significant changes. Commonly, in our programs, participants list twenty or more.

STEP 2: RATE THESE CHANGES AS THREATS OR OPPORTUNITIES.

Now go down your list of changes and put an O next to those you perceive mainly as opportunities and a T next to those you see mainly as threats. If you're like most sales representatives, you'll probably be hesitant about this. As our clients tell us all the time, practically any change can be seen as both a threat and an opportunity: It all depends on how you react to it. That's true, but we're not judging your potential reaction here. We're trying to develop an overview of your current position with your account. So as you debate the threats and opportunities, start from where you are *today*. Is the change you're thinking about, right now, primarily positive or primarily negative?

The question will be easier to answer for some changes than for others. If you're experiencing a drastic shift in customer loyalty from your products or services to a competitor's, it's not hard to identify that as a threat. If your engineers have just developed a new assembly technique that will dramatically cut your production costs, this could easily be seen as an economic opportunity. But if a major customer is moving toward single sourcing, this is a change whose impact might go either way, depending on your company's position on a preferred vendor list. Only you know your situation intimately enough to make reasonable decisions about rating the changes plus or minus. Just be sure to concentrate on how you see these changes *today*. Take about another five minutes here. When you've made your list, put it aside. We'll be returning to it in a moment.

STEP 3: DEFINE YOUR CURRENT SINGLE SALES OBJECTIVE.

Now, on the facing right-hand page of your notebook, write down your current sales objective with regard to the account you've chosen. We need to clarify what we mean by current. You always have a long-term objective with any account, which is to keep the decision-makers in that account satisfied with your relationship, and therefore ready to do more business with you. But you also have specific, short-term objectives that change from sales period to sales period, and very often even more quickly than that. Salespeople typically call these objectives "sales" or "orders" or "deals" or "pieces of business." In Strategic Selling we call them Single Sales Objectives. Pick one Single Sales Objective that you're pursuing in your chosen account right now. Define it briefly but precisely, and write it down.

In being precise, you should include in your definition exactly *what* you're trying to sell the account, *when* you expect final approval, and if possible *what quantity* you expect the customer to order. Don't say: "Get Newberry chain to buy sofas." Specify which sofas, how many, and when: "Get Newberry chain to order trial package of 100 Slumber Line sofas by June 1." It may strike you as belaboring the obvious to do this, but we have a reason for asking you to be precise. Our work as managers has taught us that many salespeople, working on a hundred things at once, often create problems for themselves by lumping together two or more Single Sales Objectives. Since even two closely related objectives may have quite different sets of decision-makers, this fusion often leads to confusion, and objectives are lost because the salesperson doesn't know what they are.

The bottom line is this: *Every piece of business is unique.*

It's easier to keep that fundamental fact in mind if you remember that every Single Sales Objective always has the following characteristics:

- It's *specific* and *measurable*. It gives numerically precise answers to the questions who, what, and how much.
- It's tied to a time line. That is, it defines exactly *when* you expect the order to close.
- It focuses on a specific *outcome* that you're trying to bring about in a specific account. It answers the question "What am I trying to make happen in this account that isn't happening right now?"
- It's *single* rather than multiple. Each Single Sales Objective can be defined in a simple rather than a compound sentence. In a sentence where the connector "and" is lurking in the middle, you've probably got two, not one, Single Sales Objectives.

We're not suggesting, when you're working in a large account, that it's desirable or even possible to go after only one piece of business at a time. In corporate selling you're always pursuing multiple opportunities. But in setting strategies, it's got to be one "battle" at a time, because each Complex Sale has its own unique configuration, and you have to design a separate positioning for each one. Breaking a complicated account out into multiple Single Sales Objectives helps you give each potential order the unique attention it deserves. This is essential to keeping your information under control and well organized.

If, like many sales representatives, you're unclear about your current objective, note this as a possible cause of your general uneasiness about the account. To help you define the immediate objective, write down briefly what you're doing with the account right now, and what you'd like to be doing with it by the end of the next sales period. Think of other objectives you could be pursuing at this time, and which of them would be most gratifying to you not only in terms of immediate commission, but also in terms of maintaining good relationships with the account. And take your time. Our program participants tell us constantly that taking a few minutes to think about what they're trying to do with their accounts almost always helps to reduce their confusion. They find out that they knew things about the account, and about their approach to it, that they weren't aware they knew. And they discover gray areas—areas where they should have information, but don't.

When you've defined your Single Sales Objective, look at it side by side with your list of "Changes." How does each change on your list affect your current sales objective? Are the changes that you've marked as threats creating problems for you in attaining this objective now? Are the ones you've marked as opportunities making it easier for you to attain it? Or can you see some way, now that you're relating these changes to a Single Sales Objective, in which they could be turned to your advantage? The purpose here is to help you define specifically the connections between general changes and your immediate goal. Doing this won't alter the environment, but it may help to reduce your uneasiness by making you more *conscious* of what's happening.

STEP 4: TEST YOUR CURRENT POSITION.

The next step in clarifying the situation is to test your current position: to find out how you feel overall about your prospects in this account and about your specific chances for making this objective work out. Ask yourself the following question: "How do I feel *right now* about closing this piece of business?" Be brutally realistic, and listen to your gut. Your feelings are not the whole story, but they're a necessary start.

To help our clients define how they feel about this question, we ask them to identify their position along what we call the Euphoria-Panic Continuum.

We've reproduced it here:

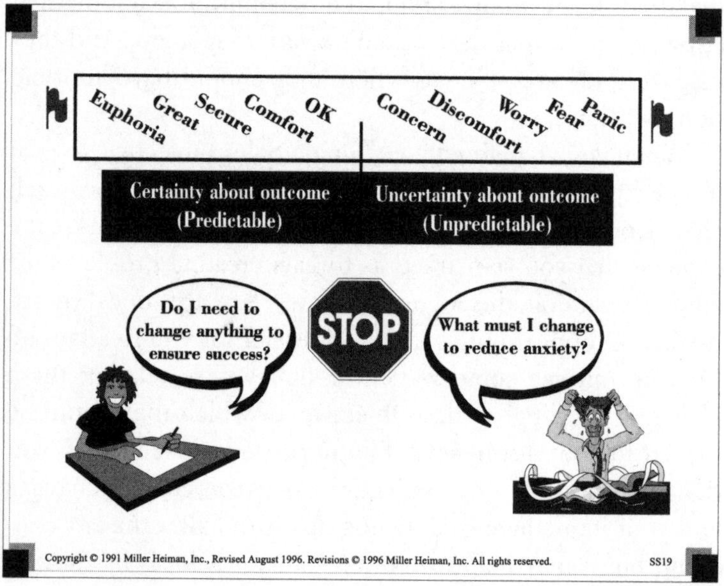

You may feel that none of the adjectives we've listed on the continuum exactly describe your feelings, and if that's so, fine: supply your own. This is not a multiple-choice test, but a guide for you to determine where, along a line from euphoria to panic, you feel you belong. Whether you use your own words or ours, the point is for you to define how good (how close to euphoria) or how bad (how close to panic) you feel right now.

The use of the Euphoria-Panic Continuum seems straightforward enough, but we do want to add a few comments so that you'll get maximum benefit from this exercise. First: Be straight with yourself. Unless there's absolutely nothing wrong with your current situation (which happens only in Never-Never-Land), identifying how you feel about it is like locating symptoms of trouble by sensing pain in your body. Your uneasy or worried feelings about the situation signal you that something is "off." Don't ignore the signal and don't kid yourself. Don't simply put on a brave front, adopt a "positive" or "winning" attitude, and forge ahead as if everything were fine. If you don't treat your feelings about your accounts seriously, you'll be like the football player who "plays through pain" with the use of painkillers, and ends up in the hospital because he couldn't feel himself being hurt.

Second: It's just as dangerous to be blissfully happy about your account as it is to be in a panic mode. If you find yourself at *either* end of the continuum, be wary: You're probably being unrealistic in your assessment. You cannot function well in either a euphoric or a panic state. In the former you tend to do nothing because you think things are already perfect. In the latter you do everything and anything you can, and most of it has no impact. In either case you're out of touch with reality.

In fact, the person who's euphoric and the one who's in a panic are really much closer than they think, in terms of how they're probably handling their accounts. We illustrate this in our programs by drawing the Euphoria-Panic Continuum not as a straight line, but as a nearly closed circle. When we draw the continuum this way, you can see that the distance from euphoria to panic can be very short. As our frantic little graphic on page 62 indicates, it is often no more than a single phone call away.

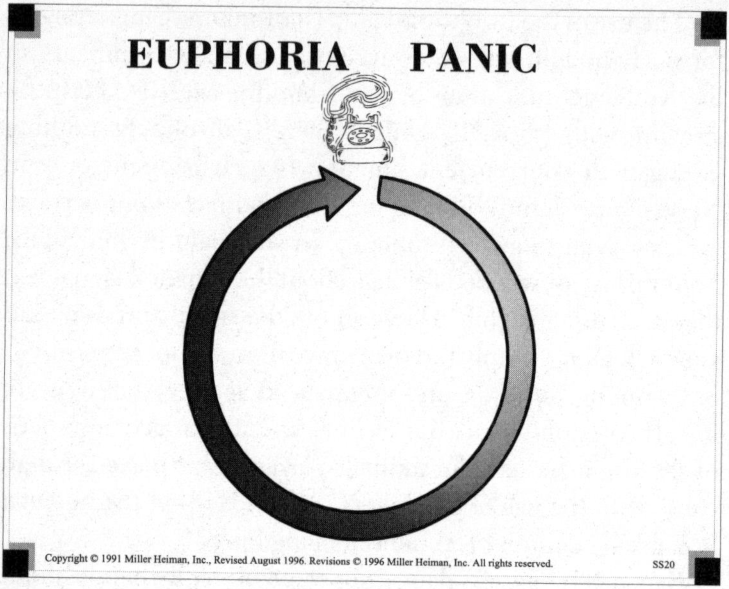

Euphoria, left unchecked, leads to complacency; complacency leads to arrogance; and arrogance inevitably leads to disaster. The cocksure sales representative always overlooks "trivial" pieces of information that indicate the sale is in danger—and soon ends up in a state of panic.

The distance *back* from panic to euphoria, unfortunately, isn't nearly so short. Once you've fallen into panic, you have to work your way back slowly, going through the whole long circle of reality until you're feeling confident again. So be very suspicious of euphoria. As a regional manager in a tough Eastern market once told us, "I want my competition to get euphoric. That's when I've got my best shot."

The final point to notice about the continuum is that it isn't a predictive device, merely a descriptive one. Its purpose is to let you test your strategy, or position, *up to this point* by allowing you to gauge your emotional reactions to the situation. Throughout the rest of this book you'll be making adjustments to your strategy that will move you to the left of the continuum if you're now far off to the right, and ensure that you stay where you are, in spite of changing conditions, if you're already feeling good. As conditions change, you'll be reassessing your position many times. The continuum is designed to help you do that efficiently.

STEP 5: EXAMINE ALTERNATE POSITIONS.

Once you know where you are, you next want to know where to go. In terms of the four steps we outlined in the last chapter, you've now finished the first one, analyzing your current position. Now you need to examine alternatives, to discover how you might *reposition* yourself to make the attainment of your Single Sales Objective more likely.

The entire rest of this book will help you to identify and take Alternate Positions. Right now, we want you to focus on what you already know, and to think about areas of possible change—areas in which something *you* do can counteract the environmental changes that are causing you distress. You'll notice that on the continuum, a predictable, successful outcome is more likely if you find yourself on the left than if you find yourself on the right. But this is only a likelihood, and it too is subject to change. The significant thing to observe at this point is that, no matter how you're feeling about your current account and sales situation, you still must consider change—that is, change that *you* bring about.

The stop sign in the diagram is meant to point you to that necessity. If you're on the right side of the continuum, you need to consider changes in your position so that you can reduce anxiety. If you're on the left, you need to consider changes that will ensure continued success. So stop now for a few minutes. Put your pencil down and look at what you have. Look over your list of "Changes" and at how they relate to your objective. Look at that objective itself: Have you identified it clearly for yourself, or is it an area for possible change? Finally, review how you feel about the account and the objective in question. What changes, in the account or in the environment, would make you feel better than you do? And what can you do right now to bring that about?

To make your options more visible, turn to another page of your notebook and write the heading "Alternate Positions." Then list the things you can do to improve your position. *Save this list.* You'll be revising it throughout the book. At this point, it's likely to be short. That's fine. Learning that you don't yet have all the answers is itself a positive strategic achievement.

Now that you've spent half an hour thinking about the effect of outside changes on your position, you should be more certain about *where* you're uncertain, even if you don't know what to do next. You're in the position of the house carpenter who knows that the south wall needs work, but needs a blueprint before he starts using his tools. Hold on to your tools and to all the information you've collected in this workshop. You're going to start building a strategy, and we're going to give you the blueprint.

CHAPTER 4

A GLANCE AT THE STRATEGY BLUEPRINT: THE SIX KEY ELEMENTS OF STRATEGIC SELLING

You've just done a Personal Workshop to make your position regarding your current sales objective more visible. You've identified areas of uncertainty and drawn up a list of Alternate Positions that you might take to broaden your strategic options. We've acknowledged that this options list is likely to be short. We're now going to give you the blueprint you need to expand and revise it, so that by the end of the book you'll have turned it into a working paper for a strategic Action Plan.

That Action Plan will grow out of not one but many Alternate Positions. There's never only one correct strategy for a sales objective, but always a choice of options. Indeed, as a sales professional you'll commonly have to adopt several strategies—to change your position several times—between your first meeting with a key player and the successful close of any sale. The blueprint we're going to give you will help you do that with a minimum of trial and error, and with the greatest possible understanding of *all* the sale's elements.

In our years of coaching sales leaders in a vast array of businesses, we've found that every good sales strategy always attends to six such elements. These Six Key Elements of Strategic Selling are the fundamental analytic tools you need to move from the position you've just defined to any Alternate Position of greater strength. The Six Key Elements are:

1. Buying Influences
2. Red Flags/Leverage from Strength
3. Response Modes
4. Win-Results
5. Ideal Customer Profile
6. Sales Funnel

Future chapters will show you in detail and with examples how to bring these Six Key Elements together into a tested, practical strategy for sales success. In this chapter we're just going to define our basic terms, to give you an overview of the entire blueprint. Treat the chapter in that way—as an overview or glance. Don't "study" it or take notes or worry about unfamiliar concepts. Just give it a quick run-through, to get a basic feel for the tools you'll be using.

As you do so, keep one thing in mind. We present the Six Key Elements to you in the same sequence we use in our Strategic Selling workshops, because we've discovered that it makes the material accessible in the most orderly fashion. Don't infer from this numerical presentation that they are ranked in order of importance. On the contrary. The element of Buying Influences is discussed first, for example, because you can't fully understand the other five elements without it. But the Six Key Elements are equally essential to your success. The only proper way to use them is *interactively, as a system.*

KEY ELEMENT 1: BUYING INFLUENCES

We've defined a Complex Sale as one in which several people have to give their approval or input before the sale can go through. Identifying *all* those people accurately, and understanding the role that each of them plays in getting you to your sales objectives, are two of the major stumbling blocks for salespeople—even very good salespeople—in the Complex Sale.

Many sales managers address the problem of identifying key players by telling their sales representatives to get in touch with "my old buddy Jim" or to find out the department manager's name. They concentrate on the individuals who have been important in previous sales, who are "friends," or whose position or title in the buying organization suggests that they're key.

We take a more sophisticated approach. Since corporate structures today are in constant flux, we tell our clients to begin their strategy by looking not for people, but for *roles*. Then, we say, look for the people playing those roles for a specific sales objective—without being distracted by their titles.

In every Complex Sale, there are *four* critical buying roles. We call the people who play these roles *Buying Influences*, or, more simply, *Buyers*.

To head off a potential misunderstanding, we need to emphasize right away that we *don't* use the capitalized word "Buyer" in the conventional sense, to indicate a department store's "dry goods buyer" or a manufacturing division's "purchasing agent." We know that "buyer" commonly implies someone whose job involves designated purchasing responsibilities, but we use the term quite differently.

When we use the capitalized terms "Buyer" and "Buying

Influence," we are referring to people who play one of the *four buying roles*. There may be four, or fourteen, or forty people in the buying organization who can influence a given sale, but each one of these people always plays at least one of the four Buying Influence roles. We define them as follows:

- *Economic Buying Influence.* The role of the person who will act as Economic Buyer for your sales objective is to give *final* approval to buy. There is always only one person or set of people playing this role for a given sales objective. The Economic Buyer can say yes when everybody else has said no, as well as veto a deal that everybody else has approved.
- *User Buying Influences.* The role of User Buyers is to make judgments about the potential impact of your product or service on their job performance. User Buyers will use or supervise the use of your product or service, and so their personal success is directly tied to the success of your solution. There may be several people playing User Buyer roles in a sale.
- *Technical Buying Influences.* The role of Technical Buyers is to screen out possible suppliers. Their focus is on the product or service itself, and they make recommendations based on how well it meets a variety of objective specifications. Technical Buyers can't give a final yes, but they can (and often do) give a final no. As with User Buyers, there are usually several people playing the role of Technical Buyer for a given sales objective.
- *Coach.* The unique and very special role of a Coach is to guide you to your particular sales objective by leading you to the other Buyers and by giving you information that you need to position yourself effectively with each one. You usually (although not always) find the other three Buyers

in the buying organization. Coaches are different. They may be found in the buying organization, in your own organization, or outside of them both. Your Coach's focus is on helping you to make *this* sale.

Understanding these four Buying Influence roles—and then identifying all the people playing them with regard to your sales goal—is the foundation of Strategic Selling.

KEY ELEMENT 2: RED FLAGS/LEVERAGE FROM STRENGTH

The story of Ray in the first chapter showed that even experienced salespeople can make fatal mistakes in positioning. When sales representatives or managers fail to spot them in time, to understand why they've arisen, or to take them seriously, they can be disastrous to the sale. Our second Key Element of strategy helps you to identify your positioning difficulties with precision *before* they throw your business in the competition's lap.

We've chosen the symbol of a Red Flag to highlight areas of strategy that need further attention. We use the Red Flag device for the same reason that a road crew does—because it means "warning" or "danger." We want you to think of the uncertainties and problems in your sales in just that way: not as minor annoyances, but as hazards that can jeopardize the sale. In our presentation of the second Key Element, we identify common sales situations that you should consider automatic Red Flag areas. And we stress that Red Flags are *positive*, because they help you identify trouble before it finds you.

The Red Flag device, which you'll be using throughout

this book, is one of two principal ways in which you will test the effectiveness of Alternate Positions. The other way can be seen as the Red Flag's mirror image. It's the principle we call Leverage from Strength, and it's represented in our programs by a barbell icon. When you lever from a Strength, you highlight areas that differentiate you from the competition as a way of offsetting or minimizing threats to your strategic position. Every sound Alternate Position either leverages from a Strength, eliminates a Red Flag, or (ideally) does both at the same time. You'll be practicing these two halves of the second Key Element interactively in all the remaining Personal Workshops in the book.

Key Element 3: Response Modes

If the foundation of your strategy is knowing who your key Buying Influences are, the next thing you need to know is how they feel about your proposal. In Strategic Selling, you determine that by identifying their current receptivity to *change*, specifically the change to their business that your proposal represents.

In the workshop you just did, you saw that change can be a critical factor in the way you view the sales environment, and that it's always possible to perceive change as positive, negative, or a mixture of the two. But change doesn't happen just to you. It impacts each of your Buying Influences as well. Understanding *their* perceptions of change is what helps you to predict their level of buyer receptivity.

There are always four possible reactions to change that a Buyer can have in a given selling situation. We call these reactions *Response Modes*. They're determined by:

1. The Buyer's perception of the immediate business situation.
2. The Buyer's perception of how your proposal is likely to change that situation.
3. The Buyer's perception of whether or not that change will close a gap, or discrepancy, between what's seen as the current reality and the results needed. No matter how good a match there is between your proposal and those "objective" needs, no Buyer will be receptive to change unless he or she first recognizes such a discrepancy.

In the first Response Mode, *Growth*, the Buyer does perceive this essential discrepancy, and feels that the gap between current reality and the desired results can be closed only if quantity can be increased, quality improved, or both. A Buyer in Growth Mode will thus be receptive to you, provided you can show that your proposal will make it possible to do *more* or *better*.

The second Response Mode is called *Trouble*. A Buyer in Trouble Mode also sees a reality-results discrepancy, but it's a discrepancy on the down side. Something in the business environment has caused a deviation from the planned course; therefore the Buyer needs help and will welcome any change that promises to take away the source of the problem. Here you have another good candidate for a sale—provided you can show that your proposal will *quickly* eliminate the discrepancy.

The third Response Mode is called *Even Keel*. A Buyer in Even Keel perceives no discrepancy between current reality and the hoped-for results, and is therefore perfectly satisfied with the status quo. Since Buyers in Even Keel have no incentive to change, the probability of selling them change is very low. Buyers in Even Keel consistently demonstrate the truth of the maxim "No discrepancy, no sale."

The same thing is true, only more so, for the Buyer in the fourth Response Mode, *Overconfident*. A Buyer who is in Overconfident Mode perceives reality as being far better than the hoped-for results. Overconfident Buyers are therefore totally unreceptive to change, and your chances of changing their minds are practically nil.

In Strategic Selling we stress that the four Response Modes are not descriptions of overall attitude or personality, but rather of the way in which individual Buying Influences see a given sales situation, and a given sales proposal, at any particular moment. Changing business conditions can move a Buyer from Overconfident to Trouble Mode extremely quickly, and the strategic salesperson has to be ready to capitalize on such shifts.

Key Element 4: Win-Results

You already know that we believe the smart salesperson never thinks of selling as a battle or of customers as enemies to be beaten. It's possible to get an order by tricking or pressuring your customers into signing, but when you do that you are making them Lose, that is, allowing yourself to Win at their expense. This is an extremely shortsighted strategy. A customer whom you've beaten in this way will get out, get even, or do both. In the short run, you may not care. But in terms of the long-range management of that customer's account, you'll be kidding yourself even more than you've kidded the customer: An order that you get by "beating the buyer" nearly always turns out to be business that you wish you hadn't sold.

In Strategic Selling we look beyond the individual order. We concentrate on the account, and we help you to develop ever widening networks of quality sales and new prospects.

We make the assumption that, as a sales professional, you're interested not only in the order, but also in:

- Satisfied customers
- Long-term relationships
- Repeat business
- Good referrals

The only way to ensure that you'll get these things—the only way to keep every one of your accounts productive over time—is to approach every one of your Buying Influences as a potential partner in your success rather than an adversary to be overcome. It's to concentrate on developing "Win-Win" outcomes.

There are only four possible outcomes to every buy/sell encounter:

1. In the first, or Win-Win, scenario, both you and the Buyer "Win." That is, you both come out of the sale feeling satisfied, knowing that neither of you has taken advantage of the other and that both of you have profited, personally and professionally, from the transaction.
2. In the second, or Win-Lose, scenario, you Win at the Buyer's expense. You feel good about the sale, but he's already looking for revenge, or at least how to avoid you and your company in the future.
3. In the third, or Lose-Win, scenario, you allow the Buyer to Win at your expense by "buying the business." You provide a special discount or free time or other services in hopes of a return favor in the future. Often, it never comes.
4. In the final, or Lose-Lose, scenario, both you and the Buyer Lose. Even though you get the order, neither of you feels good about the sale.

Of these four scenarios, only one can bring you the long-term success that you want. That is the Win-Win, "partnership" scenario. But you cannot achieve that scenario just with good intentions. Unless they're actively *managed* into a Win-Win outcome, both Win-Lose and Lose-Win ultimately, and inevitably, degenerate into Lose-Lose.

To be able to manage all of your sales into the Win-Win scenario, you have to go beyond the conventional wisdom about why people buy. Many sales-training programs act on the premise that people buy when you demonstrate to them that you can meet their immediate business needs. Such programs are product-oriented. The trainers who use them pack sales representatives' heads full of data about the features and benefits of the product, and then send them out to collect orders from people who "can't help but be impressed" with the product's advantages.

Of course you need sound product knowledge, but to a sales professional that's not enough, because the reason that people *really* buy is only indirectly related to product or service performance. For that reason, we don't focus on the product. Instead, we show you how to use your product knowledge to hook up to your Buying Influences' *personal* reasons for buying. You can't just meet their business needs. You have to serve their individual, subjective needs as well. You do that by giving them what we call Win-Results.

A *Result*, as we define it, is the impact that your product or service can have on the Buyer's business processes. The product-oriented salesperson sells Results alone.

A *Win* is a less widely recognized, but equally important, factor in buying psychology. It's a personal gain that satisfies an individual Buyer's perceived self-interest.

A *Win-Result*, finally, is a Result that gives one of your individual Buying Influences a Win. Win-Results are the real reason that people buy. We show you how to determine them, how to draft a Win-Results Statement for each Buying Influence, and why delivering Win-Results consistently is fundamental to your success.

KEY ELEMENT 5: THE IDEAL CUSTOMER PROFILE

Every sales representative you know, no matter how successful, has up to 35 percent poor prospects working at any given moment—prospects that will be impossible to close or, if they're closed, will eventually become liabilities. That may seem like a surprisingly high percentage—but just think of how many times since you began selling you've heard someone say, "I wish I'd never closed that order." Think of how many times you've said it to yourself.

Salespeople end up regretting orders for a simple reason. Somewhere during the sales cycle, they allowed themselves to be seduced by the old saw "Any sale is a good sale." They allowed themselves to believe that it's quantity, not quality, that counts. And so they ended up selling a customer with a poor or nonexistent match to their product or service.

As we've just mentioned, you *can* sell a customer who perceives the sale as a Lose, but you're risking your own neck as much as the customer's when you do so. Our fifth Key Element carries that observation to its logical conclusion by introducing a concept we call Ideal Customer. Its function is to help you in identifying your real best prospects and in separating them from the ones who will prove liabilities. Selling to everyone indiscriminately is bound to create bad matches and bad orders. Judging your actual customers against an Ideal Customer Profile will keep those bad orders to a minimum, and ensure that the bulk of your sales have a Win-Win outcome.

We use the Ideal Customer Profile both to anticipate problems in our current customer base and as a sorting device that helps us to cut down on that 35 percent of prospects that we probably shouldn't be working with in the first place. You'll do the same thing in this book. You'll make up your own Ideal Customer Profile by analyzing the characteristics common to your current and past good customers. Then you'll use it to test opportunities with your current sales prospects.

This will leave you with a shorter list of prospects than the one you have now. But the shorter list will be *real*. It will allow you to focus on those objectives that can be achieved with a minimum amount of aggravation in the shortest period of time. Concentrating on them is what is going to keep you Win-Win.

Key Element 6: The Sales Funnel

Before they come to our programs, even our most successful clients find that their sales figures tend to be way up one quarter and way down the next. They experience what we call the Roller Coaster Effect, in which a January bonanza is followed by a seemingly inevitable April slump. In the words of a West Coast regional manager who has sent us hundreds of his people, "Before I send them to you, practically every one of them dreams of putting two great quarters together back to back."

As he's discovered, and as you'll discover, this doesn't have to be a dream. There's a reason for the Roller Coaster Effect, and there's a way to avoid it. In our discussion of the sixth Key Element, we show you a method for managing *all* your sales objectives, and *all* your accounts, so that you can fulfill the dream of having regular, consistent income.

That method involves the use of a conceptual tool that we developed as sales managers, and that we have used with excellent results not only in our own business but in all the businesses that hire us to help their people. We call it the Sales Funnel.

The funnel metaphor may not be entirely new to you. Many salespeople talk about throwing prospects and leads into the "pipeline" or "hopper" or "funnel" and then waiting for orders to come out the other end. The difference between our use of the Sales Funnel and theirs is that we don't wait. We actively and methodically *work* the Funnel, so that the prospects that make it through to the order do so on a predictable basis.

The Sales Funnel enables you to use your most precious commodity, your selling time, in the wisest and most efficient manner possible. You know that selling time is a resource that's always in short supply. What you may not know—or may not have articulated consciously—is that every successful sale involves four different kinds of selling work. If you don't divide your time efficiently among these four kinds of work, you can easily end up squandering what little time you have. The Sales Funnel will help you to identify the type of work you need to be doing at any given moment on each sales objective, and to bring about a balance among the four types. It will also help you determine how much time you should allocate to each type of work, on a regular basis, to ensure predictable revenue.

A Final Word of Introduction

You'll probably recognize the use of a customer qualifying profile as an example of a marketing-oriented approach to sales. We encourage the people we work with to think in marketing terms rather than in "product first" terms because, as we've been stressing, the Strategic Selling process focuses on the *account*. We want you to be successful with your accounts not just for this sales period but for as long as you have them. You do that by really *selling to need*, not just paying it lip service. All the Six Key Elements of the blueprint are designed to help you assess your customers' needs accurately, so that you can deliver them Win-Results on a predictable, consistent basis. Satisfying their needs in this way, experience proves, is also the surest way to satisfy your own.

You've now done all the preliminary work you need to do to understand the principles of Strategic Selling. We've introduced the concept of the Complex Sale and explained why you need to plan both strategy and tactics to manage it effectively. You've made a preliminary assessment of your current position with regard to a particular sales objective, and you've started to consider Alternate Positions to make the attainment of that objective more predictable. Finally, we've presented in outline form the Six Key Elements of strategy that you'll use as a blueprint.

We know you have questions. We know you want details of the blueprint filled in, and we know you're anxious to begin applying it to your current sales objectives. So let's get started.

PART 2

BUILDING ON BEDROCK: LAYING THE FOUNDATION OF STRATEGIC ANALYSIS

CHAPTER 5

KEY ELEMENT 1: BUYING INFLUENCES

Your strategy can begin only when you know who the players are. Therefore, the first Key Element of the strategy you're going to start developing now is to identify *all* the relevant players for your sales objective. For now you'll continue to work with the objective that you chose in Chapter 3. But the methodology for using this Key Element will also apply to every sales objective you tackle from here on.

Identifying the relevant players may seem like an obvious first step. It is obvious. It's also frequently mismanaged—with predictable results. Because most sales training programs emphasize tactical rather than strategic skills, even very good salespeople sometimes find themselves cut out of a sale at the last minute because they failed to locate or cover all the real decision-makers for that specific sale. Unfortunately, most trainers pay little attention to this initial task of identification. Assuming that their salespeople already know whose approvals they need, they concentrate on explaining how to deal with those individuals when they meet them.

We don't make that assumption. Experience has taught us that, if left to find the key players on their own, many sales representatives simply end up talking to the people with whom they feel most comfortable, who have approved their orders in the past, or who have the "right" titles on their doors. None of these "methods" of identification is reliable. Even if one of them leads you to the right players for a given sale, it cannot help you understand *why* they were the right players, and why they were right *for that sale only*. They're not reliable, repeatable methods of finding out whose approvals count.

The reason this matters is that, in today's corporate sales arena, the names and faces of the players are in constant flux. You may understand who the relevant players were in a ten-thousand dollar sale you made to the Williamson Tool and Die Company in November. It doesn't follow that you know the right people to contact for a fifty-thousand-dollar sale—or even another ten-thousand-dollar sale—to the same account the following March. *Every sales objective is unique.* No matter how well you know the players in a given account, you still need a systematic method for locating the correct ones for the Single Sales Objective you're currently working on.

In Strategic Selling we do this by focusing not on what changes from sale to sale but on what is universal and constant.

Focus on Buying Roles

No matter how many people are involved in a buying decision, and no matter what official functions they play in their organization, the same *four buying roles* are present in every Complex Sale. The people who play these roles, who may number far more than four, are the key players that we call *Buying Influences*, or *Buyers*.

As we mentioned in Chapter 4, we use the term "Buyer" very differently from the way it's usually used. When you see "Buyer" capitalized in this book, don't read it as "dry goods buyer," "purchasing agent," or anything else that suggests merely a person with purchasing authority. We use "Buyer" as shorthand for the term "Buying Influence." In Strategic Selling, a Buying Influence, or Buyer, is *anyone* who can influence the outcome of your sale—whatever the title on that person's door.

True, some purchasing agents do play a Buying Influence role in many sales. But others do not. Even more to the point, *most* of the people who will act as Buyers in your sales won't have anything to do with "purchasing" or "buying" per se. In addition, in some sales scenarios, certain players may take on more than one of the four key "Buyer" roles.

In order to sort through the tangles of authority that inevitably result from situations like this, the first thing you have to do in setting an effective sales strategy is to *position* yourself effectively with *all* of the people playing *each* of the four roles. This involves three steps:

1. Understanding the four Buying Influence roles that are common to *every* Complex Sale
2. Identifying all the key players in each of these four roles for *your* specific sales objective
3. Ensuring that all of these players are "covered"—that is, that you fully understand and have dealt with their attitudes toward your proposal

To understand why we focus on roles rather than on comfort level, past contacts, or titles, consider a sports analogy. In football, the lineman who stands in front of the quarterback has a clearly defined position, or "title." He's the center, and his primary role, on most plays, is to snap the ball and then block. On a fourth-down kick, however, his role changes. After the snap, he's still called the center, but the role he's expected to play is that of defensive tackler. If you think the distinction is merely semantic, consider what would happen to a punt receiver who, confronted by a charging 280-pound lineman, said to himself, "I don't have to worry about this guy. He just snaps the ball."

In the Complex Sale no less than in football, a given player in an account can shift roles quickly and unpredictably, even though the player's title and official function on the buying "team" remain the same. A purchasing agent who has routinely approved your three previous sales objectives may suddenly be unable to do so—unable to play her usual role—if your fourth sale is for double the usual order, or for a new product or service. A financial officer who has never been remotely involved in your orders may suddenly become a key Buying Influence because corporate headquarters has just changed its capital expenditure protocols. Focusing on the four Buying Influence roles that are filled in every Complex Sale will help you weave your way through the corporate labyrinths of your accounts and get to the real Buying Influences for *your unique objectives*.

The four Buying Influences that need to be identified and covered in every sale are the Economic Buying Influence, the User Buying Influence(s), the Technical Buying Influence(s), and your Coach(es). Each has a different business focus—that is, a different point of view regarding your proposal and a different reason for considering it. And each one must be sold to close the deal.

THE ECONOMIC BUYING INFLUENCE

The Economic Buyer is the person who gives *final* approval to buy your product or service. The role of this Buying Influence is *to release the dollars to buy*. For that reason, we sometimes say that the Economic Buyer exercises the Golden Rule: "Whoever has the gold makes the rules." This person can say yes where everybody else has said no. He or she can also veto everybody else's yes.

THE ECONOMIC BUYER'S FOCUS—AND IMPORTANCE

We don't call this Buying Influence the Economic Buyer because his or her major concern is the cost of the sale. The focus is never price per se, but *price performance*. Since the Economic Buyer has a discretionary use of funds, if your product or service matches the firm's priority needs and is good value for the money, he or she can adjust the budget to find or release unallocated funds. The ultimate focus—the ultimate business reason this person will buy—is the bottom-line impact you can make on the organization

Although the identity of the person filling the role of Economic Buying Influence may change from sale to sale within the same account, there's always only *one* Economic Buyer per sale. Even though many others may give recommendations and advice, only one person gives final approval. That's why it's critical to find out who gives the final yes for *your* sale.

One clarification: The role of Economic Buyer may be played by a board, a selection committee, or another decision-making body acting as a single entity. But even when such a group is involved, there's usually one person within the group who is first among equals and whose "final final" approval is essential. You always have to determine, when you're selling to such a group, who really has direct access to the funds. It may not be the best strategy for you to contact this individual personally, but it's always your responsibility as "director of strategy" for the sale to identify accurately the single person filling the Economic Buyer role.

Failing to do so can be fatal, as an American airplane manufacturer found out recently when it tried to sell a consignment of jets to a Middle Eastern country. Everybody in that country loved them—the king, the air force generals, even the pilots who would eventually fly the planes. But when the manufacturer drew up the contract and presented it to the king for his signature, he looked both pleased and bemused. "This is very nice," he said. "Now all we have to do is to ask our friends the Saudis to lend us the money for the planes." And a multimillion-dollar "sure thing" was suddenly on hold, pending approval of an unidentified Economic Buying Influence.

We recognize that this is an extreme example. Few of us are ever going to be involved in a sale of this magnitude. But the same principle applies in Complex Sales of any size. If you don't identify the source of funds—and do it *early in the selling process*—you run the risk of handing the ball to the competition.

The box on page 87 summarizes the focus and importance of this first critical Buying Influence.

FINDING THE ECONOMIC BUYER

In identifying Economic Buyers in your sales, you have to know where to look. Almost by definition you don't find

ECONOMIC BUYING INFLUENCE

Role: **To give final approval to buy**

Only one per sale, but may be a set of people such as a team, board, or committee

- **Controls expenditure of**
- **Authority to release**
- **Discretionary use of resources**
- **Veto power**

Focus: **Bottom line and impact on organization**

Asks: **"What return will we get on this investment?"**
"How will this impact our organization?"

 SS22

people who give final approval far down on the corporate ladder. People playing the Economic Buyer role are usually highly placed in their organizations. In smaller firms the CEO or president may play the Economic Buyer role for many sales. But you don't always have to go that far up. The Economic Buyer role, like all buying roles, can shift from sale to sale, and the organizational position of the person playing it depends on several variables. Five critical ones are the dollar amount of the sale, business conditions, the buying firm's experience with you and your company, the buying firm's experience with your product, and the expected organizational impact.

1. ***Dollar Amount.*** The greater the dollar amount of your sale, the higher up in the buying organization you need to

look for the Economic Buyer. Every company has its own cutoff points at which final approval for purchases passes up or down the organizational ladder. These points relate to the dollar amount of the sale relative to the company's size. The president of the Apex Food Company, which does a hundred million dollars' worth of business a year, may feel he has to personally approve every sale over ten thousand dollars. In Multiplex Toys, where annual sales amount to half a billion dollars, the president may get involved—may be called in to play the Economic Buyer role—only in purchases over fifty thousand dollars. Sales that in a small company have to be approved at the top may, in a large concern, be handled by middle management.

2. ***Business Conditions.*** In hard times management starts counting paper clips. Therefore, the less stable the overall business environment, the more likely it is that your Economic Buyer will be found higher up in the organization. We have seen this numerous times in our client companies. One of them is a major computer firm that does several billion dollars' worth of business a year. In "normal" times, the CEO has to approve every expenditure over fifty thousand dollars. During a recent recession, however, he became the Economic Buyer on expenditures as low as five thousand dollars. This is not an uncommon practice even in Fortune 500 firms.
3. ***Experience with You and Your Firm.*** It always takes time, even for the most reliable salespeople, to build customer confidence in their firm's capabilities. Lack of trust means greater perceived risk for the buying firm, and greater perceived risk means that the final decision to buy will move up the corporate ladder. Conversely, the more experience a buying organization has had with you and

your firm—that is, the better you've established your credibility and that of your company—the more likely it is that top management will entrust final approval to middle management.

4. ***Experience with Your Product or Service.*** Even if a buying organization has had a solid history with your company, its Buyers may still be unfamiliar with the specific product or service involved in your current proposal. If that's the case, the Economic Buyer role is going to move up. The same thing is true if they've bought your type of product before, but not from you. A buying organization's initial decision to introduce robotics into its manufacturing division is obviously going to require final approval from top levels. So is a subsequent decision to shift suppliers—to start buying the same type of automation from a different supplier. Once they have experience with your particular robotics line, though, they'll be willing to entrust decisions about servicing and replacement to lower-level executives. Thus the Economic Buying role for those future sales will probably shift downward.
5. ***Potential Organizational Impact.*** Since the Economic Buyer's business focus is on long-term stability and growth, buying decisions that radically affect those areas will involve a higher-placed person playing that role. The decision to computerize all billing procedures will be made at the top; subsequent decisions about personnel retraining, service, or supplies may not have to go that high.

A critical point to remember is that there's never a single Economic Buyer for a company or account. There's no such thing as "the Apex Company's Economic Buyer." There are only people filling that role for *individual buying decisions.* Within any account, the identity of the person playing the final approval role may vary from sale to sale, depending on the above factors.

In looking for the Economic Buyer, many of our most astute clients have found it useful to ask the question *"At what level in my own organization would such a decision have to be made?"* The answer may not give you the Economic Buyer's title for your sale, but it will start you looking at the right corporate level. That's one way of focusing in on the person who actually controls the funds. Another way is to utilize your Coach. More about that critical and unique Buying Influence in a moment.

User Buying Influences

User Buyers are the people who will actually use (or supervise the use of) your product or service once the purchase is made. Their role is to *make judgments about the impact of that product or service on the job to be done.*

FOCUS OF THE USER BUYER

The key phrase here is "on the job." User Buyers are concerned primarily with how a sale is going to affect everyday operations in their own areas or departments; their focus is therefore narrower than that of Economic Buyers. People acting as User Buying Influences will ask you about areas of day-to-day concern, such as the product's reliability, service record, retraining needed, downtime record, ease of operation, maintenance, safety, and potential impact on morale.

Because the focus of User Buyers is how a sale will affect *their* jobs, their reactions to sales proposals, as well as their predictions about performance, tend to be subjective. This doesn't mean that they are either irrational or irrelevant. It means that, because their *personal* success hinges on the success of your product or service, you have to take subjectivity into account when you're selling to them. User Buyers want good performance not only because it makes their people productive, but also because better productivity makes them look good. You get User Buyers on your side, therefore, by giving them satisfactory answers to one simple question: "How will your product or service work *for me*?"

There's always *at least* one person whose central focus is the job to be done; therefore, there's always at least one User Buyer. Most Complex Sales, however, have more than one person playing this role. In fact, in certain scenarios, a majority of the people you're calling on might fall into the User Buyer category. If you're selling group insurance to a large firm, for example, User Buyers might include the employee benefits manager, a personnel manager, union representatives, or other agents of the employees being insured. If you're selling laboratory equipment, they might include a technical administrator, an R&D manager, and various lab technicians. If you're putting thirty new computers into a branch office, they might include the branch manager, a head of data processing, and individual operators. In the case of the airplane sale we just mentioned, the User Buyers were the military personnel—the pilots and their commanders—who would actually operate the planes. Because the primary interest of all of these people is the job to be done, all of them must be considered User Buyers.

The role and focus of the various User Buyers in your sale are summarized in the box on page 92.

USER BUYING INFLUENCES

Role: To make judgments about impact on job performance

Often several or many

- **Use or supervise the use of your product/service**
- **Personal since User will live with your solution**
- **Direct link between User's success and the success of your product or service**

Focus: The job to be done

Asks: "How will it work for me in my job or my department?"

 SS23

USER BUYERS CAN'T BE IGNORED

If a key User Buyer isn't sold, you'll have a very difficult time closing the sale. Management can, and sometimes does, approve orders for products that User Buyers just as soon wouldn't buy; but the eventual outcome of these sales is generally bad for everyone concerned. You have to please User Buyers because the way they use your product directly affects how that product is viewed—and, even more important, how it is implemented—by everyone else in the buying organization. That's why "going around" a key User Buyer can be so hazardous; when you do that, the chances are good that future orders to his or her department will be hampered by resentment, lack of cooperation, or outright sabotage.

A friend of ours encountered just this type of sabotage several years ago, when he sold a half-million-dollar training program to a major textile firm. The program was designed to help mechanics and other skilled laborers troubleshoot more efficiently. The textile company president was so impressed with its miraculous possibilities that he agreed to give it a trial run in every one of his twelve mills. Unfortunately, our friend neglected to contact the managers of those mills—the key User Buyers—before he closed the sale.

After the papers had been signed, when he showed up to help implement the program, the plant managers treated him like an outside troublemaker who had gone over their heads to The Boss. The not so miraculous result? A month after the program went on line, troubleshooting in every one of the twelve mills was far *less* effective than it had been before the sale. There was nothing wrong with the program itself. The User Buyer managers, annoyed at having been ignored, had just seen to it that it wouldn't work. As a result, the end of the trial period was also the end of the program.

Our friend learned a valuable lesson from the experience. Realizing that he had been done in by his own ignorance of the players, he vowed never again to overlook a User Buyer. "The next time somebody's going to use my stuff," he told us, "he's going to *want* it first!"

TECHNICAL BUYING INFLUENCES

User Buyers *can* be difficult, but Technical Buyers *have* to be. One sales representative we know describes these Buying Influences as "people who can't say yes, only no—and usually do." As is the case with User Buyers, Complex Sales usually involve several people playing different Technical Buying Influence roles. Because their input is so often negative, the combined presence of these multiple players can often pose a real problem for the salesperson.

THE TECHNICAL BUYER AS GATEKEEPER

Popular opinion notwithstanding, Technical Buyers don't say no because they're ornery. They throw blocks in your way because that's their job. The Technical Buyer's role is *to screen out*. They're gatekeepers. You might call them the professional Saint Peters of the Complex Sale. At a wedding, the Technical Buyer would be the one to stand up and say, "Hold it! I know a reason why these two should not be married!" On a hockey team this kind of person would be unanimous choice for goalie. It's the Technical Buyer's task to limit the field of sellers and to come up with the short list. They don't decide who wins, but they do decide who can play.

The objections of Technical Buying Influences may seem petty at times, but these people serve a necessary function. The screening that Technical Buyers do on candidate vendors makes it much less likely that, as a close approaches, an unforeseen technicality will get in the way. We call them Technical Buyers, in fact, because they screen out based on technicalities.

That's not the same thing as technologies. True, some Technical Buyers are concerned with technology, but many of them are not, and even one whose area of expertise is electronics, for example, may still know less about a particular electronic product than the salesperson does. Technical Buyers make judgments about the measurable and quantifiable aspects of your product or service based on how well it meets a variety of specifications. These specifications may or may not be technology-related.

Your customer's legal counsel, for example, may know nothing at all about your product from a technological point of view. But the lawyer can still screen you out based on the terms and conditions—the legal technicalities—of a contract. An accounting consultant may not be able to tell a carburetor from spaghetti carbonara, but she can still block a major automotive transaction if she deems the credit terms to be unsatisfactory.

Among the people who most often serve as Technical Buyers are purchasing agents. Even when there's a seemingly perfect match between your product or service and a potential customer's needs, a purchasing agent still can throw a wrench into the works by screening you out based on specifications—anything from price and delivery schedules to logistics and references. But purchasing agents are only one example of these gatekeeping Buyers. A personnel manager might block a sale because of a potentially harmful impact on morale. A government agency could screen you out because of regulations. In each of these examples, and in countless others, a Technical Buyer, making judgments about technicalities, can pull the plug on a sale that everyone else wants.

In identifying these gatekeeping Buyers before they shoot you down, you have to know that their principal focus—the reason they'll recommend you or show you to the door—is *the product itself*. All they really want to know is how well it meets their screening tests. Therefore, the better you know your product and understand all the tests it might have to meet in a given sales situation, the better your chances of getting your Technical Buyers' recommendations.

The box on page 96 summarizes the critical facts you need to remember about Technical Buyers.

TECHNICAL BUYING INFLUENCES

Role: To screen out

Often several or many

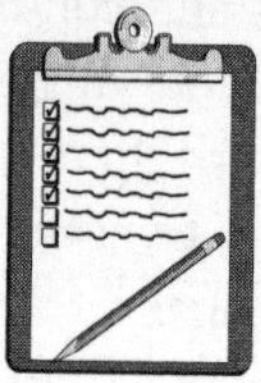

- **Judge measurable, quantifiable aspects of your proposal**
- **Gatekeepers**
- **Can't give final approval**
- **Can say no based on specs or technicalities**

Focus: Match to specifications in their areas of expertise

Asks: "Does this meet the specifications?"

 SS24

THE HIDDEN OR CAMOUFLAGED TECHNICAL BUYER

Because Technical Buyers are often more difficult to spot than either User Buyers or Economic Buyers, they pose special problems for the sales representative. It can be fatal to underestimate the power of a Technical Buyer, or to assume that because someone playing a screening role isn't immediately evident in the buying organization, that person is irrelevant to the sale. A financially troubled airline found this out recently, when it tried to use some of its grounded planes to reorganize itself as a limited entrant in the commercial carrier market.

The troubled company's creditors, the court that handled its default, and the airline unions were all in complete agreement on the reorganization, but at the last minute the Federal

Aviation Administration stepped in to inform everybody that the critical airway slots—the old firm's takeoff and landing rights—could not be made available because they had been reassigned. If the negotiating parties had thought through all the ramifications of the deal strategically ahead of time, they might have identified these government players in time. They might have realized that the FAA players were not irrelevant—that they would have to be contacted and sold before anything could be finalized. Because those Technical Buyers were ignored, the deal fell through.

While some Technical Buyers are thus seemingly invisible, others are all too visible. Technical Buyers can be difficult not only because of their screening role but because, in playing that role, they often run interference for the Economic Buyer, making it hard for you to see, or even identify, that person. In fact, the favorite game of Technical Buyers is to try to convince you that they are Economic Buyers—that *they* have the final authority to approve the sale. Believing this can get you into trouble even before you begin.

Some of the Technical Buyers who play this game deliberately lie about their role in the sale, but this isn't always the case. Some Technical Buyers actually believe that they *do* have the final say. Although the Technical Buyer's role is to say no rather than yes, that may not be clear to the person playing that role if he or she has gotten mixed signals from the real Economic Buyer. For example, an Economic Buyer, trying to save time, may ask a Technical Buyer for a "recommendation" in confusing terms: "We'll take whoever you say, Margaret. Just run it by me first." If Margaret is a totally rational person with no ego to defend, she'll read this as it is meant to be read: "You give me your input, and I'll make the decision." But if she's a normal human being, it will be easy to read it as "I trust you, Margaret. You decide." So you can easily find yourself confronted by an earnest, well-meaning Technical Buyer who misunderstands her role in the sale. If you take her at her word, you can misunderstand it, too.

It's to help you avoid problems of misidentification like this one that you need to rely on the people playing the fourth Buying Influence role—your Coaches.

Your Coaches

The role of a Coach is *to guide you in the sale* by giving you information that you need in order to manage it to a satisfactory close—one that guarantees you not only the order, but also satisfied customers, solid references, and repeat business. A Coach can help you clarify the validity of your Single Sales Objective, identify and meet the people who are filling the other Buying Influence roles for that objective, and assess the buying situation so that you're most effectively positioned with each one. To close any Complex Sale, you should develop *at least* one Coach.

Looking for a Coach is different from looking for your other three Buying Influences. The first three Buying Influences already exist. They're waiting to be identified, and you just have to find out where they are. Coaches have to be not only *found* but *developed*. The first three Buying Influences will already be playing their roles when you find them. The Coach's role is one that you, in effect, create. In doing that, you must remember that the Coach's focus is your success in the specific sales objective for which you want the Coaching.

The box on page 99 outlines the salient facts about this fourth, unique Buying Influence.

COACHES

Role: **To act as guides for this sale**

Develop at least one

Provide and interpret information about:

- **Validity of this Single Sales Objective**
- **Other Buying Influences**
- **Other elements of your Strategic Analysis**

Can be found:

- **In buying organization**
- **In selling organization**
- **Outside both**

Focus: **Your success with this proposal**

Asks: **"How can we ensure that this solution happens?"**

 SS25

THE THREE CRITERIA FOR A GOOD COACH

In searching for someone to develop into a Coach, you judge by three criteria:

1. ***You have credibility with that person.*** Usually this is because the Coach has won in a sale with you in the past. By definition, then, a good place to find potential Coaches is among your own satisfied customers. If you sold someone a product last year and he has been grateful ever since, you've got an ideal candidate for a Coach in terms of this first criterion. This person's past experience with you is that you can be *trusted*. That's what credibility means.
2. ***The Coach has credibility with the Buying Influences for your Single Sales Objective.*** Once you find some-

body who trusts you, you then have to be sure that this person is in turn trusted by the buying organization. A potential Coach who doesn't have credibility with the customer is going to be a poor liaison to its people, and the information he or she gives you about the sale may not be reliable.

Because credibility with the buying organization is so important, you'll often find good Coaches within that organization itself. We've already noted that people can play more than one Buying Influence role in a sale. A Technical or User Buyer who's on your side would be an excellent candidate to play a Coaching role. The best of all possible scenarios is to turn the Economic Buyer into a Coach.

3. ***The Coach wants your solution.*** In other words, he or she wants you to succeed—although not necessarily in your career in general. A Coach may be, but is not necessarily, a mentor or a friend. But by definition the Coach wants you to succeed in *this particular sales objective*. For some reason—it doesn't matter what the reason is—this person sees that it's in his or her own *self-interest* for the customer to accept your solution.

Coaches can usually be found among the Buying Influences in the customer organization, but because the Coach's focus is your success, you can also often find good ones within your own organization. One of the most innovative uses of a Coach that we've seen recently was demonstrated by a Midwest sales representative who dramatically increased penetration in an account by turning his own boss into a Coach. The boss had come up from the ranks and had sold in that account himself, and since his sales had been solid, mutually satisfying ones, he had good credibility with the Buying Influences. The sales representative was a sales leader himself, so he had credibility with the boss. And because the new business would obviously benefit the selling organization, the boss wanted the sales representative's solution. So on all three counts, the sales representative had developed an excellent Coach.

ASKING FOR COACHING

You may not always be lucky enough to find potential Coaches who perfectly fulfill all three criteria. But whenever those criteria suggest that someone *might* be developed into a Coach, we recommend that you test that person's potential usefulness by asking him or her for Coaching. Seldom will a real Coach refuse to give you the assistance you require.

Most people welcome the opportunity to do Coaching. Being a Coach, in our culture, has a very positive connotation, and few professionals will turn down the chance to demonstrate to a fellow professional that they are expert, and expertly placed, in their mutual field. Even a potential Coach who doesn't really have the information you need about the sale can often guide you to someone who does. As you nurture and develop Coaches for different sales over time, you'll eventually build up a network of reliable sources who can guide you to the key players in any account, no matter what your specific sales objective.

Asking for Coaching, however, isn't the same thing as asking for a referral or for assistance in making the sale. You don't want your Coach to do your selling for you, and you shouldn't give that impression. Not only are you the best person to sell your product or service, but your Coach already has enough work to do without taking on your responsibilities. When you say, "Can you help me talk to Jackson?" or "Will you recommend me?" it can easily decode as "I'm incompetent to manage this sale. Please do my work for me." You can't sustain credibility with a Coach who hears that message.

That's why, instead of asking for a referral, you should ask the potential Coach to give you information and direction. You want the Coach to help you *think through your position with the other Buying Influences*. By asking for Coaching rather than a referral, you make it clear that *you* will be the one running the plays, and that you just need some advice to help you do it. What you want the Coach to hear is "I'll take accountability for the sale, but I could use your expertise. I'll do the selling if you'll explain how a couple of things work." The irony of this approach is that, while a salesperson who asks for a referral almost never gets Coaching, the one who asks for Coaching usually gets it—and the referral besides.

Selling All Your Buying Influences

Soon after Miller Heiman, Inc., was founded, officers of one of the largest food-products manufacturers in the country began looking us over. They were considering sending hundreds of their salespeople to our programs, and the prospects looked very good. We had received extremely favorable reactions to our presentations from the president of the company himself, and were already beginning to talk about possible dates and venues.

The only hitch was a nervous sales-training manager who thought our program was a threat to his turf. He was used to running things his way, and although he couched his objections in phrases like "incompatibility of design" and "basic structural impasses," his real reason for opposing us was obviously fear. In his estimation, if we got in, he was out. Or at least (so he thought) his level of authority would be diminished.

We handled his resistance in a rather perfunctory manner, not only because we knew his fears were unfounded—in fact our entire implementation design was to let him take over once we'd introduced the process—but also because we already had the company president on our side. This cavalier attitude proved to be a big mistake. When the president heard about the training manager's misgivings, he withdrew his support. He still liked our proposal, but he wasn't willing to override a subordinate he had been relying on successfully for many years, and whose value to the organization he didn't want to jeopardize. As a result he backed off, and a "surefire" order went down the drain.

This story illustrates the important principle that, in every Complex Sale, you have to sell your proposal not just to one or two people but to *all* the people filling the four Buying Influence roles. Selling the Economic Buyer alone, as we tried to do here, can be just as disastrous as selling only someone who doesn't give the final yes—as the airplane manufacturer tried to do in the Middle East. What we should have done in this case was to turn our Economic Buyer, the president, into a Coach, and get him to help us convince the training manager (who was filling both a User Buyer and a Technical Buyer role) that his fears about his job authority were unfounded. Instead we made the all-too-common error of assuming that as long as Mr. Big is sold, everything else will fall into place. We paid a heavy price for that assumption.

Many sales representatives are still paying this price, whether they focus on the top (as we did) or on middle-range decision-makers (as the airplane manufacturer did). It's very hard to break with tradition, and traditionally salespeople build their account sales around the people with whom they feel most comfortable. Sales representatives with electronics firms, for example, are often engineers, and in fact are often referred to not as salespeople but as "field engineers." Since they're comfortable with other engineers, they become adept at selling their products to User and Technical Buying Influences who are also engineers. But because they're much less comfortable with top management, they often ignore their Economic Buyers, and find themselves losing out to competitors who cover all four Buying Influence bases.

When we make this point in our programs, someone usually objects, "But what about the sales where one person does it all? Aren't there situations where one individual plays all four roles?"

The answer is almost always no. We realize that there are still a few small firms around where The Founder seems to run everything, and we know that when you're selling to such a firm it may look as if every buying decision is made by that single individual. But before you conclude that all four Buying Influence roles are played by that one person, look further. Does he really read all the firm's legal documents himself? Is she really going to be personally involved in using every product or service you want to sell her company? Does he really dispense entirely with advice and consent? Or, when you look at how buying decisions are made for this firm, don't you find that her people play roles that are both more complicated and more fundamental than the ones they appear to be playing?

The true one-man or one-woman company is virtually a thing of the past, and the sale that can be decided by one vote is not now, and never again will be, a reality. In corporate sales today, complexity of decision-making is the rule rather than the exception. So if you find a situation in which only one Buying Influence seems to be involved, be careful. We've acknowledged that key players can play double or multiple roles, but if you can find only one key player in a major account sale, you're almost certainly misreading the situation.

DEGREE OF INFLUENCE

One final clarification before we close this chapter. When we say that it's critical to cover all your Buying Influences, we don't mean to imply that all of them, in all cases, should be considered equally important to the outcome of the sale. They seldom are. So, while it's hazardous to ignore *any* Buying Influence, it's also important to recognize that, on many sales, certain key players may be "more equal" or "less equal" than others.

That is, some players may exert such a major influence on the outcome of the sale that wisdom says you should pay them special attention. Other players may exert less of a direct influence on the outcome than their exalted titles (vice president) or roles (Economic Buyer) might lead you to believe. In setting good strategies, therefore, you need to be attentive not only to the roles that all your Buying Influences are playing, but also to the Degree of Influence that each one may exert on your objective.

As we mentioned in the introduction, Degree of Influence is one of the new concepts that we've added to this "enhanced" edition of *Strategic Selling*. A few examples will illustrate its importance.

THE TERMINATING TECHNICIAN

Suppose you're trying to place a computer system into a company that was founded by, and is run by, engineers. If it's a multimillion-dollar deal that needs top-level approval, you might imagine that the "mere" technician who is involved in appraising the system would be less important than the vice president who will sign the papers. But if the vice president routinely defers to the technician's expertise, then this "lesser" player's input may have a high Degree of Influence on the sale, and you'll have to adjust your strategy to reflect that fact. If you don't, then your chances might easily be "terminated" by this Technical Buyer.

THE LAME-DUCK ANTISPONSOR

When is a D rating actually a plus? When it comes from a Buying Influence that nobody else trusts. A client of ours ran into this scenario recently when she tried to provide a solution to a customer's inventory logjam. The inventory-control manager hated her proposal, and she saw this as a major impediment until she examined his Degree of Influence. She found that he was so disliked by the other Buying Influences that his negativity actually helped her case. As the sale progressed, his Degree of Influence spiraled downward from minimal to zero, and the organization eventually let him go. Until that moment, of course, he was still undeniably a Buying Influence—but one with a lame-duck reputation and equivalent impact.

THE ECONOMIC BUYER AS RUBBER STAMP

It is no more valid to assume that the Economic Buyer is always the most important figure in the sale than it is to say that he or she is the sole decision-maker. With the increasing sophistication of technology, it's not uncommon today for an Economic Buyer to delegate responsibility, allowing a lower-level employee (like the "terminating technician") to approve the purchase of a sophisticated system or equipment, and in effect rubber-stamping whatever decision is made. Since that rubber stamp is essential to the sale, the person using it is still the Economic Buyer, but his or her Degree of Influence is in this instance obviously minimal. A successful strategy takes that into account.

One caveat, however: While an Economic Buyer may choose to delegate responsibility—and thus diminish his or her Degree of Influence over a specific Single Sales Objective—it's important to remember that the responsibility can always be reasserted, thus restoring this Buyer's "naturally high" Degree of Influence. This type of give-and-take can happen very quickly. That is why, in covering your various Buying Influences, you should always be guided by the need for constant reassessment. Like everything else in sales, Degree of Influence is a mobile, energetic phenomenon. A good strategist takes frequent fixes on its force and direction.

In our workshops, after participants have identified all the people playing the four Buying Influence roles for their targeted sales objective, we ask them to specify, for each person, whether the Degree of Influence on the sale is likely to be High, Medium, or Low—that is, whether this individual is likely to exert a dominant, moderate, or minimal influence on the outcome. Obviously, rating players in this way is not an exact science, and we're not suggesting that it can give you rock-solid confidence about your players' importance. What it does provide is a further dimension of strategic analysis, an extra perspective for assessing how buying decisions are actually made, and how critical each Buyer will be in getting them made. As one of our own sales professionals puts it acutely, "The Degree of Influence piece makes you look harder at the situation. It's one more checkpoint that refines the quality of your information."

Five Critical Factors

In using that checkpoint, we urge you not to guess about a given individual's Degree of Influence, but to consider the impact of organizational and personal factors that can serve to heighten or diminish influence. Here are some of the factors that we have found to be important:

ORGANIZATIONAL IMPACT

Where in the buying organization is your proposal likely to have the most immediate and/or lasting impact? The answer to that question should point you to those levels in the organization where the Degree of Influence will probably be strongest. Those levels, moreover, will relate roughly to the focus areas of the Buying Influences. If your proposal promises to create an instant spike in profitability, for example, the Economic Buyer's Degree of Influence will probably be high.

LEVEL OF EXPERTISE

Which of your Buying Influences are most knowledgeable in your company's area of expertise? Which ones are the buying organization likely to turn to for inside advice? A head of shipping may have low overall influence in his company's decision-making, but if you're trying to sell his factory a new line of forklifts, it's reasonable to suspect that his Degree of Influence may rise.

LOCATION

"The three most important things in real estate," according to the old saying, "are location, location, and location." We won't go quite that far with regard to Degree of Influence, but the geographical location of Buying Influences is definitely a factor to consider. This is common sense. Say you're selling to a company that is based in Los Angeles, and there are three executives who have to approve the sale. If one of them is currently stationed in Buenos Aires, it's likely that her influence will be less than that of the others. Of course "likely" doesn't equal "certain," and you may discover, through Coaching, that her influence is high. In that case your strategy might call for a flight to Argentina.

PERSONAL PRIORITY

The higher priority your Single Sales Objective has for a Buying Influence personally, the greater likelihood that he or she will exert—or at least attempt to exert—a significant Degree of Influence on the outcome. Perhaps this is most obviously true for User Buyers, because their jobs are most directly affected by the sales proposal. But any Buying Influence can take a personal interest in a sale—especially if he or she sees it as an opportunity to defend or grow "turf."

"POLITICS"

Protection of turf is an example of internal politics, and those politics are probably the single most common—and often the single most irritating—factor involved in the ebb and flow of Degree of Influence. We'll see in the next chapter how the identification of Buying Influences can be complicated by such organizational changes as hirings, firings, and shifts in reporting structures. We'll anticipate that discussion here by mentioning just one essential caution: Whenever you're looking at a customer's decision-making and the situation appears politically charged, it's safe to assume that you had better reexamine the Buying Influences, and take a closer look at each one's potential impact on the sale.

Before you take that closer look, however, you need to locate your Buying Influences in the first place. You'll do that now, in the second of our Personal Workshops.

PERSONAL WORKSHOP 2: BUYING INFLUENCES

To give you some practice in understanding your own Complex Sales, you'll now do a Personal Workshop in which you apply the Key Element of Buying Influences to an analysis of your chosen Single Sales Objective.

STEP 1: DRAW YOUR BUYING INFLUENCES CHART.

We've defined the role of each of the four Buying Influences that appear in the Complex Sale. As a way of reviewing them and of making them constantly visible, we suggest that you write them down in a format that you can use throughout this book whenever you redefine your strategic position. It's called a Buying Influences Chart.

Turn your notebook so that the longer side of the page is horizontal, and at the top of the page write "Buying Influences Chart." Divide the page into four equal boxes. At the top of each one write the name of one of the four Buying Influence types and, next to it, the role that each one plays in the Complex Sale. You'll want to write small enough so that you can add material to this chart in future Personal Workshops. When you have the Buying Influences Chart set up, it should look something like the example here:

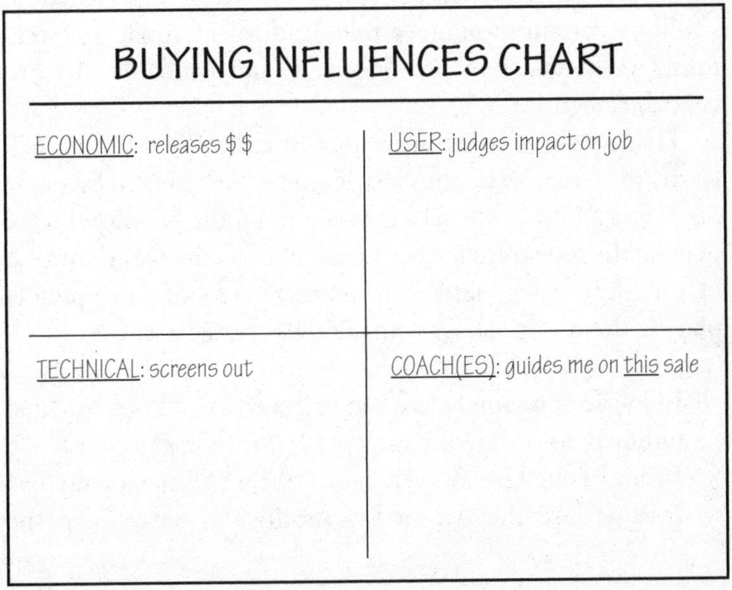

STEP 2: IDENTIFY ALL YOUR BUYERS.

Now, with your Single Sales Objective in mind, write down in the boxes the names of the people who are currently filling the four roles for your sale. Remember, there's going to be only one Economic Buyer, but in the other three boxes you may have a number of names. Remember also that a single individual may appear in more than one of the boxes, if that person is playing multiple roles.

There are two ways of identifying your Buyers, the right way and the wrong way. The wrong way is simply to list the people you're currently calling on and fit them into the four slots you've just drawn. This *labeling*, or pigeonholing, approach is a tempting but unproductive shortcut. If you start from your own current prospects, or from an organization chart of the buying firm, and paste an Economic Buyer label on Black because he's the chairman of the board and a User Buyer label on Snyder because she's head of production, you'll be certain to confuse titles and roles. You'll be force-fitting your data into preconceived (and probably misconceived) categories.

The right way to identify your Buyers—the way that will clarify for you how the buying decisions are going to be made for your specific proposal—is to *search* for the people who are playing the four roles for your current objective. You can zero in on these roles—and thus correctly identify the people playing them—by asking yourself these questions:

- To locate your single Economic Buyer, ask, "Who has final authority to release the money for *this sales objective*?"
- To find your User Buyers, ask, "Who will personally use or supervise the use of my product or service on the job?"

- To find your Technical Buyers, ask, "Who will make judgments about the specifications of my product or service as a way of screening out vendors?"
- To find the people you can most effectively develop into Coaches, ask, "Who can guide me in *this* sale?"

Write in the names of your Buying Influences in the relevant boxes of the chart, in a single column at the left-hand side of the box.

STEP 3: DETERMINE DEGREES OF INFLUENCE.

Your next step is to determine, for each of these Buying Influences, whether their likely impact on your current sales objective will be dominant, moderate, or minimal. Remember that the Economic Buyer may or may not exert a dominant influence on the sale, but that, even where he or she delegates responsibility, it's still important to cover this "rubber stamp." Remember too that it's hazardous to ignore any Buying Influence, even one whose impact on the sale will probably be slight.

Referring to the five critical factors that we discussed a moment ago, assess your key players' Degree of Influence now. Next to each of their names on the chart, write an *H* if you believe the influence is high, an *M* if you think it's medium, and an *L* if you think it's low. When you're done, the chart should look like the example on page 114.

BUYING INFLUENCES CHART

ECONOMIC: releases $ $	USER: judges impact on job
Dan Farley H	Doris Green H Harry Barnes L
TECHNICAL: screens out	COACH(ES): guides me on this sale
Gary Steinberg M Will Johnson H Harry Barnes L	Doris Green H Sandy Kelly M

STEP 4: TEST YOUR CURRENT POSITION.

Finally, look at each name in turn and ask yourself where you stand with that person right now. Remember, you always have a position even if you don't know what it is. In this step of the workshop, you're objectively assessing your current position with each key individual with regard to the role each one is playing in your sale. You're making your position visible.

In testing your position with your Buying Influences, you should ask yourself two questions, designed to locate areas of uncertainty that we've found to be extremely common:

1. Have I identified *all* the key people who are currently playing each of the four Buying Influence roles for my sales objective?

2. Have I covered the bases with every one of these key players?

The first question is self-explanatory. Since we've stressed that there may be many players filling the four Buying Influence roles, you should look at the entire situation and dig for the key players rather than say, "OK, I've got four. I'm in good shape."

The second question relates to a concept that we'll explain more fully in a moment. For now, just think of "covering the bases" as a synonym for "contacting" or "qualifying." In looking over your Buying Influences Chart, ask yourself whether you've personally contacted each person identified, or whether you've arranged for someone else to do so. A Buyer whose role you understand, but who hasn't yet been called on, is an *uncovered base*.

Next to the names of those players whose roles or Degrees of Influence you're not sure of, next to each uncovered base, and in any Buyer box for which you don't have at least one name, stick one of your Red Flags—or mark the name with red pencil. This will call your attention to uncertainties in your current position. Don't worry if your Buying Influences Chart has one or more of these Red Flags. If it didn't, you'd already have the order. We'll show you now how to use them to improve your position.

CHAPTER 6

KEY ELEMENT 2: RED FLAGS/LEVERAGE FROM STRENGTH

In a Strategic Selling program, the participants were in the midst of identifying their various Buying Influences when one of them, an energetic young man who had twice been the top sales representative in his division for the year, threw his pencil on the table and looked up with an expression of odd elation. We could see that his worksheet was covered with tiny Red Flags. "You know," he said, "I just discovered something. I thought this was one of my best accounts. Now I realize I don't even have a prospect. I guess I'm going to have to do some rethinking."

We were delighted with his discovery, and even more delighted at the conclusion he'd drawn from it. It wasn't hard to see why he'd been consistently successful. He was using the Red Flag element of strategy in exactly the way it was meant to be used: as a way of calling his attention to problems with the sale while he still had time to fix them. Consistently in our program the sales commission leaders, the people who regularly pull down 200 or 300 percent of their quotas, are those who find the *most* Red Flags in their accounts when they begin their strategic analysis. It's those people who most fully appreciate the value of the Red Flag highlighting system—and who most consistently react to the discovery of Red Flags as this top salesman did, by committing themselves to reassessing the situation.

As we mentioned earlier, we use the term "Red Flag" because in everyday language it's a signal for "warning" or "danger." That's exactly how you should view those incomplete or uncertain areas in your sales strategy. You should consider them not merely "fuzzy" areas, but areas of immediate danger, threatening to block your Single Sales Objective. We use the Red Flag symbol for the same reason that a road crew or the Coast Guard uses an actual red flag: to call your attention to a hazard before it can do you in.

"AUTOMATIC" RED FLAGS

The things that can threaten your sales are virtually numberless, and we'll be discussing many of them in this book. We want to begin, however, by discussing five things that are so prevalent and so dangerous to sales that we consider them "automatic" Red Flag areas.

MISSING INFORMATION

In the Personal Workshop you just did to identify your Buying Influences, we asked you to place a red sticker next to the name of any Buyer whose role you didn't understand, and also in any of the four Buying Influence boxes for which you couldn't find a key player. In both cases, we were asking you to highlight areas of missing information that you need in order to fully understand the sale. You should always consider such missing information a signal that *your sale is in danger*—whether the lack of data relates to your Buying Influences or to any of the other Key Elements that we'll introduce later in this book. Whenever you have an unanswered question about the sales scenario, then it's time to reassess your position.

UNCERTAINTY ABOUT INFORMATION

It's just as important to reassess that position when the answer you have is hazy or uncertain. In our Strategic Selling programs, we see a clear distinction between situations where salespeople simply lack the relevant data and know it, and those where they have some data but aren't certain what it means to the sale. The latter situation is usually worse than the former. At least when you know you're missing a piece of the puzzle, you can take steps to track it down. When you have a piece that "looks right" but doesn't quite fit, you run the risk of force-fitting what you already "know" into your analysis—and ignoring what you really *need* to know.

Because uncertainty about "known" information is such a common impediment to successful sales, we'll give you the same advice here that we give our program participants. Whenever you're "pretty sure" or "almost certain" or "90 percent convinced" that you understand a piece of information that you need to close a sale, *look again*. And reach for those red stickers.

ANY UNCONTACTED BUYING INFLUENCE

We also mentioned this Red Flag area in the last Personal Workshop, when we asked you to place a sticker next to the name of any person playing any of the Buying Influence roles who had not yet been contacted either by you personally or by someone better suited to do so. *Any Buyer ignored is a threat.* We often call such a Buyer an uncovered base. The baseball metaphor accurately suggests the trouble you'll encounter by failing to contact, or cover, every key player. You can field a team without a second baseman or a shortstop, and you can close a Complex Sale without contacting all of the relevant players. But you'll do so under conditions of extreme uncertainty—so why try?

You don't have to contact and convince each of the key players yourself. In fact, that's not always the most effective strategy. But arranging for all the people in each of the four Buying Influence roles to be contacted by *someone* is a principal element of your responsibility as a "strategic orchestrator," that is, as the manager of your Complex Sale. Like the manager of a ball team, you have to see to it that each base is adequately covered by *the person best qualified to do so.*

In some cases that person will be you. In others it will be another member of your organization, a Buying Influence who is favorable to your proposal, or one of your Coaches. Many of our clients—Aramark, Coca-Cola, and Hewlett-Packard, to name a few—employ the strategy of *like-rank selling* to cover the various bases in their sales. Since they understand that business professionals are usually most comfortable talking to people at their own organizational level, they have devised flexible protocols in which vice presidents call on vice presidents, middle-management people talk to other middle managers, lawyers talk to lawyers, and so on. No two arrangements are identical, since no two sales are identical. The successful arrangements, however, all share one element: They cover *all* the Buyers for each objective.

ANY BUYING INFLUENCE NEW TO THE JOB

The appearance of new faces is a fourth reason for an automatic Red Flag, especially if you haven't yet contacted those people. Even if you have contacted new potential Buying Influences, you should still consider them possible threats to the sale until you've determined positively what roles they're playing and how they feel about your sales proposal. This may sound overly cautious, but since Buyer roles—and therefore Buyer perceptions—change quickly and subtly in the Complex Sale, the point is really only common sense.

A friend who sells hospital supplies discovered, after he'd actually *closed* a deal with an East Coast medical center, how hazardous it can be to minimize the threat of a new player. The Economic Buying Influence was a vice president of finance named Jeffries. He'd already placed an order when the vice presidency was taken over by a woman named Cole. Our friend, wrongly assuming that the deal was solid because the ink was dry, told himself Cole was irrelevant and took a brief vacation. When he returned, the order was still sitting on the loading dock and he was out a fat commission. Cole, the new Economic Buyer, had overturned Jeffries's decision and canceled the order in favor of a less costly bid.

Ignoring a new Buying Influence like this is always the wrong way to manage a Complex Sale. The right way was demonstrated by a client of ours from a New England insurance firm. He was in the middle of negotiating a contract for group insurance with a company that employed three thousand people when the company suddenly brought in an outside consultant. Our client knew that his chief competitor for the account, one of the country's largest insurers, wasn't as well positioned with the buying company as he was. If he had rested on his laurels and forgotten that new players are hazardous, he might have ignored the consultant, and lived to regret it.

Fortunately, he was familiar with the Red Flag concept and immediately spotted the consultant as a threat. Instead of ignoring her, he approached her and was able to convince her that it was in the best interests of everyone concerned—including the consultant herself—for his company to get the order. The larger carrier, which *had* ignored the consultant, found itself strategically outclassed. It was a classic example of a strategy-wise salesperson converting a potentially dangerous Technical Buying Influence into an ally.

New Buying Influences don't have to *remain* threats. Indeed, one of your roles as a sales professional is to transform as many of those new faces as you can into sponsors. You can do that only if you consider every new player relevant—and if you refuse to take any of them for granted.

REORGANIZATION

The introduction of a new Buying Influence is a relatively easy danger signal to spot. A more difficult one is presented when the faces in a given account remain the same, their titles and supposed functions remain the same, and yet their *roles* for your particular sale shift from the ones they have played in the past.

We've stressed that the identities of the people playing the four Buying Influence roles are always in a state of flux, even in the most stable corporate environments—and that you therefore have to reidentify your Buyers every time you propose a new Single Sales Objective. This admonition is twice as important when the buying company is undergoing, or has just undergone, any internal reorganization.

These days, of course, this kind of change is more the rule than the exception. As the century draws to a close, we are being bombarded more and more by downsizing, reengineering, and "M&Aing"—one of our clients' pet terms for mergers and acquisitions. As a result, somebody is always reorganizing. Forewarned, therefore, is forearmed. Whenever you encounter hirings, firings, promotions, consolidations, or expansions—in fact, anything that alters your decision makers' organizational structure—you should reach immediately for your Red Flags.

When reorganization takes place on a corporate level, it's generally pretty easy to spot. If two billion-dollar firms merge, or if the presidency of a Fortune 500 company changes hands, you don't have to be a wizard to sense that it might affect your selling prospects. It's much harder to spot this fifth automatic Red Flag when the reorganization is subtle and internal. An especially difficult reorganization to spot is one in which the players retain their titles and their ostensible responsibilities in the buying organization, but no longer have the same authority.

We knew a vice president for a large consumer-products group, for example, who had been in the same office and had been exercising the same responsibilities for ten years. Those responsibilities included approving any sale to his division that exceeded ten thousand dollars: He was the Economic Buyer for those deals. Then he was "promoted" to senior vice president. He stayed in the same office with a modest increase in salary, and as far as the casual outsider was concerned, he seemed to enjoy the same privileges and responsibilities. But that wasn't the case. As is true in many instances of an executive being kicked upstairs, he had lost his Economic Buying Influence role when he took on the "senior" title. After his promotion, sales of ten thousand dollars and above had to be approved by a "junior" vice president down the hall. Any sales representative who casually assumed that nothing had changed might easily have wasted her time—and imperiled her sales—by presenting proposals to an Economic Buyer who no longer existed.

In these days of mergeritis and administrative razzle-dazzle, such corporate reorganization is hardly infrequent. As one of our program participants recently complained about a notoriously unstable banking client, "Their 'constant' is ninety days. Reorganization is the most important Red Flag there is." A word to the wise should suffice. Whenever the buying organization shifts gears, take a new look at the account and reidentify the players in the four Buying Influence roles.

The five automatic Red Flag areas discussed here, highlighted in the box on page 124, are the most obviously and consistently dangerous ones you'll encounter in your Complex Sales. But they're only the tip of the iceberg. Every sales objective can be blocked in countless ways. Therefore, sales success is always a direct result of constant vigilance. The Red Flag technique for locating those hazards works only when it's so fully incorporated into your strategy that you use it again and again without hesitation—in other words, when it has become second nature.

RED FLAGS

- **Critical information missing**
- **Uncertainty about information**
- **Any uncontacted Buying Influence**
- **Buying Influence(s) new to the job**
- **Reorganization**

 SS14

FEEDBACK AND OPPORTUNITY

Used in this way, the Red Flag technique is a "continuous assessment" device, a feedback mechanism that enables the strategy-conscious sales professional to maintain an effective position in the face of every contingency, because it shows, every time it's used, where you are shaky and where an Alternate Position may be needed.

Because they enable you to test and reposition yourself in the face of change, you should always consider Red Flags *positive,* not negative. Ideally they serve not only as "road hazard" signals, but as signposts to *opportunities* that you might have overlooked without them. The best salespeople understand that a strategic analysis without Red Flags is one without opportunities. Like our program participant who discovered "I don't even have a prospect," top people *welcome* their Red Flags. They know that without the constant checking of position that these devices offer, it's very easy to fall into a fool's paradise.

Sales hazards, like road hazards, are most dangerous when they're unflagged and hidden. That's why people who are afraid or embarrassed to identify what's wrong with their positions always get run off the road. They allow themselves to feel blindly confident right up to the moment when the sale falls through and they're thrown into blind panic. If you think back to the Euphoria-Panic Continuum that we introduced in Chapter 3, you'll recall that being euphoric, just like being in panic, means you're out of touch with reality. The Red Flag early warning system, by forcing you to uncover what's hidden, keeps reality visible.

THE "BETTER HALF" OF STRATEGY: LEVERAGE FROM STRENGTHS

When you know a Red Flag is there, you then can work to eliminate the problem that it identifies. You do that by using a principle we call Leverage from Strength. Leverage from Strength can be considered the "better half" of the Red Flag technique. It's what enables you to turn the weaknesses uncovered by your Red Flags into opportunities for strategic improvement.

Before you can use this principle effectively, you have to understand what we mean by Strengths. To many people in sales, a "strength" is any feature or benefit that they can crow about—any aspect at all of their product or service that an "objective" observer might think of as a plus. That's a mistake. At Miller Heiman we don't believe that any product or service has inherent benefits—only benefits *as the customer perceives them*, in a particular situation and at a particular time. To us, it makes no sense to say that a given product, service, or solution is objectively better than another. Whatever you're proposing to your customer, it demonstrates a real advantage only when the customer sees it that way—when she perceives the value that you're bringing to her business.

Given this subjective and customer-oriented perspective, it's not surprising that we are very precise—some clients have even called us picky—in our definition of strategic Strengths. In Strategic Selling, and in all Miller Heiman processes, a true strategic Strength meets the following criteria:

1. A STRENGTH IS AN AREA OF DIFFERENTIATION.

That is, it enables the customer or prospect to identify a *difference* between the solution you're offering and all alternative options. It's fine to say that the personal computer you're selling has four billion megabytes of Random Access Memory, but if every other PC on the market does too, then your RAM capacity is not a Strength as we define it. In addition, even if you're the only supplier who can offer that alleged advantage, you have a Strength only if this matters to your customer. If the customer doesn't see why your "difference" *makes a difference* to him or her, then your snazzy feature or benefit may be worthless.

2. A STRENGTH IMPROVES YOUR POSITION.

The use of a Strength increases your chances for success in the immediate sales objective for which you're setting a strategy. If it doesn't do that, by definition it isn't a Strength. As we've said, "position" is just another term for strategy, and the point of strategy is to help you understand where you are, so you can take steps to move yourself and your company toward the close. Thus anything that increases your understanding of the selling situation—provided it's also a relevant area of differentiation—might be seen as a strategic Strength. Anything that inhibits your understanding should be seen as a Red Flag.

3. A STRENGTH IS RELEVANT TO YOUR CURRENT SALES OBJECTIVE.

That is, it matters to the customer with regard to the specific sales objective you're pursuing right now—what we've called your Single Sales Objective. In setting out strategic Action Plans, we always focus on one manageable piece of business at a time. Those plans have got to incorporate Strengths that are just as focused. If you're a clothing supplier and your down jackets are widely acknowledged to be the warmest in the industry, that may well be a Strength when you're selling to retail chains in Minnesota. It probably won't be if you're cracking a new market in the Caribbean.

By measuring your areas of supposed advantage against these three criteria, you'll be able to determine which ones are in fact Strengths. Once you've done that, you'll be able to use them as leverage against your Red Flags.

STRENGTHS

- **Areas of differentiation**
- **Opportunities that can be used to improve your position**
- **Must be relevant to this sales objective**
- **Diminish importance of price competition**

 SS13

Eliminating Red Flags: Dos and Don'ts

As effective as it is in improving position, it's surprising how infrequently Leverage from Strength is employed, even by very good salespeople. Many sales representatives, faced with an obvious roadblock, choose either to hammer away until it moves or to run around it as if it weren't there. Both these reactions are ways of skirting the unknown, and they both generally have a boomerang effect: They send the sales representative hurtling *into* the unknown, and often give the order to the competition.

To see how these reactions fail, and how Leverage from Strength works, consider a typical sales picture. Suppose you're working with an account where two of the principal players are a production manager acting as a User Buyer and a financial vice president serving as the Economic Buyer. The User Buyer is clearly on your side; he's ready to put in your order. But the Economic Buyer won't sign. Moreover, you can't even get close; like many Economic Buyers, this one is insulated from salespeople and won't even return your calls. Consider three approaches you could take.

SCENARIO 1: HAMMERING AWAY

In this common scenario, you assume that the reason you've been unable to see the vice president is that you haven't tried hard enough. It's *your* fault that the Economic Buyer is inaccessible. If you only adopt a more positive attitude and keep leaving phone messages, your persistence will eventually be rewarded. We've already told you how worthless we've found this kind of "better mental attitude" approach. Even if the fates (or a secretary) should smile on you and you get five minutes with the vice president, it's extremely unlikely that you'll be able to turn it to your advantage: You'll still be the same unknown quantity that you were before you were given the privilege of getting in the door. Thus you'll probably end up only advertising your weakness.

SCENARIO 2: IGNORING THE ROADBLOCK

In this scenario you forget about the Economic Buying Influence entirely. You accept the fact that you can't get in and focus your presentation on the User Buyer, who's already favorable to your proposal. Of course there's nothing wrong with talking to a User Buyer who wants you in (in fact, by not doing so you could easily create a new roadblock). But since no sale can go through without a release of funds, you're still going to be weakly positioned to close the sale if you settle for talking *only* to the User Buyer. An uncovered Economic Buyer is a major Red Flag in any sale. Relying on your good relationship with the User Buyer to offset that serious weakness is like playing stud poker with a deuce in the hole.

SCENARIO 3: LEVERAGE FROM STRENGTH

A strategy that would most likely succeed in this sales situation would use Leverage from Strength. Using this principle, you would go to the User Buyer for assistance in getting the Economic Buyer covered. By turning the User Buyer into a Coach for the sale, you would be relying on an established Strength (his desire for you to make the sale) to eliminate a Red Flag (the vice president's reluctance to see you). "This sale is obviously good for the two of us, Jill," you could say. "But the money is tied up in Finance. How can we show them up there that buying will increase productivity?"

Jill will have her own ideas about that. She may simply offer to introduce you to the vice president. She may offer to make a presentation for you or suggest that the two of you go in together. In any event, as a production manager in the vice president's own company, Jill already has better credibility with Finance than you do; since you also have credibility with her, and since she wants you to make the sale, she's an ideal candidate for a Coach.

The User Buyer may or may not become your Coach for this sale. But involving her in your approach to the Economic Buyer at the very least consolidates your position with her. Ideally, you can capitalize on that Strength to improve your overall position in the sale. The point is that the Economic

Buyer, as a Red Flag, has to be covered by *somebody;* a friendly User Buyer can help you find out who's best qualified to do that.

Referring to the mechanical advantage of a simple lever and fulcrum, the Greek mathematician Archimedes is supposed to have said that with a lever long enough and a place to put the fulcrum, he could move the world. His extravagant conjecture illustrates an important principle. Leverage enables us to move by indirect force objects that we could never budge with an equal, or even greater, amount of direct force.

That principle is as applicable to sales as it is to mechanics. You gain a distinct strategic advantage when you apply indirect rather than direct pressure on tough Buying Influences. Much of your repositioning in Strategic Selling involves looking, as Archimedes might have said, for a place to put your "fulcrum." Invariably you'll find that that place is one where you're already solidly positioned.

Summarizing our second Key Element, we can say that the dual principle of Red Flags/Leverage from Strength involves three sequential techniques:

1. Locating areas of weakness (Red Flags)
2. Locating areas of Strength
3. Using those Strengths to remove or reduce the impact of the Red Flags

You'll use this combined principle now in a Personal Workshop to assess your position with the Buying Influences for your stated sales objective.

Personal Workshop 3: Red Flags/Buyers

In the Personal Workshop that you did in Chapter 3, you assessed your feelings about your current position with regard to the selling world's only constant, rapid change. Now that you've been introduced to the first two of our Six Key Elements, you can reassess that position using objective criteria. So get out the Buying Influences Chart that you drew up in the last chapter, and your Red Flags and Strengths highlighters or stickers.

STEP 1: IDENTIFY RED FLAGS AND STRENGTHS.

Take out your Red Flags and use them to identify uncertainties. Place one in any box of the Buying Influences Chart for which you have not identified at least one player. Then, remembering the automatic Red Flag situations we discussed in this chapter, put a Red Flag next to the name of any of the following players:

- Anyone about whom you have insufficient data—about whom you have a question you can't answer
- Anyone about whom the information you have is unclear or uncertain
- Any uncovered base—any Buying Influence that nobody has yet spoken to
- Any new player
- Any player involved in a recent or current corporate reorganization

Once you've identified your roadblocks, start looking for areas of Strength from which you can use Leverage to remove them. Which of your Buying Influences are most enthusiastic about your proposal? Which of them could best be utilized as a Coach? Have you spoken to these people yet about helping you move to a stronger position? On your Buying Influences Chart, place a Strength marker at any place that you think your position is particularly solid. Then test each of those positions by asking the following questions:

- Does this Strength clearly differentiate us from the competition in a way that matters to the customer?
- Does this Strength relate directly to my current Single Sales Objective?
- Will leveraging from this Strength improve my position regarding that objective?

Unless you can answer yes to each of these questions, you may not really have identified the Strength that you need. Reconsider whether any of your Strength markers should be removed.

As you look for places to put your "fulcrum," *be alert to your positioning patterns.* Observe whether you're consistently well positioned with one category of Buying Influence and out of touch with those in another category. We've mentioned the danger in adopting the traditional approach to Complex Sales, which is to build the sale around the people whom you've known the longest, whom you can contact most easily, or with whom you feel most comfortable—and to ignore other critical Buying Influences. Identifying the *patterns* in how you cover your Buyers will help you determine whether or not you're falling into this trap.

The bottom line here is this: To close a quality sale, you have to cover *all* the key players filling *all four* of the Buying Influence roles.

Take about five or ten minutes to analyze your Buying Influences Chart as a whole. Think about each Red Flag in turn, considering what specific opportunity it offers you to improve your position. And for each one, locate a possible Strength from which you can work toward the improvement.

STEP 2: REVISE YOUR ALTERNATE POSITIONS LIST.

You now have much more information about your account situation than you did when you first drew up your Alternate Positions list in Chapter 3. Now you're going to begin a process that you'll be carrying through all the remaining Personal Workshops in the book. You're going to use the information you've just acquired to revise and expand on that list. By Part 6 of the book, where you draft an Action Plan for your chosen sales objective, you will have worked over the Alternate Positions list several times, and will have transformed it into a working paper for the Action Plan.

Since you'll be performing this revision process continually throughout the book, we want to lay out a few basic guidelines here that will enable you to do it effectively. As you go down the list point by point, we want you to be *inclusive*, to be *specific*, and to *test* your Alternate Positions.

By being *inclusive* we mean you shouldn't worry too much right now about whether every one of your Alternate Positions is ideal for the situation. The Key Elements of strategy that we have yet to introduce will help you to thin out the list so that only the best options remain. But right now don't throw out too much. It's still too early to put all your eggs in one basket.

Be *specific* because you're not making out a list of theoretical sales principles; you're developing the basic working paper for *your* chosen sales objective. In listing alternatives, you can't just give yourself a cheery pep talk and resolve to "do better" with Dan Farley. If he's the Economic Buyer for your sale but he won't let you in the door, then "getting to Farley" is not an effective Alternate Position. You need to write down something like this: "Get Doris Green (my enthusiastic User Buyer) to show Farley how we can increase their productivity by 15 percent."

Of course, using friendly Doris to get to the boss won't make the sale for you. It will just deal with one Red Flag. Once you see Farley, you may find new Red Flags (maybe he's had bad experiences with your company in the past, or maybe productivity isn't a high priority at the moment), and you'll have to reassess your position again. Take it one step at a time. And use the leverage principle again and again as you work your way toward your sales objective.

Finally, *test* each Alternate Position. Don't make an unwarranted assumption that *any* change at all in a bad position will necessarily be a change for the better. Every Alternate Position you list should do one of two things:

1. Capitalize on an area of Strength
2. Eliminate a Red Flag—or at least reduce its impact

Of course, the best Alternate Positions do *both* these things. In the example given above, for instance, getting Doris Green to see Dan Farley both capitalizes on a Strength (a friendly User Buyer) and eliminates a Red Flag (the Economic Buyer's reluctance to be seen). Don't bother listing Alternate Positions that don't accomplish *at least* one of these two objectives.

We introduce the Red Flags/Leverage from Strength principle early in our programs because we want our clients to use it in analyzing all the rest of our Key Elements. The checking mechanism you've applied to your sales objective here will be useful to you throughout your selling cycle. We'll return to it periodically throughout this book.

So put your Buying Influences Chart and your Alternate Positions list aside, but keep them handy. You'll be adding to them both very soon.

CHAPTER 7

BUYER LEVEL OF RECEPTIVITY

Up to now you've been focusing largely on your own perceptions of the sales situation, as a way of making your position regarding your current objective more visible and of highlighting areas of uncertainty in your strategy. Now you're going to shift your focus to the perceptions of the various Buying Influences for that objective. We've said that after you determine who all those individuals are, the next thing you have to do is to find out how each of them feels about what you're trying to accomplish in his or her account. The third Key Element of strategy—Response Modes—is designed to help you do that more effectively, by zeroing in on their levels of buying receptivity.

You need to be able to gauge your Buyers' receptivity to your proposals because, without an understanding of this factor, you can easily end up trying to sell someone who isn't really there—one whose perception of reality is so different from your own that he or she is utterly incapable of appreciating why *any* transaction ought to occur in the first place. In addition, if you don't have a reliable method of gauging receptivity, you can easily fall into one of three fatal traps:

1. You can take your *own* perceptions of reality as the key to the sale.
2. You can assume that your perceptions of reality are the *same* as those of your Buying Influences.
3. You can recognize that the Buying Influences' perceptions of reality are different from yours, but nonetheless conclude that their perceptions are *wrong* or *irrelevant*.

Our third Key Element of strategy is designed to help you avoid these common errors of judgment by focusing on what really counts in the sale: how each Buyer is likely to react to the *change* that your proposal is offering.

Change: The Hidden Factor

In the Personal Workshop that you did in Chapter 3, you listed the changes that are influencing your current sales environment and then analyzed your feelings about them with regard to your Single Sales Objective. You'll recall that some changes seemed to be primarily positive, while others appeared mostly as threats. You'll also remember that, no matter what the external "facts" of your sales environment, most changes could be seen as either threats or opportunities, depending on your response to them.

The same thing goes for the people playing Buying Influence roles in your sale. The elements of change that you listed are impacting their business environments too, and like you they can have a variety of responses to those elements. In addition, however, they have to respond to *one* significant change that you by definition see as an opportunity, but that they can easily see as a threat. That change is *your sales proposal itself.*

You probably don't like to think of your sales proposals as threats, but Buyers can, and often do, see them in just this way. The strategic sales professional understands that *any time you ask someone to buy something, you're asking that person to make a change.* Neither the seller nor the buyer may consciously identify the sales proposal as an offer to make a change, but change is nonetheless a *critical hidden factor in every sale.* Since people react to change in different ways, and since virtually every change can be viewed as either a threat or an opportunity, there's always the chance that a Buying Influence will perceive your sales proposal as threatening even when it's "obvious" to you that it's not.

The nonstrategic salesperson often ignores the hidden factor of change. Dazzled by the elegance of your own presentation or impressed by the "perfect fit" between your product and a Buying Influence's objective needs, you may overlook the Buyer's potential perception of the proposal as an unwanted or threatening change, and assume that she will respond in the "obviously" sensible manner—that is, affirmatively.

Experience has proven to us and to our clients that this is a dangerously myopic approach. No matter how good the "facts" of a given sales situation, they may still look terrible to one or more of your Buying Influences. If that's the case, it's the facts, not the Buyers' perceptions of them, that are irrelevant. Only by understanding each of your Buying Influence's perception of reality will you be able to predict accurately his or her response to your proposal.

THE BUYER'S PERCEPTION OF REALITY

By "perception of reality" we don't mean the Buyer's general outlook on life, philosophy, or overall approach to business. We mean his or her perception of the *immediate* business situation and of what will happen to that situation if the change that you are offering is accepted.

A Buying Influence can bring four different reactions, or Response Modes, to a sales situation. Each of these four modes derives from a different perception of the immediate business reality. And each one leads to a different level of receptivity to incoming sales proposals.

Because each of the four perceptions of reality leads to a different Response Mode, and because each mode leads to a different level of receptivity, the strategic sales professional has to develop *a different sales approach for each of the four perceptions.* We're going to show you how to do that now, as we introduce the four Response Modes.

We need to stress, however, that these Response Modes are *not* descriptions of attitude or personality. They don't refer to categories of people, but to different ways in which Buyers can perceive immediate, specific situations. They show you where the person is coming from in relation to the specific change you're offering. That's all. You can speak of a given individual being in a certain mode with regard to a given business situation. It makes no sense to say that someone is *always* in that mode.

This is a critical point, because in many account situations you'll find yourself selling to a positive, growth-oriented person who, at the moment your call is scheduled, happens to see your proposal as nothing but trouble. If you focus on what you see as this person's difficult personality, you may conclude, erroneously, that your cause is lost. If you use the Key

Element of Response Modes to assess his or her reaction, however, you may find that it's only your timing that's off. You may find that, if you adopt a strategy that takes timing into account, this Buyer could become your strongest ally. As we'll see now, your Buying Influences' perceptions of reality, like most things in the Complex Sale, are often notoriously unstable. Understanding our third Key Element of strategy will help you turn this fact to your advantage.

CHAPTER 8

KEY ELEMENT 3: THE FOUR RESPONSE MODES

Predicting the best time to call on a Buying Influence is one of the great unknowns in the world of selling. Knowing *when* to approach a customer is often just as important, but usually not as predictable, as knowing *what* the customer and her company needs. As a result, you can have a product that's tailor-made for someone's apparent business needs, but if you approach that person at the wrong time of the month, or week, or selling cycle, you can easily find yourself—through no fault of your own—going up against a blank wall.

In this chapter, we take some of the uncertainty out of knowing when to approach your Buying Influences. We start by giving you a simple rule of thumb:

People buy when, and only when, they perceive a discrepancy between reality and their desired results.

In spite of the many nuances that can affect a buying decision, we've found this rule to hold true in *all* buying situations. Understanding it can be of more value to you than reading any number of texts on buyer psychology, because perceived discrepancy is the key to buyer receptivity. As we've said, that receptivity can appear in four different modes. The first, and most welcoming, of the four is what we call Growth.

THE FIRST RESPONSE MODE: GROWTH

The perception of the Buying Influence in Growth Mode is represented by the chart on page 144.

The bottom line here illustrates the way the Buyer perceives the *reality* of the current business situation. The top line shows where he or she would like that situation to be—his or her desired *results*. The space between the two lines is a reality-results gap, or *discrepancy*. Because that discrepancy exists, the probability of the Buyer taking some action—including the action of agreeing to your proposal—is high. We indicate that at the top of the chart, and to visually drive home the point we add the small barbell icon that we use in Miller Heiman processes to indicate a Strength.

A Buyer in Growth Mode is always ready to say yes to *somebody's* proposal—though not necessarily to yours. This person perceives the essential discrepancy and, being in this Response Mode, believes that it can be eliminated only by more or better results. There may be a rising production quota to fill, more orders to fill than products, or a recent memo to step up quality control. Whatever the individual's reason for wanting to do *more* and/or *better*, you have a good probability of getting a commitment—*provided that your pro-*

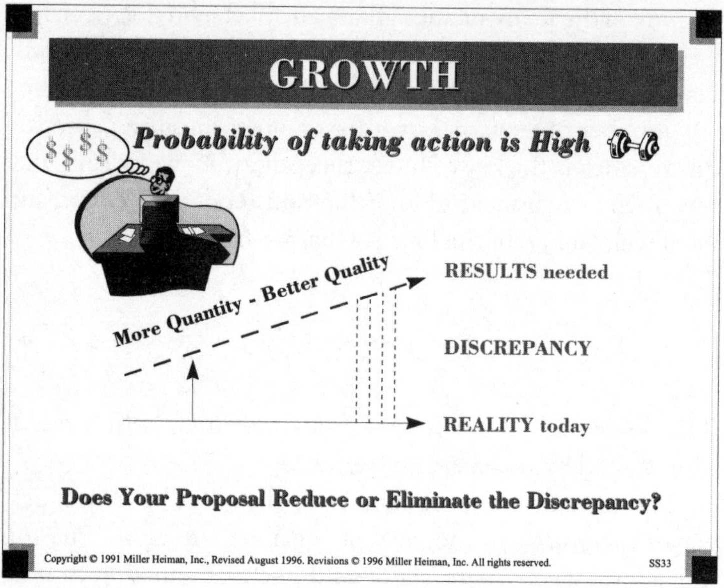

posal is seen as the change that will reduce or eliminate the discrepancy.

Buyers in Growth Mode typically use trigger words like "more," "better," "faster," and "improved" that serve as signals that they're receptive to change. This mode is usually the easiest of the four to sell to. For that reason sales representatives are often attuned to Growth themselves—and are instantly ready to comply when a Buyer is in this mode.

But there's a danger here in confusing corporate growth with the very *personal* Growth Mode of an individual. When we speak of Response Modes, we mean the personal, individual reactions of the people acting as Buying Influences for your sales proposal, not the "growth profiles" of their firms. Since you always have to adopt an individual selling approach for each of these people, you can run into serious difficulty if you assume that all the Buyers in an obviously expanding company are in an expansive Growth Mode themselves. That won't necessarily be the case.

Remember the salesman we described in Chapter 5 who lost an important contract because he sold a textile company's president a troubleshooting program without also contacting the mill managers who would be the program's User Buyers. Ignoring these key Buying Influences wasn't his only error. He also assumed incorrectly that, since the company as a whole was growth oriented, all the Buyers wanted to do more and/or better too. In fact the User Buyers in this situation wanted nothing to do with the growth he was offering them; they wanted things to remain as they were. The salesman's failure to address this fact was a major reason that the contract fell through.

No matter what the current financial picture of a customer's organization, selling to it will always involve addressing the perceptions of individual Buying Influences for your sale—*not* the "perception" of the company at large. In Strategic Selling there's no such thing as a company's perception of reality. Only individuals can have perceptions. And all of them must be taken into account for a quality sale.

THE SECOND RESPONSE MODE: TROUBLE

The probability of action being taken is also high when a Buying Influence is in Trouble. Don't be put off by the name. As the barbell icon suggests, when you confront a Buyer who is in Trouble Mode, you're facing an opportunity that is a potential Strength. It's not you who are in Trouble. The chart on page 146 shows why.

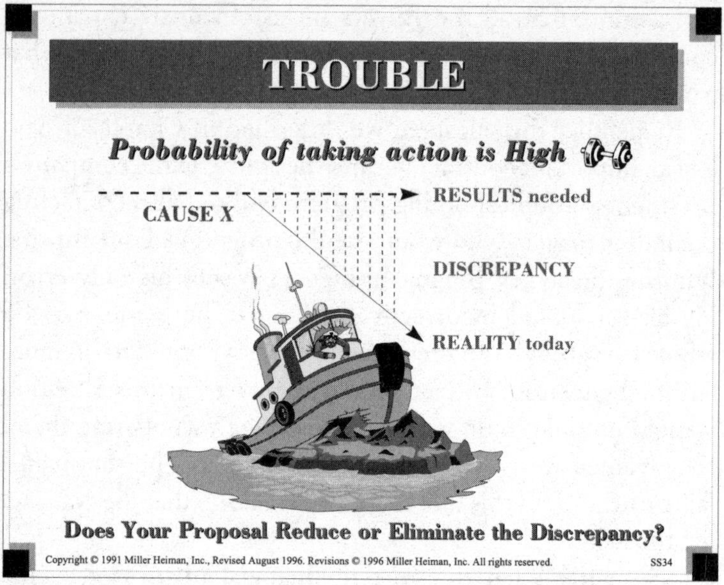

Again, the bottom line shows the Buyer's perception of current reality and the top line her perception of the results she needs in order to "win." Again there's the necessary discrepancy between reality and results that indicates the Buyer will be receptive to change.

The discrepancy here, however, is different from the discrepancy perceived by the Buyer in Growth. The Buyer in Growth Mode welcomes incremental change as a way of improving an already good situation; the Buyer in Trouble Mode is begging for immediate change as a way of reversing or preventing a defeat. Things had been going along well, but then came a crisis that created the discrepancy. All the Buyer wants is to fix whatever it is that's wrong—to get things back to normal. As the picture suggests, his basic plea—whether it's spoken or unspoken—is the business equivalent of "Get me off these rocks and back on course."

This means that a Buying Influence in Trouble Mode is ready, indeed eager, to buy—*but not necessarily from you.* The proposal that will be approved is not going to be the most beautifully presented one, or the cheapest bid, or the most technically advanced solution. It's going to be the one that will *most quickly* remove the cause of the Buyer's perceived problem.

THE URGENCY OF TROUBLE

Many people forget this. We constantly run across salespeople who are so attuned to Growth and "improvements" themselves that they have difficulty understanding, and selling to, the real needs of a Buying Influence in Trouble Mode. This is especially common in high-tech industries, where the latest, state-of-the-art product developments are a major component of the selling arsenal. You'll probably recognize this exaggerated devotion to technical improvements as part of the "bells and whistles" approach to sales. It's also part of the product-oriented approach, which, as we've already pointed out, is of only limited value in Strategic Selling.

The sales representative who relies on this approach is continually stressing the latest features of the product or service, the most recent technical refinements—the bells and whistles that make the company's line always three days ahead of the competition's. This usually works fine with Buyers in Growth Mode, but selling technical improvements to Buyers in Trouble is almost always an error, because Buyers in this mode are hurting. They're on the panic end of the Euphoria-Panic Continuum. And when people are up to their ears in alligators, they don't want to hear about the sophisticated pumping system that you're going to use to drain the swamp. They want out of the swamp, fast. When people are in Trouble Mode, you don't talk about how your product will improve their lifestyle. You sell survival. Period. The moral here may be stated as an axiom:

Trouble always takes precedence over Growth.

This doesn't mean that Growth is unimportant, only that, to a Buyer who's feeling pain (remember, it's the *perception* that counts), doing more and/or better can *wait* until you've fixed the cause of the pain. Selling Growth to a Buyer who feels in Trouble is like selling a new roof to a farmer whose barn has just caught fire. Even if the barn needs a roof, it doesn't need one *now*.

WHEN GROWTH FEELS LIKE TROUBLE

The truth of the axiom "Trouble always takes precedence over Growth" becomes immediately apparent when you confront someone who's frantically asking for "more" with an urgency that suggests Trouble rather than Growth. Although Buyers always display one Response Mode more dominantly than the others at any given moment, their feelings about their business situations are also constantly in flux. Therefore you frequently have to sell to individuals who are in the process of moving from one Response Mode to another. A common example is the case of the person who has just received a directive to increase production or quality, but without an immediate increase in the necessary resources.

A production manager we know in a West Coast appliance

plant was once faced with this exasperating situation. Sales management had just closed a deal with a catalog house that would require him, within a matter of months, to increase his factory output by 30 percent. The company was obviously growing—but our friend definitely wasn't in a Growth Mode. "I need everything yesterday," he told us. "We're moving so fast, if I don't get the parts I need by next week, I'm sunk."

There are two ways to interpret a statement like that. Either you can see it as a pure Growth statement— "I need to do *more* right now"—or you can see it as a desperate Trouble Mode plea: "I need to do more *right now*!" The difference in emphasis is crucial. If you try to sell simple Growth to a person in this situation—if you emphasize the state-of-the-art aspects of your product or service without addressing the customer's problem—you're likely to lose out to a competitor who understands that the first order of business is to get the guy away from the alligators.

We've said that Trouble Mode perceptions arise because something has happened to the Buyer to change his or her reality from what it was to something worse. The cause doesn't necessarily have to be something bad. There's nothing bad about a 30 percent increase in orders. But that development becomes a source of Trouble when it's perceived by one of your Buyers as a personal difficulty. In this case, such an increase *was* perceived by our manager friend as a problem—and he was therefore, by definition, in Trouble Mode.

Because nobody will say outright to you, "I'm in Trouble Mode here," or "We're doing terrific; all I need is better results," you have to be attentive to nuance whenever you're uncertain whether an individual Buying Influence feels himself to be in Trouble or Growth. If your product or service answers the needs of both Trouble *and* Growth, of course, you're home free. But you still have to design your approach to each individual based on which of the four Response Modes that person is in when you lay out your proposal. As always, the bottom line is that you stress those aspects of your product or service that speak to that individual Buyer's *perception of immediate reality*.

The Third Response Mode: Even Keel

The first two Response Modes provide relatively easy selling situations. The next two do not. When a Buying Influence is in Even Keel, your chances of making a sale are low because the Buyer doesn't perceive the essential discrepancy between current reality and desired results. In fact, the probability of a Buyer in Even Keel taking *any* action is low; that's why we identify this scenario as a Red Flag.

The perception of a Buyer in Even Keel can be represented by the chart on page 151.

Here the top line, representing results, and the bottom line, representing reality as the Buyer perceives it, coincide. (For visual clarity, we've drawn two separate lines. You should think of them as the Buyer does—as superimposed, or identical.) There's no gap for your proposal to close and therefore no receptivity to change. Buyers in Even Keel consistently demonstrate the truth of the maxim "No discrepancy, no sale."

To someone in Even Keel Mode, moreover, your proposal will very likely be seen as a threat. Since results and reality already coincide, this person can perceive the change you're offering only as a potential undoing of that coincidence. The Buyer in Even Keel is by definition wary of *any* change. What this person is usually thinking—and will often say to you—is "Go away. Don't rock the boat."

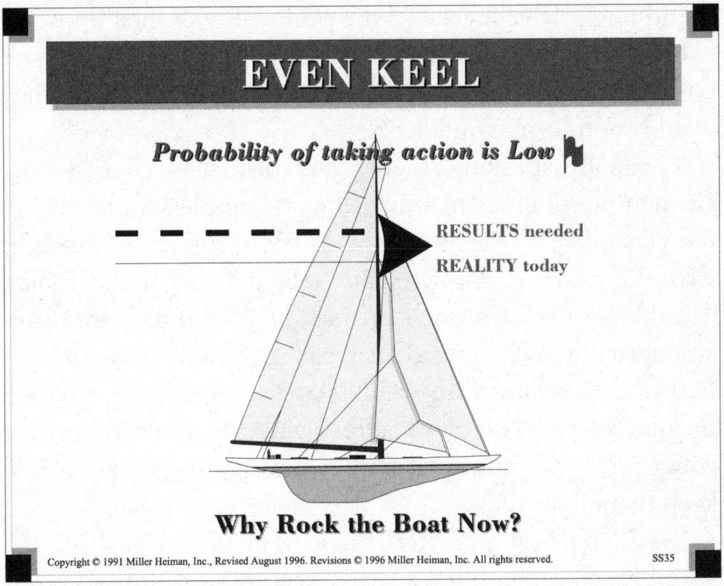

When a Buyer is firmly entrenched in Even Keel, only three things can raise the probability of your making a sale. The Buyer can see Growth or Trouble coming, he can be pressured by another Buyer who is already in Growth or Trouble, or you can demonstrate a discrepancy that the Buyer doesn't see.

THE BUYER SEES GROWTH OR TROUBLE COMING.

The User Buyers in the textile plant sale we mentioned earlier were clearly in Even Keel Mode. They saw the troubleshooting program that our friend had sold without their approval as an unnecessary and potentially unsettling change—one that would undo a comfortable status quo. Our friend might have increased the probability of their approval if he'd convinced them either that his proposal had great Growth possibilities, or that, without his program, they would soon be in Trouble.

Generally speaking, there's less risk involved in selling Growth possibilities than in selling "Trouble avoidance," so the general rule here would be to try to move the Buyer in Even Keel toward Growth. But selling Growth and selling Trouble avoidance to such a person aren't mutually exclusive strategies: Trouble avoidance can be seen as a kind of Growth. By selling a Buyer in Even Keel something that will prevent *future* Trouble, you're saying, "I know things are going great with you right now. And I have a way for you to keep them that way."

You'll be best prepared to do that if you can see the Trouble coming. That's why keeping on top of your prospects' objective needs is just as important when there's no possibility of a sale as when the signing is just around the corner. If you know how your product can help a Buyer, you also know how being without it will eventually create problems. Knowing that, you can plan your "I can get you out of this mess" presentation while the person is still in Even Keel. Probably she'll beg you to deliver it when reality breaks in.

YOU USE PRESSURE FROM ANOTHER BUYING INFLUENCE.

Buyers in Even Keel generally listen much more attentively to the views of their own Growth or Trouble superiors than they do to the most well-meaning salesperson's "warnings." Therefore, one effective way of getting someone in Even Keel to reassess a position is to get another Buying Influence—

preferably someone senior —to put pressure on him or her to reassess the situation.

Often the best candidates to exert this kind of pressure are people playing the Economic Buyer role—precisely because Economic Buyers are usually quicker to spot Trouble coming than individuals in the other roles. Because of their relatively narrow focus, for example, Technical Buyers and User Buyers are often notoriously slow to recognize storm signals. Sometimes they just don't want to know that, six weeks from now, their boat will be under water. Economic Buyers, on the other hand, are paid to forecast the future; it's their job to be well attuned to coming storms, and when they sense Trouble coming, they're generally more open than others to making drastic changes. (In addition to that, they have the authority to do so.)

Therefore, one useful strategy is to sell Growth or Trouble avoidance to the Economic Buying Influence and then get that person to convert the Buyer in Even Keel Mode. This is a way of circumventing resistance by employing the principle of Leverage from Strength. Buyers in Even Keel often cycle out of their sit-tight condition as a result of such pressure even when a sales representative isn't involved. Anything you can do to intensify that pressure—without alienating the Buyer in Even Keel—is probably going to work to your advantage.

If the Economic Buyer is in Even Keel, however, the probability of making the sale in the short term is remote. Don't count on getting an order soon in this situation.

YOU DEMONSTRATE A DISCREPANCY.

Since people will buy only when they perceive a discrepancy between reality and desired results, a third way to increase the probability of sales to Buyers in Even Keel is to show them discrepancies that they haven't already perceived. You can do this in one of two ways: You can show them that reality actually isn't as satisfactory as they currently believe, or you can show them that the results they've settled for are far short of those they can achieve. In either case, if you can demonstrate that current reality and possible results do *not* in fact coincide, you'll have created the discrepancy that's a prerequisite to any sale.

For example, a production line manager who is used to turning out 500 units a day and who's now turning out 510 won't readily see that there might be Trouble on the horizon; most likely, such a person will be in Even Keel. But if you demonstrate that one of this manager's competitors, with equipment that you've sold it, is turning out 700 units a day of an equivalent product, the manager will probably understand that the competitive results needed are in excess of current production. And receptivity to change will naturally rise.

These three strategies for selling a Buyer in Even Keel frequently prove effective. But they also have their risks—risks that derive from the fact that Buyers in Even Keel Mode find their sit-tight posture *comfortable*. Very few of them look forward to being disillusioned. Because it's difficult to break down the comfort zone of people in Even Keel, the wisest strategy to adopt with them is often the one that Woodrow Wilson adopted when Pancho Villa was threatening the New Mexico border: He gave it the voter-friendly tag "watchful waiting." Remember that while there may be no match between your product or service and an Even Keel Buyer's perceived needs today, there could well be one in the future, if you watch and wait.

THE FOURTH RESPONSE MODE: OVERCONFIDENT

The same principle applies to Buyers in Overconfident Mode. This is the most difficult of the four Response Modes to sell to. In fact, the probability of making a sale to someone who's in Overconfident Mode is, for all practical purposes, zero. The figure below indicates why a key Buyer's overconfidence is a giant Red Flag.

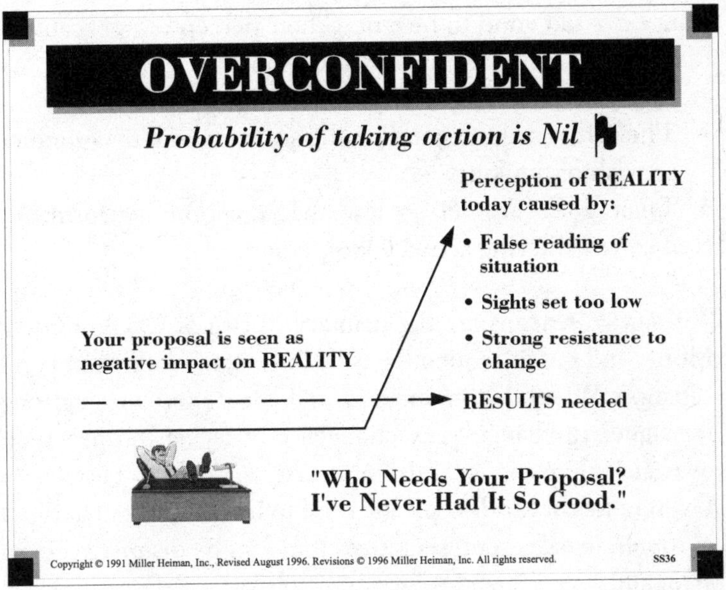
OVERCONFIDENT
Probability of taking action is Nil
Perception of REALITY today caused by:
• False reading of situation
• Sights set too low
• Strong resistance to change
Your proposal is seen as negative impact on REALITY
RESULTS needed
"Who Needs Your Proposal? I've Never Had It So Good."
Copyright © 1991 Miller Heiman, Inc., Revised August 1996. Revisions © 1996 Miller Heiman, Inc. All rights reserved.
SS36

When a Buyer is in this fourth mode, there's clearly a *kind* of discrepancy between reality and perceived results, but in this case the discrepancy works against rather than for the selling organization. An Overconfident Buyer perceives reality as outstripping the desired results. Because this person is already doing much *better* than anticipated, he or she feels no incentive to change. Like the Buyer in Even Keel Mode, this one doesn't want you to rock the boat—and that boat, in the Overconfident Buyer's view, is not only watertight, but winning the America's Cup. When you suggest a change, therefore, you'll be treated as if you were crazy. "I never had it so good," the Buyer will boast. "Things are too good to be true. You want to sell me something that could change that? Get lost!"

What Buyers in Overconfident Mode don't realize is that things *are* too good to be true. Their perception of reality is distorted, usually for one of two reasons:

- They are misunderstanding the situation, out of ignorance or wishful thinking.
- Their goals are set so low that the poor performance they're achieving actually looks good.

These two reasons are the primary causes of Overconfident Mode, and not infrequently you'll find them working in combination. When that happens, you'll encounter such a strong resistance to change—any change—that trying to open their eyes is almost certainly a waste of time. People in Overconfident Mode typically tend to be complacent and out of touch; to sales representatives they can be dismissive, even arrogant.

We've all seen the dangers of Overconfidence, in and out of the business world. Examples of this self-delusion are common enough in our recent history. Look at numerous celebrities' falls from grace or the phenomenal losses that "unassailable" U.S. manufacturers have suffered at the hands of foreign upstarts. Such examples illustrate the hazards of counting on a "sure thing," or what might be called the impotence of positive thinking. They remind us of how close euphoria is to panic on the Euphoria-Panic Continuum. And they show that, given enough time, *Overconfidence always cycles into Trouble.*

KILLING THE MESSENGER

Being in Overconfident Mode, in spite of the fact that it feels great, is really a kind of perceptual disability. It's an illness whose only cure is massive doses of reality. But as we constantly caution our clients, to a Buyer in this mode, as to one in Even Keel, you may be the worst person in the world to offer that cure. Buyers in Overconfident Mode are even more difficult to budge than those in Even Keel. Firmly entrenched in their delusions, they don't welcome the news that they're reading the situation all wrong. Therefore, when you try to "convert" an Overconfident Buying Influence to reality, you always run the risk of being seen not as helpful but as intrusive.

In ancient Greece, according to legend, messengers who brought a king bad news were sometimes put to death for causing the ruler pain. If you announce an unwelcome reality to someone in Overconfident Mode, you're taking a risk with your commissions, if not your head. We're sure you can think of many sales situations in which an overeager, honesty-smitten salesperson ruined his company's chances for future business by badgering an uncooperative Buyer into "facing facts."

WAITING FOR REALITY

Because it's so difficult to dislodge people in Overconfident Mode from their misperceptions, our general advice is not to try. Our most successful clients tell us that, when they're faced with a Buying Influence in this intransigent mode, a wise strategy is simply to maintain a low profile and to wait, as long as it takes, for reality to intrude. As a sales professional, you should keep the lines of communication open, keep the pressure off, and, when the Buyer inevitably cycles into Trouble, be sure that you're in a position to fix the problem.

A client from a West Coast computer company recently used this strategy to good effect in managing a major software sale. The buying organization, which produced a line of multiplex boards for telephone construction, was experiencing an upsurge in orders. It was producing only fifty boards a day, and because of increased demand wanted to up that figure to five hundred. There was concern about quality control at this new pace, however, and that was how our client got involved: She was widely respected as a specialist in QC systems.

The program that was already in use, she knew, wasn't doing the job well enough. It was barely capable of detecting errors efficiently when the line ran at fifty boards a day. At the new rate of five hundred a day, it would become virtually useless. She said as much to the quality control supervisor—a combination Technical and User Buyer—and was met with arrogant disbelief. "Surely you jest, Diane," the Buyer told her testily. "The system's nowhere near its breaking point. We could run it to a thousand a day and still not hear it creak."

The supervisor's cocky attitude was a classic example of Overconfidence, and so Diane managed the sale with the waiting strategy we'd recommended. For three months she bided her time, quietly keeping in touch with the supervisor and letting him know that, if he ever needed her help, it was available. Then the weak system started not only to creak, but to crack. First in a trickle and then in a steady flow, defective boards started to slip through, and soon the company was hit with a deluge of service orders. Suddenly the know-it-all supervisor was in deep Trouble. "I've got a 27 percent return rate on these boards," he complained. "How soon can you get me a better system?" "Right away," Diane replied. And she proceeded to put in the system she knew had been needed all along.

The moral of the story is simple: Don't waste your precious selling time working on an Overconfident Buyer. This mode is highly unstable. It always, eventually, cycles into Trouble. Just plan to be there to fix things when it does.

MATCHES AND MISMATCHES OF MODES

The salesperson's ideal situation is to have all of the Buying Influences in either Growth or Trouble Mode at the same time. When all your Buying Influences are saying, "I want to do more now," or "I need better results," they're obviously ripe to be sold. Similarly, when all your Buyers are hurting, you also have a golden opportunity—if you can convince them that your proposal will eliminate their problems. Whenever there's a match of perceptions among your Buyers in Growth or Trouble—or Growth *and* Trouble—there's a higher probability of a sale than when the modes are mixed.

However, given the volatility of sales situations and the personal idiosyncrasies that can influence Buyer perceptions, you aren't likely to come upon these perfectly matched fields of Buying Influences very often. More commonly, you'll be confronted with a mixed or mismatched field, in which, for example, four different Buyers have four distinct perceptions of the same business "reality."

The salesperson unskilled in strategy often mishandles these mixed fields. As we've mentioned, a natural tendency among those salespeople who like to play things by ear is to focus on the Buyers they like, or who like them, rather than to see to it that all the relevant bases are covered. You see this all the time with regard to Response Modes.

A sales representative who sees Growth possibilities, for example, might approach the ABCO company with a proposal designed to boost production. He finds that only a lone User Buyer sees the situation as he does; all the other Buyers are in Trouble, focusing on a "trivial" problem. But because he and the User Buyer agree, the sales representative concentrates on him—and quickly loses the order to a competitor who addresses the Trouble seen by the other Buying Influences.

Or the same sales representative might approach ABCO six months later with a surefire cure for absenteeism—a problem revealed by a Technical Buyer in personnel. It turns out that all the other Buyers are now in Even Keel. They're willing to live with the time loss because productivity has never been higher, and they don't want to jeopardize what they have by fiddling with the system. Crying Trouble in this kind of situation might bring the sales representative closer to the personnel manager, but it would alienate everyone else.

To avoid falling into the "single Buyer" trap that these scenarios indicate, you've got to recall our advice about covering all the bases. The strategic pro doesn't simply play ball with the person whose perception he shares. He adopts an approach that realizes that truth, like beauty, is often in the eye of the beholder—a strategy that takes into account with equal seriousness the perceptions of all the Buying Influences involved in the sale.

Covering All the Bases—Again

One of the most serious errors you can make in a Complex Sale is to ignore or abandon a key Buying Influence because that person's perception of current reality doesn't match yours. You don't have to see eye to eye with your Buyers in order to sell them. You do have to respect each one's perception, since it's to that perception, ultimately, that you're selling.

We've emphasized the importance of covering all the Buying Influence bases and of managing the contacts with the key individuals in such a way that each one is covered by the person best qualified to do so. It's also important that the people you arrange to have covering those bases understand that it's the individual Buyer's perceptions of reality, not their own, that determine the best approach to take with each one. The starting point is always the same: It's how the individual Buyer *feels* about the current situation.

The various Buyers' feelings will almost always be at variance with each other, not to mention with your own feelings, even when the "facts" are obvious to you. Frequently, a situation that spells Trouble to one Buying Influence will simply reinforce the Overconfident attitude of another Buying Influence in the same company. Therefore, you have to manage each sale on the admittedly unconventional assumption that there's no such thing as reality—only individual perceptions of reality. And you have to see that each base is covered by a person who's willing to take individual feelings about the situation as valid starting points for discussion.

You, as the manager—or what we have called the "strategic orchestrator"—of the sale, need to survey the entire field of players, and to work toward a match of modes whenever that's possible. Generally the best way to do that—the way that most effectively employs the principle of Leverage from Strength—is to first approach those Buyers who are in Trouble and Growth, and then get them to work with you on their Even Keel and Overconfident colleagues.

In summary, it's possible to sell a proposal to a mixed field of Buying Influences, but only if you employ the basic principles of Response Modes:

1. The starting point for approaching each individual is to understand his or her current perception of the business situation and his or her perceived discrepancy between reality and results.
2. Each base must be covered by a person who accepts this as the starting point, and who is best qualified to approach that individual Buyer.
3. When working with a mixed field of responses, always use Leverage from Strength to bring about a match of modes.

You'll practice these principles now, in a Personal Workshop.

Personal Workshop 4: Response Modes

STEP 1: IDENTIFY EACH INDIVIDUAL'S RESPONSE MODE.

Take out the Buying Influences Chart you started in Chapter 5 and focus now on how each Buyer feels about the *immediate* situation, with regard to the specific change you are offering to introduce to that person's business environment—that is, your sales proposal. Ask yourself how that proposal affects the environment, and whether or not it can close a perceived gap (discrepancy) between reality and results. Then, on your chart, write in the letters *G* for Growth, *T* for Trouble, *EK* for Even Keel, and *OC* for Overconfident,

BUYING INFLUENCES CHART

ECONOMIC: releases $ $ Dan Farley H G	USER: judges impact on job Doris Green H G Harry Barnes L EK
TECHNICAL: screens out Gary Steinberg M T Will Johnson H OC Harry Barnes L EK	COACH(ES): guides me on this sale Doris Green H G Sandy Kelly M T

depending on how each Buyer perceives the situation. Your Buying Influences Chart should now look something like the example shown above.

You may find—in fact you almost certainly will find—that identifying your Buyers' modes isn't an entirely straightforward process. Inevitably you'll come across someone you can't figure out, or someone who seems to be straddling the fence between Growth and Even Keel. That's all right. Since Buyers can be erratic in their perception, and thus in their responses, it would be unreasonable to expect them to fall into slots like pegs into prearranged holes. It would also be unrealistic to expect them to stay there throughout the selling cycle. In reality the Response Modes often appear as permutations and combinations away from the "norm."

Furthermore, they are *dynamic,* not static. That's why we emphasize the need for constant reassessment of position.

But you can still identify where your Buying Influences are right now, with regard to your current proposal. The emphasis is on *this moment.* Remember that the four Response Modes aren't categories or types of people; they're *situation perceptions.* All we want you to do is to identify each of your Buyers' responses today to the change you're offering. Ask yourself how each one is talking at this point in the developing sale:

- If Dan Farley is asking for faster delivery or bigger orders, he's by definition in Growth Mode.
- If Gary Steinberg has an inventory problem, he's by definition in Trouble Mode—even if he's "usually" oriented toward Growth.
- If Harry Barnes is saying, "I like things just the way they are," he's in Even Keel; if he's smugly self-assured about how great things are, he's probably Overconfident.

If after about five minutes on this step you can't determine a Buyer's current Response Mode, place a Red Flag by that name. Then move on to the next step.

STEP 2: RATE YOUR BUYERS.

Now that you've identified and listed on the Buying Influences Chart all of the key individuals and their Response Modes, assess where you stand with each of them by asking yourself this question:

How does each person feel right now with regard to my current sales proposal?

Notice that you're not trying to find out how the Buyers feel about *you* as a person, or about *your company,* but how they feel about *your current sales objective.*

In our programs we ask our clients to rate their Buyers on a scale of –5 to +5. You should do the same thing now. Each of your Buyers will be somewhere on a scale between wildly enthusiastic about your proposal and vehemently opposed to it. Next to the names of those who are enthusiastic sponsors, place a +5 on your Buying Influences Chart. Next to those who are strongly opposed or who won't even see you, place a –5. For the people who are somewhere in between, place appropriate numerical ratings (+1, –2, +4) next to their names.

Rating your Buyers in this fashion isn't an exact science. It's not meant to be. What you're trying to do is to determine *how well each base is covered,* based on how you perceive each person to feel about the change you're trying to bring into his or her organization. Trusting your gut reactions here is just as important as it was in the workshop on position, when you concentrated on your own feelings about the sale. We realize that your feelings are not infallible, but they remain a necessary guide in assessing your Buyers, and we urge you, again, to accept them as a valid beginning.

STEP 3: TEST THESE RATINGS.

In our programs we use the informal scale on page 166 to test our participants' assessments of how their Buying Influences feel.

RATINGS

+5 Enthusiastic Advocate
+4 Strongly Supportive
+3 Supportive
+2 Interested
+1 Will Go Along
-1 Probably Won't Resist
-2 Uninterested
-3 Negative
-4 Very Negative
-5 Antagonistic Antisponsor

Measure your Buyer ratings now against this scale. Look at the numbers you've placed next to their names and then ask yourself the following questions:

- If I've rated this Buyer as +5, is the person really an enthusiastic advocate of my proposal?
- If I've rated someone as +1, will the person definitely at least go along with the proposal?
- If I've rated someone as –1, will that Buyer at least stay out of the way? Will any resistance be slight?
- If I've rated a Buyer as –5, is this a major impediment to the proposal? Will the person work actively to block the sale?

Ask yourself similar questions about the people who fall elsewhere on the informal scale. And note two important points:

One: It's only theoretically possible for a Buying Influence to be neutral to your proposal. You see that we have no zero on our rating scale. The reason is that, in our experience, Buyers are always at least slightly positive or slightly negative about sales proposals. If you have a Buyer who seems firmly planted on the fence, the chances are good that you're misreading that person's feelings.

Two: The same thing is true of those Buying Influences whom you haven't yet contacted at all. Remember, this is an exercise in testing how well you've covered the bases; an uncontacted Buyer is by definition an uncovered base. Don't guess about how such people feel. Until you know for sure how each one feels, you should consider every one a Red Flag. They may not turn out to be strong antisponsors; but *in terms of your current position* with them, you have to consider them so.

After you've rated your Buyers and tested those ratings against the scale, your Buying Influences Chart should look something like the example on page 168.

STEP 4: ANALYZE YOUR INFORMATION.

You now have each Buyer assessed twice, once in terms of modes and again in terms of overall feelings about your proposal. Now compare these two assessments. Looking at the modes and numerical ratings together, determine your current Strengths and weaknesses (Red Flag areas) based on the composite picture. Note that ratings in the +4 and +5 range may themselves be considered Strengths, while severely negative ratings should be seen as Red Flags.

Look especially for inconsistencies. For example, if you have a Buyer in Overconfident Mode whom you've rated as +3, there's something logically inconsistent in your analysis.

BUYING INFLUENCES CHART

ECONOMIC: releases $ $. Dan Farley H G +2	USER: judges impact on job Doris Green H G +3 Harry Barnes L EK −2
TECHNICAL: screens out Gary Steinberg M T −4 Will Johnson H OC −4 Harry Barnes L EK −2	COACH(ES): guides me on this sale Doris Green H G +3 Sandy Kelly M T +4

That Buyer is either Overconfident *or* +3, not both. Label that kind of inconsistency with a Red Flag: You need to learn more about this Buyer to develop an effective strategy.

Similarly, if you have a Coach who isn't *strongly* in favor of your proposal, look at your data again. The best Coaches are generally in Growth Mode, but to be really effective—to fulfill their role of helping you to make the sale—they *have* to be in either Growth or Trouble. If you've labeled your Coach EK or OC, or given that person a rating of less than about +3, then you don't really have a Coach. You might want to think about "firing" this Coach and finding somebody else.

In comparing the two assessments, finally, remember that Buyers you've rated with a plus must by definition be in either Growth or Trouble. You can mark any +4 or +5 person in

Growth or Trouble mode as a Strength. However, Buyers in Growth and Trouble Mode can also rate as minuses—they might, for example, still like your competitor's proposal better than yours. Individuals in Even Keel and Overconfident Mode are by definition negative: There is no such thing as a +3 Buying Influence in Even Keel.

Look also for matches of mode—both those that already exist and those you might be able to create. Think about not only how the various Buyers relate individually to you, but how they're integral parts of a composite response to your proposal. Which Buyers share a current Growth or Trouble level of receptivity? These people constitute one of your most significant areas of Strength. How can you use them to overcome the poor receptivity to change that's evident from the Buyers in Even Keel or Overconfident Mode?

STEP 5: REVISE YOUR ALTERNATE POSITIONS LIST.

You should now have a pretty good idea of how receptive each of your key individuals is, right now, to your current sales proposal. Now take out your Alternate Positions list again and use the data you've uncovered in the last two chapters to revise it. Go over each option on the list and ask yourself this question:

How does the level of receptivity of each of my Buying Influences affect the viability of this option?

Based on the answers you get to that question, drop those options that no longer seem workable. Modify those that should be modified. Add any new options suggested by the lessons of these two chapters. We'll make the same provisos here that we did in the previous workshop:

- Continue to be *inclusive,* listing less than ideal options as well as those that you consider right on target. You're not ready yet to identify a first-choice Alternate Position.
- Continue to be *specific.* Be sure that every Alternate Position you list relates to your specific sales proposal, as it stands right now.
- Continue to *test* your Alternate Positions by making sure that each one capitalizes on a Strength, eliminates or reduces the impact of a Red Flag, or does both.

Since our current focus is Response Modes, you'll want to pay special attention to this Key Element as you assess your list. For example, consider the option we suggested you might employ to get to the hypothetical Dan Farley: getting your friendly User Buyer, Doris Green, to show him that you could increase his productivity by 15 percent. Remembering that this option has to be inclusive, specific, and testable, you might judge its current value to your strategy by asking yourself questions like these:

- Is productivity increase a high-priority item for Farley right now? I have him down as moderately interested (+2) and in Growth Mode; do I need to reassess those judgments?
- Is Farley's reluctance to see me evidence that he's not in Growth Mode at all? Might he be in Even Keel—and therefore uninterested in the Growth points of my proposal?
- Does Doris Green have all the information *she* needs to sell Farley on the 15 percent increase?

- If Farley is less enthusiastic about Growth than he appears to be, can I show him that ignoring my proposal will eventually get him into Trouble? Can I sell him my Growth proposal as a means of avoiding Trouble?
- What feedback do I need to get from Doris Green to be sure she's the right person to cover Farley for me? Is *she* as enthusiastic about my proposal as I need her to be?

These questions, of course, are only samples. But they should give you the general idea we're stressing. *Every selling strategy is only as good as its most recent reassessment.* Our point in asking you to test all the items on your Alternate Positions list in this way is to ensure that this list—which will be so vital to your Action Plan—continues to be up to date and realistic.

In a sense this entire book can be seen as an analytical machine designed to produce one meticulously tested product—your Alternate Positions list. By now you should have already begun to work out some of the bugs in its design. But you'll be testing and revising it again very soon.

CHAPTER 9

THE IMPORTANCE OF WINNING

We began this book by analyzing your Single Sales Objective in terms of your needs as a seller. In a Personal Workshop in Chapter 3, we asked you to assess your current feelings about that objective and to begin considering Alternate Positions that would make you feel more certain about its outcome. For the past few chapters, we've been analyzing your objective in terms of your various Buying Influences' needs. We've given you a framework for analyzing their feelings and for predicting the likelihood of your proposal's success based on those feelings.

Now we're going to bring these two forms of analysis together and consider how the sale can fulfill both your own *and* the Buying Influences' needs. We're going to present a model of selling that takes *mutual satisfaction* as the foundation of long-term success.

The emphasis here is on "long-term." By using the Win-Win model we present in this chapter, you'll be able to count not just on meeting your current Single Sales Objective, but on building incremental business way down the line. This is important because, as any professional knows, getting an individual piece of business can be a relatively simple task—if all you want is that one piece of business. We're betting that you're not content with closing individual orders and pocketing immediate commissions. Like our most successful clients, you understand that *getting the order, while it's essential, is never enough*. Like our clients, you also want:

- Satisfied customers
- Long-term relationships
- Repeat business
- Strong referrals

As a Strategic Selling professional, you want every sales objective, no matter how large or how small, to move predictably toward an outcome that delivers on *all* of these goals. The key to getting all your sales objectives to do that lies in understanding the concept of Winning.

WINNING: A KEY TO LONG-TERM SUCCESS

A lot of fluff has been written about Winning, and much of it can be fatal to the sales professional. If you think, for example, that Winning has anything to do with intimidating or gaining "victory" over your Buying Influences, you're going to be in for a rude shock when you look for new business and referrals. If you suppose that you Win every time you close a deal (as in the misnomer "We won the order"), then you're the victim of another common misinterpretation. Or if you think that a Win can be measured in simple monetary terms, you're going to be shortchanging your customers—and eventually yourself as well.

Our definition of Winning is different from the others you've encountered. The heart of it is the notion of *self-interest*. We've said that you Win in a buy/sell encounter when you come out of it feeling positive. The *reason* you feel positive is that you perceive that encounter as having served your personal self-interest.

Self-interest is misunderstood and unfairly criticized by many well-meaning people. Many sales professionals, even though they strive energetically to Win, are still reluctant to admit the importance of Winning in their lives, and some of them actually feel guilty about wanting to Win. The common result is an internal tension that psychologists call cognitive dissonance, which comes from confusing self-interest with self-centeredness or simply selfishness.

Aside from Ayn Rand and a few die-hard social Darwinists, few of us are about to give any hearty toasts to selfishness. But to take selfishness and self-interest as equivalent terms is to distort their true meanings. Selfishness is a kind of social pathology: It's what happens when someone thinks and cares *only* about himself—whatever the long-term consequences for himself or others. Self-interest, on the other hand, is a social necessity: It's what you honor when you judiciously assess your own needs within the dynamic context of competing needs.

In nature, self-interest is an absolutely necessary and beneficial instinct. The biological truth is plain: All living things either serve their self-interest or die. Human beings in all social situations serve their self-interest by attaining what they see as personal Wins. In selling, they do this by agreeing to business transactions that they feel will be to their *personal* advantage.

If you think about your past experience in selling, you'll see that this is true. You know that the sales where you leave feeling satisfied are those in which you have Won because some aspect of your self-interest—financial, personal, social—has been served by the transaction. And you know that you have felt cheated—have felt that you lost—in scenarios where your self-interest was violated or ignored.

The same thing is true of your Buying Influences. They enter the buy-sell encounter hoping to Win, too. And they leave the encounter satisfied when, and *only* when, they feel that it has served their personal self-interest.

THE FOUR QUADRANTS OF THE WIN-WIN MATRIX

Even though both buyers and sellers enter sales encounters hoping that they will Win, that isn't always the way things turn out. Every buy-sell encounter can have one of four possible outcomes. They are represented in the quadrants of what we call the Win-Win Matrix, shown on page 176. At the conclusion of any face-to-face buy-sell encounter, you're always positioned in one of these four quadrants.

As we describe these quadrants, keep two interrelated points in mind:

First: Each quadrant of the matrix describes a relationship between you and *each* of your Buying Influences—not between you and "the account" or "the customer" as a whole. Winning, like buyer receptivity, is a personal matter. Therefore, logically you cannot manage a sale so that a company Wins. You can and must manage each sales objective so that every one of the Buying Influences in that company sees a personal Win in adopting your solution. Your goal in utilizing the Win-Win design is to achieve mutual satisfaction between you and *each*

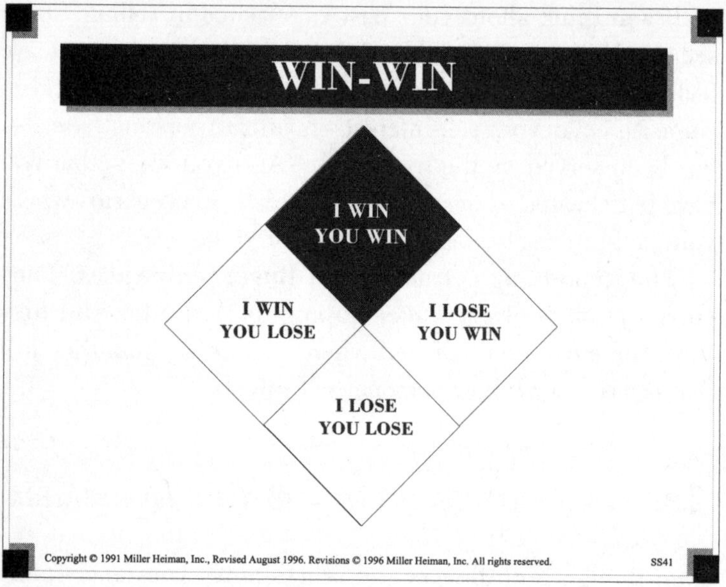

one of your Buying Influences. If you leave even one of them with the feeling of losing, you'll be severely hurting your chances of maintaining good relations with that person—and therefore his or her account—over time.

Second: The matrix describes not only how you're *currently* positioned with each Buying Influence, but also how you're positioned *after the sale is made.* The assumption behind each quadrant of the matrix is that you've already gotten, or soon will get, the piece of business. You might be tempted to interpret that fact itself as a Win, but that would be a mistake. Even after you close a deal, you can still Lose, and so can any or all of your Buying Influences. Therefore, we use the Win-Win Matrix to describe the probable *long-term* outcome of your relationships, after you have successfully closed a transaction.

For optimum sales results over time, you have to try to direct every sales objective into the same quadrant of that matrix—the Win-Win, or "joint-venture," quadrant.

I WIN–YOU WIN: THE JOINT-VENTURE QUADRANT

Our dictionary defines adventure as "an undertaking involving danger and unknown risks." The Arctic explorer Sir Ernest Henry Shackleton put an interesting spin on this definition when he called one of his adventures "the result of poor planning."

The naive salesperson—not to mention the salesperson who is allergic to planning—often welcomes adventure. He sees the Buyer as an adversary, the order as a prize, and the selling cycle as a fascinating, unpredictable contest with the customer. This adventurous approach to selling frequently leads to trouble because it intensifies uncertainty—precisely the element that the good strategist, like the good Arctic explorer, wants to avoid.

We tell our clients that, rather than seeking *ad*venture, they should strive to develop *joint* ventures in which their Buying Influences are seen not as threats from the outside but as members of their own teams. Those of us who have prospered by using Strategic Selling know that good selling is never an adversarial game in which the Buyers' Losses are our Wins, but one in which the Buyers' Losses are our Losses too, and where their Wins always serve our self-interest too. We understand that only by enlisting our Buying Influences as *partners* in mutually supportive joint ventures can we hope to achieve mutual satisfaction over time.

MUTUAL DEPENDENCE

This isn't true of all social situations. Certain inherently adversarial encounters cannot be managed as joint ventures. In a baseball game or a lawsuit, for example, you can't reasonably expect the opposing sides to cooperate. But in any situation where *mutual dependence* is important, you must learn to hang together or, as Ben Franklin once observed of the bickering American colonies, you will hang separately. American labor and management have recently (and belatedly) begun to apply this lesson in their dealings with each other—thus softening the traditionally bitter atmosphere of collective bargaining.

How does this work on the personal level? To answer that, think about your own best sales: the ones from which you've come away feeling both emotionally and financially satisfied. Think about a sale in which (a) you satisfactorily served *your* self-interest, (b) you also served the self-interest of your *Buying Influences,* and (c) those individuals *knew* that you had done this. That sale was by definition one with a Win-Win outcome. There's nothing more satisfying. Every real professional wants *all* of his or her sales to end up there.

Why? The answer isn't altruism. We're not advising you to adopt a joint-venture approach to your customers out of "niceness," politeness, or ethics. Those reasons are gravy. The meat-and-potatoes reason is purely pragmatic. When your Buyers Win, *you* Win, because you get the repeat business and new leads that you're looking for. Serving your Buying Influences' individual self-interests is ultimately the best way for you to serve your own.

I WIN–YOU LOSE: BEATING THE BUYER

This is the quadrant into which the general public seems to believe that everyone in sales wants to manipulate prospects. Examples of the I Win–You Lose scenario abound in popular stories—from the used-car salesman who sets the odometer back to the appliance dealer who reneges on his warranty, from the messenger service that delivers your package two days late to the mail-order house that doesn't deliver it at all. Whether it follows from outright dishonesty or mere incompetence, the I Win–You Lose outcome has never been in short supply.

The Federal Trade Commission and the postal service are continually tracking down and imprisoning those lovers of the Win-Lose approach who have actually broken the law—the countless scam and bunko artists who agree with Charles Dickens that the "true business precept" is "Do other men, for they would do you." But these outright thieves are only the scum of the crop. Unfortunately, it's easy to play I Win–You Lose without ever breaking the law. You can, for example, fall into these common traps:

1. You can sell someone something at an inflated price at a time when that person's urgent business needs make it impossible for him or her to negotiate or refuse.
2. You can describe the service capabilities of your firm unrealistically, leading the customer to believe that you'll instantly correct any problem that might arise with your product.
3. You can place a model in the Buyer's firm that's more (or less) sophisticated than what's really needed.

In each of these adversarial, and adventurist, scenarios, you're sticking it to the Buyer in exchange for a quick commission.

But in spite of what the public has been led to believe, this "common" and "traditional" selling approach is actually neither common nor traditional—at least not among successful salespeople. The *best* companies and the *best* sales representatives have always understood that, wherever repeat business is important, playing I Win–You Lose is a disastrous policy. The only positive thing it can get you is an initial order. Often it also gets you the last thing any professional salesperson wants: a customer who is hell-bent on revenge.

BUYER'S REVENGE

The principal reason that you should avoid playing I Win–You Lose is that the Win-Lose quadrant is short-term and *unstable*. Given enough time, it always degenerates into Lose-Lose. Playing Win-Lose with anyone with whom you expect to have future business contacts isn't in *your* self-interest because, sooner or later, the people you've allowed to Lose are going to discover that you've done them wrong. To refer back to the examples we've just given, they'll discover:

1. That the competition's price was 35 percent lower than yours for a similar product
2. That service requests aren't being answered as you promised they would be
3. That your product, in spite of its technical capabilities, isn't suited to their particular needs

These things may not happen right away, but if you've really ignored a Buyer's self-interest, eventually that person is going to find out. The *best* you can hope for, when that happens, is that she will simply walk away and forget about you, nursing a case of Buyer's Remorse in private. What's much more likely is that she will counterattack, by spreading the word around that you can't be trusted. That's Buyer's Revenge. It can be deadly to your business years down the line.

Sometimes, of course, the payback is immediate. Consider the sale to the textile company of the troubleshooting program that never made it past the trial period because the sales representative had ignored the User Buyers. Ignoring them was tantamount to saying, "I don't care about your self-interest. I can Win here even if you Lose." Their Buyer's Revenge came very quickly, as they simply saw to it that the program didn't perform as promised. And the ultimate outcome just as quickly became Lose-Lose.

Sometimes Buyer's Revenge can take a little longer. About fifteen years ago, a writer friend of ours coauthored a book with an aspiring actor. The book bombed, largely because the editor, who was frying much larger fish at the time, assigned it the lowest of priorities in her advertising budget. Our friend never forgot what he considered her mismanagement of the project, and a year ago, when the actor—now a rising soap opera star—asked him to do a second book, he got his revenge. The editor naturally wanted to sign the television personality, but our friend told his collaborator, "Nothing doing. I'd love to do another book with you, but I won't work with her again." So they brought the book, with considerable fanfare, to another publisher.

We realize that our writer friend wasn't a "buyer" in the technical sense. But he was, very clearly, a Buying Influence. By playing Win-Lose with that Buying Influence—all of fifteen years ago—the editor had closed off a business opportunity for herself that at the time she didn't even imagine existed. The lesson is clear. Failing to consider every individual Buyer's self-interest is, in the long run, a self-defeating proposition. Or, to paraphrase a line from one of English literature's greatest psychologists, William Shakespeare: "Hell hath no fury like a Buying Influence scorned."

I Lose–You Win: Doing the Buyer a "Favor"

Every professional knows that playing I Win–You Lose is actually far less common than playing I Lose–You Win. Here the seller plays martyr, doing the buyer a "favor" at his or her expense. "I will deliberately Lose," the salesperson says in effect, "so that you, Mr. Customer, can Win."

You've probably seen this many times in your work. One of our program participants complained that it was so common in his firm that it was "practically a company policy." Every time a sales representative gets an initial order by selling at a ridiculously low price, every time your company offers an extraordinary discount for bulk sales, every time free service, free samples, or some other loss-leader fringe benefit is thrown in with the order, the game that your company is playing is I Lose–You Win.

The rationale behind this approach is that the customer will be impressed with the selling organization's generosity and reciprocate in the future. "I'll scratch your back now," the sales representative implies, "and you can scratch mine later." Unfortunately, it doesn't always work out that neatly.

The underlying problem here is one of perception. When you play Lose-Win, you give the customer *a false sense of reality*, one that is represented falsely as the norm and that can be maintained only on a limited basis. When you "buy the business" by giving away your product, services, time, or other resources, *you set your Buying Influences up to Lose* in the future by unrealistically raising their expectations.

No company is going to keep giving away its products or services forever. When your company decides it's time for the devil to be paid, you're going to have to give your "Win" customer a decidedly unpleasant message: "Now it's your turn to Lose." Typically, Buying Influences who hear that message forget all about the "favors" you did them in the past. They see you playing Win-Lose with them *now*, and they set out to take revenge. When that happens, you both Lose—just as surely as if you'd been playing Win-Lose.

Ultimately the Lose-Win quadrant, just like the Win-Lose quadrant, is *unstable*. It too always *degenerates* into Lose-Lose. Therefore, it isn't in your self-interest.

WHEN—AND HOW—TO PLAY LOSE-WIN

We're not saying that you should *never* play Lose-Win. In certain situations it can be a useful *short-term* strategy. There's nothing like an introductory discount, for example, to interest a customer or prospect in a new product. But if you play Lose-Win, do it right. *Let the customer know that's what you're doing.* And make sure it's understood too that the supposedly free lunch you're offering is a limited offer.

The most common uses of the Lose-Win strategy in our society occur in the consumer products market. There manufacturers don't have to explain to their customers what they're doing, because it's common knowledge. When the local supermarket stops using Barko dog food as a loss leader and reverts to the normal price, nobody cries, "Why are you trying to scalp us?" When the Super Sudzee Soap Company hangs a free sample of a new product on your front door in January, you don't call up a month later and say, "Where's my February freebie?" In the consumer-products field, customers understand just as well as retailers and suppliers that "invites" like sampling and loss leaders are short-term gambits.

But in your field of business, that may not be common knowledge, and you should never assume that your Buying Influences understand it. The most serious mistake you can make in playing Lose-Win is *failing to tell your Buyers that they're getting a special deal.* This leads to constant resentment among those Buying Influences who mistakenly think that the special deal is the norm—and who therefore react to the real norm, when it's reintroduced, as if it were inflated or unfair. You can avoid this unwelcome situation only by spelling out clearly what you're doing.

Another piece of advice: *Put it in writing.* Don't rely on "friendship" to keep things on a sound footing when you know that, somewhere down the line, you're going to have to reintroduce a "most favored trading partner" to reality. Unless the specialness of the Lose-Win scenario is stipulated on paper—either in the contract, on the invoice, or in a separate letter of understanding—it will be easy for a once favored Buyer to balk at your future terms.

Even if you play Lose-Win "properly," however, it's still only a short-term strategy. Your ultimate goal should remain to position yourself in the Win-Win quadrant with all your Buying Influences, all the time.

I Lose–You Lose: The Default Quadrant

We've said that each quadrant of the matrix describes a situation both during the selling cycle and at the sale's end, *after* the order is taken. The Lose-Lose or default quadrant might also be called the "catchall" quadrant because, sometimes well after the final papers are signed, it catches all the sales that you haven't consciously and actively *managed* into Win-Win outcomes.

This is true for Win-Lose and Lose-Win scenarios, for the reasons we've explained above. It's also true for that very small number of sales that, at some point in the selling cycle, are already operating in the Lose-Lose quadrant. For example, a customer who desperately needs a product he sees as overpriced might insist on extraordinary delivery schedules as a way of justifying the extra expense. The high price would translate as a Lose for the customer, while the seller would Lose because of the rush-rush scheduling.

Such scenarios, however, are rare, because only a minuscule proportion of the selling population *sets out* to play Lose-Lose or continues to play it once it's obvious that this is what's happening. Except for the occasional masochist and assorted neurotics, people in sales generally understand that nobody has anything to gain from mutual destruction. Your Buying Influences understand this too, which is why, if you find yourself in an obvious Lose-Lose situation, you should let them know that you're not any happier about it than they are. Once Buying Influences in this situation understand that you're not *trying* to Win at their expense, they'll usually be willing to work with you so that no one Loses.

YOUR CURRENT WIN-WIN POSITION

The best sales professionals understand intuitively the importance of the Win-Win dynamic. We all know people who seem to have a gift for making things happen: people who are always in the right place at the right time, who always know the right players to contact for a given objective, who always know what to say to each player—and whose revenue figures reflect their uncannily consistent "good luck."

When you examine how they operate, though, you find that their success has nothing to do with luck. They're successful because they understand the fundamental biological and psychological law that *everyone must serve his or her self-interest*. They put that law into practice by striving constantly to serve their own and their Buyers' self-interest. And they make sure that every one of them knows it.

Each time you serve someone's self-interest, you enlist that person as a member of a joint-venture team whose basic goal is mutual satisfaction. When you and your Buying Influences practice teamwork in this way, you make it that much easier for all of you to Win together. After that has happened once, you've established the expectations and necessary conditions for it to happen again, in every new sales objective you undertake.

This is an ongoing process. Your position in the Win-Win Matrix must be constantly reassessed throughout the selling cycle to ensure that, as business conditions and key players change, you're continually moving toward Win-Win outcomes with all your Buying Influences.

You may begin this process of assessment now, by making a preliminary survey of the Buying Influences for your chosen sales objective. We've said that you serve your self-interest best when you serve the self-interest of each of your Buying Influences. Test whether or not you're doing that by assessing each one in turn. Start, for example, with the Economic Buyer (Dan Farley on our sample Buying Influences Chart) and ask yourself these questions:

- Am I sincerely and earnestly trying to serve Farley's self-interest in this sale? That is, do I really *want* him to Win?

- Does Farley understand that I'm trying to serve his self-interest? That is, does he *know* I want him to Win?

Then ask the same questions about each of the other Buying Influences on your chart.

If the answers here are negative, or if you're not *sure* of the answers, note that as an element of risk—a Red Flag area—in the sale. Perhaps you aren't yet in the Win-Win quadrant of the matrix with this Buying Influence and you need to manage your relationship with him or her toward a Win-Win outcome.

The places where your answers are clear and positive you can identify as areas of strategic Strength. But even where that is the case, you still need to remember that your current Win-Win position is only that—a current position. You need to *maintain* that position, so that you and your Buying Influences are still in the Win-Win quadrant at the end of the selling cycle, and beyond. One invaluable tool in helping you do that is our fourth Key Element of strategy, Win-Results.

CHAPTER 10

KEY ELEMENT 4: WIN-RESULTS

Many of our clients—including such Fortune 500 leaders as Coca-Cola, Hewlett-Packard, and Price Waterhouse—find our Win-Win concept so useful that they have made it an integral part of their own corporate cultures. Working toward Win-Win outcomes has become for them, as for us at Miller Heiman, not just a technique or process, but the operational core of the way they do business. Some of these companies have even adopted the Win-Win Matrix itself into their sales presentations. As a marketing executive for one of them told us recently, "Not only are we philosophically committed to the joint venture approach, but we've made your matrix a standard visual aid in our presentations; it's an ideal tool for showing our customers that we're on their side."

To use the Win-Win concept as effectively as these business leaders do, you need the same philosophical commitment as this manager—and something more. You need a practical, tested method for implementing the Win-Win philosophy in the real world. We're going to present that method now.

Implementing the Win-Win philosophy means making the Win-Win quadrant of the Matrix *operational* for each and every one of your Buying Influences—in other words, making each one realize that he or she has Won. How, practically, do you accomplish this? The answer is to give each Buying Influence something that will demonstrate you've served that person's self-interest. That something is what we call *Win-Results*.

WHAT ARE WIN-RESULTS?

"Win-Results" is a term that we coined early in the development of our processes. In the several years that we've been presenting them, we've found that the Win-Results concept always generates more discussion, more confusion, and more ultimate enlightenment than any other concept. We've also found that our program participants grasp it most quickly if we begin with a few definitions. The Win-Results concept rests on the following terms:

- *Selling:* Selling is a professional, interactive process directed toward demonstrating to all your Buying Influences how your product or service serves their individual self-interest.
- *Product:* A product is designed to improve or fix one or more of your customer's business processes. In Strategic Selling, "product" is taken to mean either a product or a service—whatever *you* are selling.
- *Process:* A process is an activity or series of activities that converts what exists right now into something else.

Examples of business processes would be shipping, invoicing, production, research and development, and quality control.

- *Result:* A Result is the measurable *impact* that a product has on one or more of your customer's business processes. Results are objective and corporate—that is, they generally affect many people at the same time, although they don't necessarily affect all of those people in the same way.
- *Win:* A Win is the fulfillment of a subjective, personal promise made to oneself to serve one's self-interest in some special way. Wins are always *different* for different people.
- *Win-Result:* A Win-Result is an objective business Result that gives one or more of your Buying Influences a subjective, personal Win.

Since you can position yourself in the Win-Win quadrant of the matrix *only* by delivering Win-Results, it's essential to understand both halves of the Win-Results concept. You can't ignore Results because a Result must take place *before* a Buyer will perceive a Win; it's a *precondition* to any Win. On the other hand, if you concentrate *only* on Results, sooner or later you're going to bring one of your Buying Influences a Result that you think is terrific, but that's irrelevant to his or her personal situation—or even worse, that he or she interprets as a Lose.

This happens *constantly* in the Complex Sale. We'll give you just one example to demonstrate the problem. A client told us recently that he was having a difficult time understanding why he couldn't push a certain sales objective through. It was an "ideal" sales possibility but, for reasons he couldn't fathom, it was being blocked by the president of the buying firm. "It's a perfect fit with their needs," we were told. "We've got a solid, approved payment schedule. We're even giving the lowest bid. If I were that guy, I would have signed three months ago. But he just won't budge."

"Tell us about the president," we said. "What's he like?"

"You mean personally?" our client asked.

"Yes. Personally."

He proceeded to describe an incredibly hardworking individual who had founded his company on a shoestring and built it from scratch, who had directed it energetically for thirty years, and who in another two months was about to begin a long-postponed retirement. As he talked, we got the picture of an exhausted, preoccupied executive who had to force himself to come to work each morning. It gradually became apparent that, however good the Results our client was offering him, they were unlikely to have an effect on the man himself, because in a sense he'd already stepped down from the presidency.

"It sounds like all this guy wants," we suggested, "is to be left alone. Is there a Win in this sale for him?"

No, our program participant suddenly realized. And once he realized that, he adopted a strategy that, given the president's intransigence, was the only reasonable one for the situation. He decided to wait the old man out.

In three months, our client knew, the company would have a new president—and the sales objective he was pursuing would have a new Economic Buyer. So he bided his time, adopting the "watchful waiting" strategy that we recommended for dealing with an Even Keel individual, and kept up regular, low-profile contacts with the buying firm.

When the new president came in, our client's patience paid off. The new president, eager to start off with a success, was delighted to approve a low-bid, perfect-fit order. Approving that order not only got her company the Result she wanted, but also served her personal self-interest in a way dn't have served that of the retiring president: It made her look immediately like a go-getter and problem solver.

Same Result, different Wins. The lesson is clear. Although a given Result may have a single, clearly defined impact on a business process, it will always have different personal impacts on the Buying Influences involved in making decisions about that process. And the personal impact can be negative even with the best of Results. We feel so strongly about this lesson that we state it as an axiom:

Companies get Results, but only people Win.

Since your basic goal as a sales professional is to show each of your Buying Influences how your product or service can serve his or her self-interest, delivering Results alone obviously isn't enough. You've got to understand how each of them, *personally,* Wins, because understanding that is what will put you in the Win-Win quadrant.

To make the distinction between Results and Wins more visible to you, the chart below presents the basic characteristics of each.

RESULTS	**WINS**
1. Impact of a product on a business process	**1. Fulfillment of promise made to oneself**
2. Tangible, measurable, quantifiable	**2. Intangible, not measurable, not quantifiable**
3. Corporate	**3. Personal**

Using this chart as an overview, we'll explain the two halves of the Win-Results concept more fully. Since Results must happen *before* any Buyer perceives a Win, we start with Results.

CHARACTERISTICS OF RESULTS

1. A RESULT IS THE IMPACT OF YOUR PRODUCT OR SERVICE ON ONE OR MORE OF YOUR CUSTOMER'S BUSINESS PROCESSES.

You need to affect your customer's business processes because process is the ultimate reason that anything happens, in or out of business; process is what *changes* one set of conditions into another. As the cooking process converts uncooked meat and potatoes into a prime rib dinner, as the exercise process transforms flab into muscle, so too your customers' business processes are designed to convert one set of conditions into another.

We've mentioned that such activities as shipping, invoicing, and quality control can all be seen as processes. In fact, virtually any business activity, from the sweeping out of a stockroom to the highest-level boardroom debates, can be viewed as a process, designed to convert some "raw material" into something of use.

Naturally everyone involved in the conversion would like that something of use to be something better as well. That's where you come in. You are important to your Buying Influences when, and only when, your product or service makes a *positive and measurable* impact on one or more of their business processes. You can do this in one of two ways:

- You can *improve* a process that is already functioning properly.
- You can *fix* something that has gone, or might go, wrong.

Recall our discussion of Response Modes in Chapter 8, where we said that people are receptive to change, and therefore likely to buy, only when they're in either Growth or Trouble Mode. The "why" of this fact relates to what we're saying here. When they're in Growth, people want you to *improve* things. In Trouble, they want you to *fix* something. In both cases, you become valuable to them because they expect your product or service to have a positive impact on their business processes.

2. A RESULT IS TANGIBLE, MEASURABLE, AND QUANTIFIABLE.

If you sell Doris Green an inventory control system to reduce her overtime by 16 percent, you don't have to know anything about her, or about her perception of reality, to determine the Result you've delivered: By definition the Result here is 16 percent overtime reduction.

Green, of course, may not *want* this reduction, and if that's the case, then you'd be foolish to offer her this particular Result. But for the purposes of objective definition, her *impressions* of the Result don't matter. Results are impersonal and value free; they exist "out there," objectively. That 16 percent is a fact you can see, feel, and count.

3. RESULTS ARE CORPORATE.

By "corporate" here we don't mean that they're necessarily seen as Results on the corporation level (although that's often the case), but simply that they're *shared* by various people in the buying organization. Since processes are interrelated in the modern corporation—and therefore in the Complex Sale—any Result you deliver is likely to impact more than one process at the same time. But even when it alters only one process (say, Green's inventory control), there will still be *many people* involved in that process (Green's whole department), and all of those people may share the Result you've contributed.

CHARACTERISTICS OF WINS

1. A WIN IS THE FULFILLMENT OF A PROMISE MADE TO ONESELF.

We've said that when people feel they've Won, it's because they've fulfilled conscious or unconscious promises to themselves to serve their own self-interest. But such promises aren't fabricated out of thin air. They evolve for each person from the general *culture*, and the many specific *subcultures*, in which the individual grows up; the dreams and designs each of us has reflect our basic *values and attitudes* toward life—and these values and attitudes are, to a great extent, culturally determined. You wouldn't expect a Tibetan mountain dweller, living close to the subsistence level, to see a Win in a dishwasher or a library card. Nor would a Mormon see a Win in a gift case of scotch. We all Win within the context of our cultural environments.

In addition, our promises to ourselves *change* as our values and attitudes change, and sometimes they become outmoded even before they're fulfilled. This is especially true in a culture such as ours, where rapid change is such a constant presence. The middle-aged man who in his youth promised himself a Florida condominium and a Rolls-Royce may find, once he's in a position to get them, that they've lost their importance to him: Getting them is no longer seen as a Win. In assessing Wins, therefore, you always have to be attentive to the *current* perceptions of the potential Winner involved.

2. WINS ARE INTANGIBLE, NOT MEASURABLE, AND NOT QUANTIFIABLE.

For most human beings, the most important things in life are subjective rewards such as family feeling, a sense of security, and the subtle pleasure of knowing you've done your best. Satisfying and enriching those feelings are the ultimate Wins.

Psychologists are always "discovering" this about people in sales. You've probably seen the attitude surveys that these social scientists periodically give members of our profession. In every one we've seen, the researchers reach the same "surprising" conclusion that what really turns good salespeople on is not their six-figure commissions but job satisfaction, recognition, and challenges. The popular belief that the top salespeople are in it just for the money always turns out to be a misconception. In every assessment of "sales motivators" we've seen, sales representatives put money far down on their lists, behind a host of less tangible, less concrete rewards.

The same thing is true of people on the "other side" of the buy-sell encounter. Like you, your Buying Influences remain in their professions not because they're pulling down six-figure salaries (although that probably doesn't hurt), but because their jobs allow them to reap the intangible satisfactions that they need in order to Win. Focusing on these "priceless" rewards is thus indispensable for anyone involved in the delivery of customer solutions.

The intangible rewards that may generate Wins for individual Buying Influences are enormously varied. The list below suggests their range and variety.

SAMPLE WINS

- **remain in power**
- **achieve control over others**
- **get more leisure**
- **remain in a given location**
- **increase skill development**
- **increase personal productivity**
- **be an instrument of change**
- **be looked on as a problem solver**
- **contribute to the organization**
- **increase mental stimulation**
- **gain recognition**
- **increase growth potential**
- **improve social status**
- **have more time with family**
- **get more power**
- **increase self-esteem**
- **be more flexible**
- **feel more secure or safe**
- **put in a quality performance**
- **be seen as a leader**
- **offer uniqueness**
- **pay a debt**
- **increase responsibility and authority**
- **pursue a lifestyle**
- **get more freedom**

Of course, this list is only a sampling. *People Win in countless ways*. One of your responsibilities as the strategic orchestrator of your sales objectives is to determine what those ways are for each of your Buying Influences.

3. WINS ARE PERSONAL.

We said that Results are corporate, or shared, and we used the example of Doris Green's inventory control to show how a single Result can benefit many people. But, no matter how solid that Result, these people *will not benefit in the same way*. This is the most important single distinction between Wins and Results. Even though an objective Result can generate Wins for many people, no two of those Wins will be identical. Each one will be linked to the *personal* perceptions of an individual Buying Influence.

Take the hypothetical Result that we're delivering to Green's department: a 16 percent reduction in overtime. Green herself may see this Result as a Win because it will help her run a tighter ship and thus satisfy a need for control. A member of Green's staff may appreciate this Result for an entirely different reason: To him, the overtime reduction may be a Win because it enables him to spend more time at home with his family. Same Result, different Wins.

Furthermore, another member of Green's staff may not see the Result as a Win at all. A staff member who *needs* the overtime to keep her budget balanced won't see her self-interest being served by a 16 percent reduction. For her, this objectively "great" Result will translate as a Lose.

This basic distinction between corporate Results and personal Wins underscores a fundamental lesson of the Strategic Selling process: *It's never enough to sell Results alone*. To manage each Complex Sale into the Win-Win quadrant with each of your Buying Influences, you *have to determine* how each individual Wins.

DETERMINING YOUR BUYING INFLUENCES' WINS

To make the Win-Win quadrant of the matrix operational you need to do two things. First, you need to identify which Result or Results each of your Buyers needs to get from your sales proposal. Then you need to show each of them how that Result can bring him or her a personal Win. When you accomplish these two tasks, you're delivering Win-Results.

It isn't always a straightforward task to understand and address your Buying Influences' subjective needs in this way. But determining their Win-Results needn't be all guesswork either. Years of working with sales professionals in various fields have taught us that there are three reliable methods for doing so:

1. You can *infer* your individual Buyers' Wins, either from the Results they're likely to want or from what you know about their attitudes and lifestyles.
2. You can *ask* them directly what's in the sale for them.
3. You can get *Coaching*.

INFERRING THE WIN

Even though each of your Buying Influences Wins in an individual way, *categories* of Buyers tend to look for similar Results for their organizations. Knowing this can help you assess whether or not a particular Buying Influence is *likely* to Win with a particular Result. True, determining Results alone is never enough. But if you start with the Results that Harry Barnes wants in a given situation, you'll be in a better position to *infer* the different Wins that each of those Results can give him.

ECONOMIC	**USER**
• low cost of ownership • good budget fit • ROI • financial responsibility • increased productivity • profitability • smooth out cash flow • flexibility	• reliability • increased efficiency • upgrade skills • fulfill performance • best problem solution • do job better/faster/easier • versatility • super-service • easy to learn and use
TECHNICAL	**COACH (WINS)**
• specs best and product meets them • delivery timely • best technical solution • discounts/low bids/price • reliability	• recognition • visibility • get strokes • make contribution • be seen as a problem solver

The chart above lists a number of sample Results. It has been useful to many of our clients in getting a handle on Results that typically produce Wins for people in each of the four Buying Influence categories.

Notice that the Results in each case relate directly to the Buyer's business concerns as outlined in Chapter 5. Economic Buyers, for example, look for results addressed to the bottom line and organizational stability, such as return on investment. User Buyers concentrate on workplace performance, and the Results they usually want for a Win enhance it. Technical Buying Influences are interested in having the product pass their screening tests; they're most likely to Win when you deliver Results that meet or surpass those tests. Notice, finally, that Coaches don't have their own Results—only Wins. *Your success in the sale* is the result that will give your Coach a Win.

There's an element of speculation in inferring Wins from Results, so you need to double-check your inference by looking at other data. It's likely that you already have access to that data. If you've called on Green three times, you already know something about her Wins. If her office is full of golf trophies and community plaques, she's probably got a strong need for achievement and recognition. If pictures of her children dominate the walls, security or family approval might be a key. If her appointment schedule is a model of regularity—if your one-hour meeting scheduled for 10 A.M. begins promptly at 10 and ends precisely at 11—then she probably values precision and efficiency. The more you know about your Buying Influences' lifestyles and attitudes, the better you'll be able to infer their personal Wins.

You can pick up other data from the company culture in which the individual works. As numerous observers of corporate life have pointed out, each large company today has its own internal culture, comprising attitudes and values that both reflect and influence those of its employees. For example, recognition for public service is more likely to be seen as a Win by people in a company that projects a high community profile than by those in one that prefers isolation. Being seen as an innovator or a maverick is more likely to be appreciated as a Win in a company that sees itself as the leading edge of an industry than in one that has been doing business the same old reliable way for fifty years.

We're not saying that individual Buyers' values are ever

merely a reflection of their companies' values. But company cultures are still a valid standard against which to check your impressions of a given person's Wins.

One caution: Remember that inferring is only a sophisticated form of guessing. Your inferences should always be *checked* by asking the Buying Influence directly, and/or by getting Coaching.

ASKING THE BUYING INFLUENCE DIRECTLY

The second way to uncover your Buyer's Wins is simply to ask. We don't mean you should sit the inscrutable Mr. Kratchit down and blurt out, "What are your Wins in this sale?" Instead, you should ask what we call attitudinal, rather than objective, questions.

An *objective* question seeks to find out what the Buying Influence wants or needs. Most sales representatives concentrate on objective questions—or, worse, try to guess the Buyer's Wins—because they don't like to "pry," they want to stick to the facts, or they just don't want to hear the answer that they expect to get to a question about attitude. Whatever reason they may have for limiting themselves to objective questions, they get out of them just what they put in: the facts. And the facts are never enough to make a quality sale.

Attitudinal questions, on the other hand, seek to find out how the individual *feels* about the situation: "What's your opinion of this system?" "Are you comfortable with the way this solution will work for your department?" Or, even more directly, "How do you feel about the current proposal?"

The given wisdom notwithstanding, questions about attitude are almost always appropriate. And not only appropriate, but essential. Because they help you to probe beyond the product to each individual's Wins, they can be invaluable in helping you to check your own reactions to the changing sales situation, and also in tracking your Buying Influences' changing needs.

Attitudinal questions can give you valuable feedback, for example, on the numerical ratings that you assigned in Chapter 8. If you've identified Doris Green as a +3 User Buyer and a subsequent attitudinal question reveals that she feels "uneasy" about the pending sale, then you've uncovered the fact that she's not really a +3. Such questions are extremely useful in providing continual assessment of the "inner sales" you need to make before any papers will be signed.

One reason that many salespeople feel wary about asking attitudinal questions is that they realize getting honest answers to them can be difficult. The smart strategist is alert to the difficulties and doesn't back away from them. A main thrust of Strategic Selling—and particularly of our Red Flag highlighting system—is to *uncover* difficulties in achieving your sales objective so they can be dealt with before they derail you. Attitudinal questions are a means of helping you do that.

We don't mean to minimize the difficulty here. True, when you ask your Buyers questions about how they Win, you'll find that the road is often blocked by both *ignorance* and *deception*. Some people who would like to tell you how they Win just don't know themselves. And others don't want *you* to know: They're happy to talk about Results, but they feel that their personal feelings about the sale are really none of your business.

In such cases you may be able to interpret the visible Results by reading between the lines to find the hidden Win. For example, a friend of ours just bought a new Porsche.

When we asked him why he bought the car, he went on and on about its being a great investment; he was particularly impressed, he said, with customer satisfaction surveys and the high Porsche resale value. You'll recognize these things as Results. They may have been factors in the sale, but they certainly weren't as important as one less measurable, less tangible fact—the fact that driving the car made him feel like an Indy 500 superstar. You only had to see him behind the wheel to realize that *that* was his Win. It was also the bottom-line, decisive reason for his purchase.

Or take the example of the Economic Buying Influence who has a need to play it safe, but wants you to interpret her timidity as executive prudence. We know of one such person who consistently buys everything she needs from the industry leader. Often the leader is a little higher in price than the competition, but this Buyer feels that she can't get into trouble if she sticks with number one—and, for her, staying out of trouble is a major priority. If you ask her why she takes the price beating, she doesn't say, "I'm afraid to make a change. My biggest Win is security." She tells you how great number one's service record is, and claims she can't get such reliable service anywhere else. Again, you can infer her Wins from what she says about Results.

Because Buying Influences often disguise their Wins like this, we advise our clients to *beware* and *compare* whenever they ask for a person's feelings about a sale. *Beware* of answers that focus only on Results. *Compare* what you're told with other information you have about this individual's needs—both business and personal needs. Finally, in reading between the lines to get at Wins, be careful not to guess.

GETTING COACHING

One way of avoiding guesswork—or at least of double-checking your speculations—is to utilize a network of reliable Coaches. Since a good Coach is by definition credible to the other Buying Influences, they may entrust information to this person, both objective and subjective, that they wouldn't entrust to you. So if someone is difficult to read, a good Coach—or Coaches—might be the key.

Remember, your basic selling goal should be to serve each Buying Influence's perceived self-interest. Zero in on that self-interest by asking your Coach, *"What Results should I be stressing with Dan Farley to show him what's in this sale for him?"*

In Chapter 12 we'll discuss your Coach in more detail and explain a number of ways in which this critical and unique Buying Influence can help make your management of the Complex Sale more predictable. One of the most important of those ways is in helping you to find out how each of your individual Buying Influences will Win.

TWO WAYS *NOT* TO DETERMINE WINS

The three methods of determining Wins that we've just described—inferring the Win, asking the Buying Influence, and getting Coaching—have been used reliably by thousands of salespeople and their managers, in countless business situations. Two other common "methods" are *not* reliable. They are:

- To interpret the Results as the Win
- To assume that your own Win is the same as your Buying Influence's

INTERPRETING RESULTS AS WINS

Examine Results first, by all means. You can't deliver a Win without a Result. But it doesn't follow that a good Result *equals* a Win. A Result is a precondition, *not* an equivalent.

Remember the case of the sales representative who had such trouble convincing an aging president to approve his sale? The salesperson had a whole string of good Results. His product would save the buying firm money, it would raise productivity—it was, as the salesman complained plaintively, "a perfect fit with their needs." But the president still wouldn't buy because the salesman had failed to demonstrate to him that the sale was in *his* self-interest.

The lesson is clear. Always start, but never *stop,* with Results. Unless you understand each individual's personal reason for buying, you can easily find yourself, even after you've sold a person many times, presenting a great Result in a situation where he or she sees only a personal Lose.

CONFUSING YOUR WINS WITH THE BUYING INFLUENCE'S WINS

When the salesman who had such trouble with the retiring president told us about his plight, one phrase stuck in our minds. *"If I were that guy,"* he said, "I would have signed months ago."

Maybe that was true. But, true or not, it was irrelevant. In fact, it was worse than irrelevant. Realizing that he himself would have signed caused the sales representative here to make what is probably the single most common error among people just beginning to use the concept of Win-Results. That error is in *projecting their own Wins onto their cus-*

tomers—in assuming that the way the Buying Influence will Win is identical to the way the sales representative would Win in the same situation. Making this assumption almost always leads you to misidentify Wins.

Salespeople who make this miscalculation do so for a logical enough reason. They confuse their own self-interest with that of the Buying Influence by asking themselves, with all the empathy in the world, "How would I Win if I were Doris Green?" Generous question. The trouble is, empathy will not give you the answer you need. All it will give you is a refried version of your own desires—a picture of how Doris would feel if she were you. Since she's not you, and never will be, that's not much help.

What you always have to do, therefore, is to focus *first* on Results and then ask, "Given the Results I can offer, how can *this Buyer* Win?"

PERSONAL WORKSHOP 5: WIN-RESULTS

In applying the Key Element of Win-Results to your chosen sales objective, we suggest that you first develop a list of corporate Results that you can use to give each of your Buying Influences a Win, and then use those Results to identify Wins for each person.

STEP 1: IDENTIFY RESULTS FOR YOUR TYPE OF BUSINESS.

The purpose of this step is to give you a fix on the Results concept as it operates *generally* in your business. You can get that fix by first going back to the sample Results that we listed earlier in the chapter, and then making up your own chart, using that one as a guide.

Open your notebook flat, so that you have two blank facing pages in front of you. Working first on the left-hand page, write the heading "Results" at the top. Then divide the page into three columns, under the subheads "Economic Buying Influence," "Technical Buying Influence," and "User Buying Influence." In each column write down as many Results as you can that those Buying Influences typically look for *in your business*.

In identifying these corporate Results, remember that Economic Buyers focus on the bottom line and organizational stability, that User Buyers want to know how you can improve their on-the-job performance, and that Technical Buyers are most interested in the product per se. You don't need a Coach column since, as we've mentioned, Coaches don't have their own Results.

If you're like our program participants, many of the Results you write down will be identical to those in our sample Results chart. Fine, but don't stop there. Add to the list whatever Results you can think of that are specific to *your* industry or product line. Your goal here is to generate a list of Results that tend to be typical for the different categories of Buying Influences in *your* selling arena. If you spend about five or ten minutes on this step, you should be able to come up with at least six or eight typical Results for each of the three categories.

STEP 2: TEST THESE RESULTS.

The next step is to test this list objectively. Do that by asking yourself the following questions about each item on the list:

- Is this Result measurable, tangible, and quantifiable?
- Is it corporate—that is, can it be shared by more than one Buying Influence?
- Is it business related—that is, does it positively affect one or more of this customer's business processes?

If you can't answer yes to all these questions, what you're looking at may be a "feature" or "benefit" rather than a true Result. If that's the case, reassess the situation, digging for the impact that you can make on your customer's business. If you cannot find such an impact, you may not have a sale.

STEP 3: IDENTIFY RESULTS FOR YOUR CURRENT SALES OBJECTIVE.

You now know what Results the three categories of Buyers generally look for in your business. Now get more specific and generate a list of Results that the individual Buying Influences want or need with regard to *the particular sales objective* you've been working on in this book.

Use the right-hand page of the open notebook to make out this list. At the top of the page write "Win-Results Chart," and then divide the page into three columns, under the subheads "Buying Influences," "Results," and "Win-Result Statements." Take out your Buying Influences Chart and copy down the names of all your Buyers in the left-hand column. As you know, you may have four of these, or fourteen. Then, in the middle column, next to the name of each Buyer write down the one or two *key* Results you believe that he or she wants from this particular transaction.

In doing this, you can start with the Results list that you just drew up, using it as a bank from which to draw out this new list.

You're performing a process of distillation—starting with the Results that are universal in your business by Buying Influence category, and narrowing the focus to identify the Results relevant to *this* sale, and *these* Buying Influences, right now.

STEP 4: TEST THESE INDIVIDUAL RESULTS.

Once you've listed the one or two most important Results for each individual, test them objectively. Your goal here is to see that you've identified Results that are *specific* and *relevant* to each person's situation. It's not enough to say that one Result you can give to Dan Farley is to "make his job easier." Look at the Result you've identified for Farley and ask yourself the following test questions:

- What business *process* of Farley's does this Result address?
- How does the Result *improve* or *fix* that process?
- How does the Result relate to *the specific business concerns* of Farley's category of Buying Influence? Since Farley is your Economic Buyer, this means asking how your Result will impact his organizational growth and stability.

Then ask the same questions for each of the other Results, and all the other Buying Influences, on your chart. Remember that the specific business concerns of your User Buyers will be linked to on-the-job performance and that those of your Technical Buyers will be linked to their screening tests of your product or service.

It should take you a minute or two for each Buying Influence to complete this step of the workshop. If you're uncertain about a given person's Results, put a Red Flag in the middle column near that person's name.

STEP 5: DRAFT A WIN-RESULTS STATEMENT FOR EACH INDIVIDUAL.

Now turn back to the sample Wins chart that we presented earlier in the chapter. Using that chart as a guide—but only as a guide, not as a definitive catalog—go down the list of your Buying Influences again, this time trying to identify the Wins that each one will get from the Result or Results that you've recognized as important to him or her. For each Result, ask yourself the following question:

How will this Buying Influence Win if my product or service delivers this Result?

In uncovering answers to this question for each person, you're seeking not the person's "general" Wins or Wins in the abstract, but a cause-and-effect connection, or linkage, between each person's desired business Results on *this* sale and the personal satisfactions that those Results will ensure. In our Strategic Selling programs, clients make that linkage visible by drafting what we call a Win-Result Statement for each individual. You should do the same thing now. Taking each Buying Influence in turn, identify how that person will Win if you successfully deliver the relevant Result. Note the Win in column three. Then, for each person, write a brief statement spelling out the connection between Wins and Results.

For example, consider the Result that you expect to deliver to our hypothetical User Buying Influence, Doris Green—that 16 percent reduction in departmental overtime. Suppose you know that she wants this reduction to counter charges that her departmental budget is overextended. For her, a sample Win-Results Statement might read as follows: "The Result of overtime reduction will give Doris Green the Win of appearing more efficient to her superiors." Or say that you have a product that will ensure the continued reliability of one of Harry Barnes's manufacturing processes—and you also know that Barnes puts a high premium on reliability and stability. A statement of his Win-Results might be "Increasing the reliability of his manufacturing system (a Result) will give Harry Barnes the Win of heightened security."

In doing this exercise, you'll probably come up against one or more Buying Influences whose Wins you can't readily determine. You may also discover that, while you know something about their subjective attitudes, you're not certain how those can be most effectively addressed with the available Results. In either of these cases, you'll want to put a Red Flag in the third column of your Win-Results Chart. That's to remind you that you need more information on this point before you can draft an effective Win-Results Statement. On the other hand, if you find that for one of your Buying Influences you have a perfect understanding of the linkage between Wins and Results, it would be appropriate to mark that on your chart with a "barbell," for Strength.

When you're finished with this step of the workshop, your Win-Results Chart should look something like the example on page 213.

STEP 6: ANALYZE YOUR CURRENT POSITION.

Now investigate both your Win-Results Chart and your Buying Influences Chart with an eye to discovering what further information you need to improve your position. Look at each Buyer in turn, assessing your areas of Strength and your Red Flags. Test whether or not there's information you

WIN-RESULTS CHART

BUYERS	**RESULTS**	**WINS**
Dan Farley (EB)	**Productivity increase**	
Doris Green (UBC)	**Less overtime; performance**	**Appear more efficient**
Harry Barnes (UB, TB)	**Continued reliability**	**Security**
Gary Steinberg (TB)	**Move inventory faster**	
Will Johnson (TB)	**Easy credit arrangements**	**Enhance reputation with management**
Sandy Kelly (C)		**Recognition**

haven't yet uncovered, but can, by asking yourself questions like these:

- What *else* do I know about Green—aside from her Results—that can help me understand how those Results might help her Win?
- What do Steinberg's lifestyle, values, and attitudes tell me about how he might Win?
- Have I asked Farley both objective and attitudinal questions to determine his Wins?
- If I haven't seen Barnes myself, have I arranged for someone else to do so?
- Can my Coaches help? Have I asked *them* to explain to me how the overconfident Will Johnson might see a Win?

Use the answers to these questions to consider revisions of your Alternate Positions list. Remember especially that, wherever you have *a lack of data* about a given Buying Influence, you have a significant Red Flag. Always make the uncovering of such data a new option on that list. Ask yourself, too, if you can leverage from an area of Strength to help you uncover it.

STEP 7: DETERMINE YOUR PRESENT WIN-WIN STATUS.

Knowing something about your various Buying Influences' Win-Results, you can now start managing your Single Sales Objective into the Win-Win quadrant of the matrix. First, test whether or not you're currently positioned in that quadrant with each individual, asking yourself:

- Have I delivered or can I deliver the Results that each Buyer needs to Win?
- Does every Buying Influence have confidence that I can do this? In other words, do they all *know* I'm playing Win-Win with them?

If the answer to either of these questions is no, then you can't really count on stability in your position. You may or may not be in the Win-Win quadrant.

For example, if you deliver Barnes a Result but don't really know how it will help him Win, you may be setting yourself up for a Lose, if not in this sale, then in future ones. Or if Farley doesn't believe there's a Win in your sale for him, then as far as he's concerned you're playing Win-Lose with him—

and you're therefore risking the loss not just of this sale, but of future business as well.

Look at the Red Flags you've placed both on the Win-Results Chart that you prepared in this Personal Workshop and at those you placed on your Buying Influences Chart. Where are you solidly positioned and where do you still lack information that you need to serve each person's self-interest? Answering such questions realistically will give you a firmer grasp on how close you actually are to the Win-Win strategy you want.

STEP 8: REVISE YOUR ALTERNATE POSITIONS LIST.

The next step in managing your sale into the Win-Win quadrant is to use what you've learned about Win-Results to revise your current position. As in previous workshops, you do that by sharpening, cutting, and adding to the options on your Alternate Positions list.

In Step 6 of this workshop we advised you to consider revisions of the Alternate Positions list based on your current position with regard to Win-Results. Incorporate any relevant revisions now and *test* each one against the concept of Win-Results. Ideally, you want every item on this developing list to help you *understand* the Win-Results of your Buyers better, to help you *deliver* those Win-Results more effectively, or to help you do both. Revise your list with this in mind.

For example, in getting rid of that Red Flag next to Gary Steinberg's name, the "position" of "Take Gary to lunch" may or may not get you any closer to the information you want. A good Alternate Position in this situation might be

"Get Doris Green to explain to me why Gary is so personally concerned about inventory." That leverages from a Strength—Green's enthusiasm about your proposal—and it focuses in on the specific lack of data you need to correct.

In previous workshops, we advised you to be *inclusive* about your Alternate Positions, to be *specific,* and to *test* them against the Strategic Selling rule that every good Alternate Position eliminates a Red Flag, leverages from a Strength, or does both. You should continue to be specific and to test your options. But it's time to get a little less inclusive and more discriminating. Since the concept of Win-Results is so central to an effective sales strategy, we urge you to look over all the items on your Alternate Positions list with it in mind. Consider dropping any option that does not, directly or indirectly, help you deliver to at least one of your Buying Influences a Result that person will personally translate as a Win.

Most important of all, remember *self-interest.* Because it determines all buying decisions, it will remain a benchmark for you in assessing all future Alternate Positions.

Summary of Win-Results

Since our fourth Key Element of strategy so often proves difficult for our program participants, we close this chapter with a summary of its major points. You should use it as a reference as you continue to refine your sales strategy.

- Any *product* (or service) provides the tools and knowledge needed to improve a *process.* The process, in turn, produces the *Results* through which a person Wins.
- Your Buying Influence Wins when his or her *self-interest* is

served. That's why Winning is important and why you need to understand *how* your Buyers Win in order to sell them.

- People buy because they perceive a relationship between your sales proposal and their individual self-interest. The art and craft of selling is in demonstrating the connection between your proposal and their self-interest.
- It's often difficult to *ask* someone how he or she Wins. Therefore, focus first on the person's Results and then ask how the person will Win with those Results. *Coaching* can help you to understand the Win.
- Serving your customers' self-interest is ultimately the best way of serving your own. Therefore, the only acceptable conclusion to a buy-sell encounter is a *Win-Win* outcome.

PART 3

COMMON PROBLEMS, UNCOMMON SOLUTIONS

CHAPTER 11

GETTING TO THE ECONOMIC BUYING INFLUENCE: STRATEGIES AND TACTICS

You've now been introduced to the four cornerstones, as it were, of Strategic Selling: the Key Elements of Buying Influences, Red Flags/Strengths, Response Modes, and Win-Results. By the time we reach this point in our programs, our clients are usually flooding us with questions, and we'd be surprised if you didn't have questions at this point too. In this third part of the book, we'll try to anticipate some of those questions, by going into more detail in those areas where our clients often tell us they experience problems.

Among the questions they present to us, these three probably stand out as most common:

- "How do I get to the *Economic Buying Influence*?"
- "How can I effectively utilize a strategic *Coach*?"
- "What about the *competition*?"

These are all reasonable questions, and we devote this section of the book to providing some answers. We begin, in this chapter, with what is probably the single most frequently identified problem area: what to do with that singularly important, yet often inaccessible, individual called the Economic Buying Influence.

The heart of Strategic Selling is managing every one of your sales objectives so that you end up in the Win-Win quadrant of the matrix with all your Buying Influences. Frequently this proves to be most problematic with regard to Economic Buying Influences, because this role differs from the other Buying Influences in two significant ways:

- Economic Buying Influences are more difficult to *identify* than the other Buying Influences.
- Economic Buying Influences are more difficult to *reach*, both physically and psychologically, than those who play User and Technical Buying roles.

For these reasons, establishing a Win-Win outcome with the Economic Buying Influence is a common area of concern, even among salespeople who are extremely competent in establishing such outcomes with other Buying Influences.

Yet failure to cover the Economic Buying Influence adequately, or to see to it that he or she perceives a personal Win in every sale, can undermine even the most "straightforward" sales scenario. Since the Economic Buyer can by definition veto the sale at any point in the selling cycle, it's only common sense to cover that key player as *thoroughly* as possible, and as *early* as possible in the selling cycle.

WHY IS GETTING TO THE ECONOMIC BUYING INFLUENCE SO TOUGH?

When we cover the Economic Buying Influence in our Strategic Selling programs, we begin by asking our participants this pointed question. Here are a few of their most common responses:

- "I don't know who he is."
- "I don't know where in the buying organization to look for that kind of authority."
- "A purchasing agent says I should deal just with her."
- "It's like being called into the principal's office when I meet him."
- "She refuses to see me."
- "I don't have any credibility with people at that level."
- "No one wants to assume the authority to sign for the order."
- "All her calls are screened."
- "He makes me nervous—I don't know what to say to him."
- "I don't know what his needs are."
- "She just doesn't talk to salespeople."

You'll probably recognize some of the responses on this list as being relevant to your own selling situations. We'd be very surprised if you didn't—these are typical responses.

Just as typical is the fact that, like all the responses we get, they can be broken down into three basic categories. In the thousands of programs we've presented, and in our own business as well, we always see this same pattern. No matter what industry our clients are in, and no matter what the average size of their Complex Sales, their complaints about getting to the Economic Buying Influence are always variations of three root problems:

Problem 1: They can't *identify* the Economic Buying Influence.
Problem 2: They're *blocked* from getting to the person playing this role.
Problem 3: They're *uncomfortable* about talking to him or her.

If you look at the responses given on the list above, you'll see that this pattern holds true:

- Responses such as "I don't know who he is" and "I don't know where to look" and "No one will assume the authority" decode as "I can't *identify* the Economic Buying Influence."
- Responses such as "A purchasing agent says talk to her" and "She refuses to see me" and "All her calls are screened" decode as "I'm being *blocked* from seeing her."
- Responses such as "He makes me nervous" and "I don't have any credibility" and "It's like being in the principal's office" decode as "I'm *uncomfortable* talking to the Economic Buyer."

If you review your past sales and think about the problems you experienced in getting to your Economic Buying Influences, we're certain that you'll see the very same pattern.

Throughout the rest of this chapter, we'll be giving you strategies and tactics for overcoming each of these three basic problems. We'll begin by briefly reviewing who the Economic Buying Influence *is*, and what this person *does* in your sales scenarios.

PROFILE OF THE ECONOMIC BUYING INFLUENCE

In helping our clients become more skillful in identifying the Economic Buyer for each of their sales objectives, we've found it useful to emphasize three concepts:

- The Economic Buyer, like all the other Buying Influences, is *sale-specific*.
- The person playing the Economic Buying Influence role is often *highly placed* in the buying organization.
- People acting as Economic Buying Influences are generally paid very well for their ability to *see into the future*.

THE "SALE-SPECIFIC" ECONOMIC BUYING INFLUENCE

We call the Economic Buyer "sale-specific" because that person plays the Economic Buyer role for a specific sales objective, *not* for an account. There's no such thing as "the Giant Soap Company's Economic Buyer," but only a number of key individuals in that company who have the appropriate level of authority to play that role. There's no guarantee that the person who plays the Economic Buying Influence role for one sale will also play it for a second sale to the same company—even if the second sale involves the same product and the same dollar amount. That's why it is critical for you to identify the Economic Buying Influence anew as you're starting to plan each new sales objective.

THE ECONOMIC BUYING INFLUENCE'S ORGANIZATIONAL POSITION

Because they have direct access to and discretionary use of the required funds, people playing the role of Economic Buyer are often highly placed in their organizations. In smaller, entrepreneurial companies, the president will often serve as Economic Buyer on many sales. In large multinationals, final authority may seldom have to go that high, yet even here most Economic Buyer decisions—that is, decisions to release restricted funds—will still be made by upper-level managers. Especially in these days of downsizing and cost-conscious reengineering, very few companies will allow junior managers to act as Economic Buying Influences for major purchases or critical policy decisions. And the more money involved in the sale, the higher you have to look for the release-of-funds decision.

READING THE FUTURE

Since Economic Buying Influences are often senior-level managers, they're typically highly paid; most of the Economic Buyers we and our clients deal with take home high six-figure salaries. But they aren't paid solely for the day-to-day management of the business. That may be a part of their responsibility, but the real reason for their high salaries is their proven ability to forecast future business conditions and to see to it that their companies profit from them. They earn their keep because of the clarity of their crystal balls.

The Economic Buying Influence can therefore be considered roughly analogous to the captain of a ship. We say roughly because, unlike ship captains, Economic Buyers aren't always at the top of the organizational ladder—as we've just mentioned, they're not necessarily their company's CEOs. But like captains, they do have ultimate responsibility for their "ships" on a given voyage. Also like ship captains, most of them aren't really paid to *do* anything. This isn't a cute snap at the brass. What we mean is that they don't necessarily navigate, manage the engine room, or personally hold the wheel. Their responsibility is much broader. They are expected to know exactly where the ship is headed, and to make decisions that will ensure it gets there on time.

Keeping this profile of the Economic Buying Influence in mind, you can now address more effectively the problems of *identifying* the Economic Buyer for a Single Sales Objective, of being *blocked* from seeing that person, and of overcoming your natural *discomfort* in his or her presence.

SOLVING PROBLEM 1: IDENTIFICATION

In identifying the Economic Buyer accurately for each specific sales objective, you have to be attentive to the Complex Sale *float factor*. By "float factor" we mean the fact that the Economic Buying Influence role can shift, or float, up or down the corporate ladder, between one sale and the next, and sometimes even *during* a given sales cycle. Even experienced salespeople often ignore this factor and assume that Farley, who gave final approval for their last Single Sales Objective, must also be the Economic Buyer for the one they're working on now. This makes misidentification a constant threat.

THE FLOAT FACTOR AND PERCEIVED RISK

In Chapter 5, we described five variables that can cause the role of Economic Buying Influence to shift up or down the corporate ladder. If you're having difficulty identifying the final authority for a given sale, you might start by asking yourself how that sale is likely to be perceived by the buying organization in terms of these five variables

1. ***The Dollar Amount of the Sale.*** Generally speaking, the higher the dollar amount of the sale, the higher the Economic Buyer role will float. Remember, though, that we mean dollar amount *relative to the size of the buying organization*. A five-thousand-dollar sale to a small firm might bring in the president as Economic Buying Influence; the same size sale to General Motors would not.

2. ***Business Conditions.*** Hard times cause the Economic Buyer role to float upward. When a firm is suffering setbacks or slow activity, buying decisions that are normally made by middle management pass to the managers at the top. The reverse happens when the economy is good.

3. ***Experience with You and Your Firm.*** For first sales to a new account, you should look high up in the organization for final approval. Once you've established a history of Wins with at least some of the Buying Influences for a given account, you may be able to get final approval for the same type of sale further down the corporate ladder.

4. ***Experience with Your Product or Service.*** This variable illustrates the same principle. The less a potential customer knows about the specific product or service you're

selling, the more likely it is that approval will have to come from high up. With experience, the final approval role will float down.

5. ***Potential Organizational Impact.*** Since Economic Buying Influences are generally concerned with long-range effects, the role may float upward whenever the buying organization feels that your sales proposal will have a significant long-term impact on its organizational growth and stability.

All five of these variables have one thing in common. The reason that each of them has the capability of generating float is that behind all five is the same fundamental business factor: *perceived risk* on the buying organization's part.

More than any other category of Buying Influence, Economic Buyers are paid to take calculated risks that they hope will lead to financial and developmental rewards. The entire focus of their decision-making is to maintain a balance between risk and reward. *And the greater the perceived risk, the higher the role of Economic Buying Influence floats.*

In identifying who is playing the role of Economic Buying Influence for your sales objective, therefore, we suggest that you ask yourself two questions. The first is one that we mentioned in Chapter 5:

At what level in my own *organization would final approval for a sale of this type have to be made?*

The answer to this question will suggest to you the general level at which you should look in the buying organization for the person acting as the Economic Buying Influence. That is, it will suggest to you whether you should be looking at the departmental or middle-management or vice-presidential level. Remember, though, that the likely level for final buying approval is always *relative to the size of the buying organization*. So, if your company and the buying company are the same size, approval will probably come at about the same level. If your company is significantly smaller than the buying organization, you may have to look *lower* than you would if you were selling something similar to your own firm. If your company is larger, you may have to look *higher*.

The second question relates to the underlying element in our discussion of the float factor—the element of *perceived risk*. Once you know at which level in the buying organization you're likely to find your Economic Buyer, ask yourself:

Considering the level of perceived risk involved in my sales proposal, should I be looking higher up the corporate ladder or lower?

If the level of perceived risk is high, adjust your sights upward. If it's low, adjust them down.

As you perform this searching process, remember that we specify *perceived* risk. Just as it's your *Buying Influence's* perception of reality, not yours, that's critical in determining Response Modes, it's the *buying* firm's perception of risk, not yours, that will help you identify the probable organizational level of the Economic Buyer. Suppose you're trying to sell the Mammoth Company a fire prevention system that *you* know has never failed. In other words, you know the risk is practically nil. That's nice for you—but totally irrelevant, unless the Mammoth Company's people also see it that way. If they have never done business with you before, if they've never installed such a system before, or if the system would mean a major commitment of their budget, then your "no risk" product might be seen as very risky indeed. And final approval for the purchase may have to come from the top.

One caution: In searching for Economic Buying Influences, it's very common for salespeople to look at too *low* a level. They are content to seek approval from a plant manager when they really should be positioned at the division level, or they settle for speaking with a director when they should see the president. Such "settling"—which kills countless opportunities—is a result of the discomfort that many sales people feel when they find themselves in the presence of senior management. This is a problem that we'll address more fully in a moment.

Because identifying the Economic Buyer too low on the corporate ladder is such a common cause of mismanaged sales, and because nobody wears a sign around his or her neck saying "I am the Economic Buying Influence," we offer two quick tips to help you avoid the blunder of looking too low.

- First, be attentive to what your suspected Economic Buyer says about big-picture organizational issues such as profitability and return on investment. If she never raises such issues, you're probably looking too low.
- Second, make it a rule of thumb to cover the bases with your customers *one level above* where you believe the Economic Buyer to be situated.

This is particularly important on an initial sale to a new account, or when you're trying to sell a significantly higher dollar amount than usual to an old account. Identifying the Economic Buyer accurately as each new sales objective begins is basic to good strategy, and it's less hazardous to start off too high than too low.

ZEROING IN ON THE ECONOMIC BUYING INFLUENCE

Once you've located the *level* in the buying organization from which approval must come for your sale, you need to confirm that the person you *think* has final approval will actually wield that authority on *this* sale. There are three ways you can do this. You can:

- *Ask* the suspected Economic Buyer directly
- Get *Coaching*
- *Guess*

Only the first two ways are acceptable. Representatives who "think" they know who the Economic Buyer is for their sale, or who have a "pretty good idea" who controls the funds, very often guess wrong. If you don't *know* who the Economic Buying Influence is for the sales objective you're working on, put a Red Flag in the Economic Buyer box on your Buying Influences Chart. Then zero in on the actual Economic Buyer by asking and/or getting Coaching. If you do know who the Economic Buying Influence is and have covered that base well, you can regard that crucial piece of information as a Strength.

1. ***Asking the Buyer Directly.*** An abrupt colleague of ours zeroes in on the Economic Buying Influence by addressing the "suspect" in the most straightforward manner possible. "Once I've covered the bases with all my other Buying Influences," he says, "I go to the guy I think is the Economic Buyer and put a close on him. If he signs the order, I know he's the Economic Buyer. If not, either I've got more work to do, or I've got to look someplace else."

It would be hard to get more direct than that, and if you're comfortable with such blunt methods, fine: "Put a close" on your suspected Economic Buying Influence and see if he or she comes up with the money. If, like us, you prefer a little more finesse, you can ask less direct questions. In framing them, remember what the Economic Buyer actually does. By definition this is the person who releases the dollars to pay for *your particular sales objective or proposal.* If you're fairly certain that Dan Farley has the authority to do that, but you want to test your perceptions, you might ask questions like these:

- When the decision is made, Dan, whose budget will the funds come out of?
- Is there anybody who can veto this proposal?
- After you give your OK, Dan, how does the final decision process work?
- Is there anybody at a senior level whose approval we need?

Such questions are designed to cut through the baloney of "referrals" and "recommendations," "tentative approvals" and "provisional orders," by focusing on this key individual's actual role in the sale. If Farley actually is the Economic Buying Influence, his responses—words or actions—will let you know that.

But only, of course, if he tells you the truth. Because that isn't always the case, we recommend a second method of identification.

2. ***Getting Coaching.*** Asking your suspected Economic Buyers if they really have the authority to release the needed funds may or may not get you a straight answer. Not only are ultimate authorities adept at hiding within

corporate structures, but, as we mentioned earlier, Technical Buyers are occupationally addicted to passing themselves off as Economic Buyers, and some of them are very good at the game. If you asked a Technical Buying Influence the above questions, for example, the person could easily tell you, with a straight face, "It's my budget, and I alone make the decision. There's nobody else you should see or need to see."

Because people who are that defensive about their authority are almost never true Economic Buyers, such an answer might well make you suspicious. But you'd still need a second opinion to help you sort things out. That's the significant advantage of having good Coaching. By asking a reliable Coach questions like these, you will often get clearer information than you will from the suspected Economic Buyer (or those Economic Buyer wannabes) about who actually releases the money for your sale.

Solving Problem 2: When You're Blocked

It's not uncommon to identify an Economic Buying Influence correctly and then be frustrated in your objective because she's out of reach. The individual may, for example, be in a remote geographical location: the real approval for your sale may have to come from a home office located hundreds of miles from your territory. Or the Economic Buyer may be isolated from outside calls by a professional screen—the secretary who tells you, every time you try to get to the boss, "Ms. O'Reilly is still out of town." Or you may be blocked by one of those Technical Buying Influences who specialize in masquerading as Economic Buyers.

Dealing with geographical remoteness and protective secretaries often requires merely the use of good proxies. You can often get to an "inaccessible" final authority by letting someone else in your organization cover that particular base for you. The best choice for that someone else is often a person at the *same organizational level* as the Economic Buying Influence. We'll return to this point in a minute, when we discuss like-rank selling.

Dealing with a Buying Influence who's actively trying to block you from seeing the Economic Buyer can be a more difficult scenario. And it's an extremely common one.

If you get to the Economic Buying Influence early enough in the selling cycle, you can often avoid this problem. No Technical Buyer is going to be able to throw an effective block at you if you've seen the Economic Buyer first. But let's assume you haven't already covered the Economic Buyer base. In that case, how do you handle the block?

HANDLING THE BLOCK: THREE METHODS

In handling a person who's actively blocking you from seeing the Economic Buying Influence, you should begin by understanding *why* another Buying Influence would want to do this. When we ask our clients to explain how they have been blocked from getting to Economic Buyers, they give answers like these:

- "The Technical Buyer wants to handle everything personally."
- "He's strong for my competition."
- "They told me that was a lower-level decision."

- "She says the Economic Buyer wants her to make the final call."
- "He just doesn't want us to make the sale."

When you examine these answers closely, you find that there's an underlying theme. No matter what the *given* reason is—no matter what the apparent motivation of the blocking Buying Influence—there's always the same root cause. It relates to what we said in the previous chapter about giving *all* of your Buying Influences individual Wins. When another player attempts to block your access to the Economic Buying Influence, it is always because the blocker sees the proposal you're offering as a personal *Lose.*

Because leaving a Buying Influence with the impression that he or she has lost is so dangerous—it's practically a surefire setup for Buyer's Revenge—your first step in dealing with a blocking Buyer should always be to determine *why* this person feels so negatively, that is, why he or she is convinced that your proposal is a Lose. You need to do this not only as a prerequisite for overcoming the negative perception, but also because the strategy you adopt toward this person's account may have to change dramatically depending on the reasons you discover.

For example, if Harry Barnes is down on your proposal because his sister is a Salesperson of the Year for your competition, you'll have to adopt a totally different strategy from the one you'd adopt if you discovered he's afraid your solution will put him out of a job. Unless you determine the nature of his "Lose" perception, you can easily say all the wrong things every time you meet him.

Once you've determined why a blocker feels that he or she is losing, there are three ways you can deal with the strategic impediment. You can:

- Show the blocking Buyer how to *Win* in the sale by getting you to the Economic Buying Influence
- Go *around* the blocker to get to the final authority
- Go *along* with the block

Each of these three choices could be valid, depending on the situation.

1. ***Showing the Blocker how to Win.*** Of the three strategies, showing the blocker how to Win is by far the best. We recommend that you always try it *first*, resorting to the other two strategies only if it fails. Since the blocking Buyer's "Lose" perception is the cause of the block, you can sometimes turn the situation around by demonstrating that this perception is mistaken. In order to become a sponsor rather than an antisponsor of your proposal, the blocker has to see that it's *in his or her self-interest* for you to get to the Economic Buying Influence.

   Ideally, you want to go one step beyond this. You want to show the blocker how to Win not just by *letting* you get to the Economic Buyer, but by *taking* you there personally. The best way of handling a blocking Buying Influence is to show that you have something the Economic Buyer needs—and that the blocker can get the credit and recognition for delivering it. If you can show a blocking Buyer that you have something of *value* to bring to the Economic Buying Influence, you'll very likely be able to convert a "Lose" perception into a "Win" perception, because there will be a realization that cooperating with you will enhance the blocking Buyer's *own* perceived value. Your goal here is to help him see that he can make an impression by being seen as the person who was smart enough to bring you on board.

The something of value that a blocker can help you give the Economic Buying Influence is always the same thing. The single most valuable contribution you can bring to any Economic Buyer is *knowledge*. Specifically, it's knowledge that will help this key player do what he or she is paid to do: predict the future and set appropriate agendas. If you and the blocking Buyer together can increase the Economic Buyer's *predictive capability*, everybody will Win. We'll speak more in a minute about this critical type of knowledge.

2. ***Going around the Block.*** No matter how earnestly you work to show a blocking Buying Influence how to Win by helping you in your sale, you may still come up against someone who just won't be moved. When you confront a User or Technical Buying Influence whose Lose perception cannot be turned around, you'll be forced to consider the second option—going around the block.

We've mentioned the advantage of using proxies in getting to an Economic Buyer whom you can't reach personally. This technique can often effectively circumvent a blocking Buying Influence. But there's a danger here. In spite of its apparent elegance, this end-run approach to a blocked sale is actually a high-risk strategy.

The risk is that, in your eagerness to reach the Economic Buyer, you'll simply *ignore* the blocking Buyer's resistance as irrelevant or unimportant. In our story of the mismanaged textile-plant sale, we showed what serious long-term repercussions this approach can have. The danger is simply stated: Whenever you make a sale *in spite* of a key player's disapproval, that person perceives you as playing Win-Lose. Inevitably, you turn that player into an enemy because you're seen as serving your interest at his or her expense.

Circumvented blockers have the memory of elephants. Ten or twenty years later they'll remember your going over their heads, and get even. Therefore, we advise our clients that they should employ this damn-the-torpedoes strategy *only when they have little or nothing to lose.* If your position with the Smith account isn't very solid anyway, or if the potential Win for you is huge, you may be justified in going around a blocker. But, since *any Buying Influence ignored is a threat,* watch out for revenge down the line. Even when you feel such a strategy is the only choice left, we still advise you to discuss the matter first with your district or regional sales manager, and with your Coaches, to determine what actions you might take that would neutralize the revenge.

3. ***Going along with the Block.*** Going along with someone who's keeping you from getting to the Economic Buyer can often cause you to lose the immediate business. Therefore, it may look like a very bad strategy. Admittedly, it's not an attractive proposition. But there are special situations that warrant it.

A friend of ours in advertising sales, a man we'll call Gary, had to make this difficult choice last year. He was the account executive for a firm that brought in five million dollars a year, a firm that accounted for about half of Gary's own income. For a holiday season promotion, Gary suggested an advertising package that one of the firm's middle managers found offensive. Gary had excellent relations with that manager's superior, and the manager's approval wasn't essential to the closing of the deal. But Gary knew that if he went around the blocker to his boss, the Economic Buying Influence, the end run would jeopardize future sales.

So he withdrew the proposal. It cost him a ten-thousand-dollar commission but, as he told us some months later, he never regretted the decision. "I had learned in your programs," he explained, "never to leave a Buyer feeling beaten. I just couldn't afford to gamble half my income on that one campaign. And you know something? That guy really appreciated my respecting his feelings. He's become my best ally in that account. I'm doing a promotion for them this year that will let me double the ten thousand I lost."

The lesson is, if you already have a good relationship with the buying organization and if your current sales objective doesn't warrant alienating one of your Buying Influences, you may want to let the immediate order go in favor of protecting the business that you already have—and of keeping open the possibility of larger future sales. Behind such a decision would be a basic goal of Strategic Selling: ensuring not just immediate but *long-term* success.

Of course, this is still at best only a temporary solution—like waiting at a roadblock until the road ahead is fixed. You can't manage an account over time by going along with resistant Buyers' blocks. Therefore, your first plan should always be to show *all* your Buying Influences how they can Win.

Solving Problem 3: The Discomfort Zone

An eager but green sales representative decided to make a cold call—without even the courtesy of a prior phone call—on a vice president in an account he had recently acquired. He hadn't sold anything to the account yet, but he'd heard that the vice president's approval was essential to virtually all sales. So, to "save time," he went straight to the top, determined to feel out the terrain. He was extremely nervous about meeting the high-level executive, but he decided to adopt a positive mental attitude and just do his gung-ho best in the lion's den.

The vice president, who was part of a company that valued ready access to its executives, was at his desk when the young man arrived.

"Hello, there," he said. "I'm George Grant. From the Webster Group? I happened to be in the neighborhood and thought I'd see how things were going here. As long as I'm here, I'd be happy to take any orders you might have."

The vice president looked up from his papers, gave George a quick, astonished once-over, and replied dryly, "Good. I have two orders for you. Get out and stay out."

You'll recognize this as almost a textbook case of amateur selling. Not only didn't George have an appointment, he didn't even call before dropping in. And, when he did drop in, he had no particular reason to be there: no sales proposal to follow up, no referral, no questions that needed answering. No wonder he was nervous. He had good reason to be. And the vice president's "orders" were just what he deserved.

The story illustrates not only the fact that preparation *before* every sales call is critical to strategic success, but also the related fact that, in preparing yourself to meet an Economic Buying Influence, your *psychological readiness* is just as important as your knowledge of your product or your observance of the common amenities such as making an appointment.

There were two related reasons that George felt uncomfortable about meeting the vice president. They are the same reasons that you might feel uncomfortable in the presence of your Economic Buying Influences:

- You might feel *intimidated* by someone who appears too busy or too successful to care about what you have to say.
- You might feel *uncertain* about what this person wants or needs to hear—uncertain, in other works, about what you're doing there.

WHEN YOU'RE INTIMIDATED

There's only one sure way we've found to overcome feelings of intimidation when you confront a high-level executive. That's to remember that, although the Economic Buyer for your sale might have a three-inch carpet and a four-car garage, he's still a human being—and it's to that human being that you're selling.

We don't mean that he's "just an ordinary Joe." He's not. In corporate America, people who play the role of Economic Buyer *are* different, if only because they make more money than the rest of the population. But if you focus on the differences, social or economic, between yourself and your Economic Buying Influences, you'll only intensify your feelings of discomfort. You want to minimize those feelings. One way to do that is to remember the man or woman behind the glamorous role.

You may think of Dan Farley in simple functional terms, as the person who puts you in fear and trembling for your career because he has the power to release the funds for your sale. But maybe he's also a doting father, a lousy tennis player, a guy who danced in his socks at his high school reunion, a homeowner who waters his lawn on Saturdays and watches football and orders in Kung Pao Chicken, just like you. Just like you, too, he's got regrets about the past and hopes for the future and needs, both business and personal, that have to be attended to right now.

Here's the most important thing of all to remember: Since you're offering him a proposal, *you are in a position to fulfill some of those needs*. In order to do that, though, you have to learn whatever you can about him as an *individual*.

Again, as is so often the case when you're clearing away difficulties that stand in the way of your sales objectives, a reliable Coach can be a valuable asset here. A good Coach can help you turn those difficulties into opportunities by providing answers to questions about the Economic Buyer's business needs, and about his or her personal interests as well.

Answers to the first type of question will help you identify which corporate Results your product or service can provide to the buying company. Answers to the second type of question will help you determine the Economic Buying Influence's personal Wins. Having your Coach brief you, *before* you make that first call, on what your Economic Buyer is like as a person is an excellent way of zeroing in on likely Win-Results—and thus of reducing your uneasiness in this key individual's presence.

WHEN YOU'RE UNCERTAIN

The ultimate reason you want to talk to an Economic Buyer, naturally, is to get approval for your sales proposal. But that's not necessarily the reason this person will want to see you. It's up to you to make sure that this individual has as good a reason as you do for wanting the two of you to get together.

It's the Buying Influence's perception, not yours, that

we're talking about now. Every time you call on an Economic Buyer, his or her unspoken question is always going to be "What reason do you have for taking up my valuable time?" If you can't answer that question to his or her satisfaction before you go in, don't count on remaining comfortable after you get there.

Therefore, if you want to reduce your discomfort with an Economic Buyer, you have to make sure, every time you call on such a Buying Influence, that you have a *valid business reason* for doing so.

What the Economic Buying Influence Wants

What does the Economic Buyer consider a valid business reason? We've just said that the one thing the Economic Buyer always wants is *knowledge* that will increase his or her predictive capability—the ability to plan ahead for the organization. This fact leads to the following Strategic Selling axiom:

You have a valid business reason for contacting an Economic Buying Influence when you can present knowledge that will make a contribution to the way he or she is doing business.

This observation surprises many people who are new to selling. Sales representatives who have had limited experience with Economic Buyers often tend to place these top executives on a pedestal, assuming that, when it comes to business, they know *everything*. This is a misconception. In fact, Economic Buyers almost always know less than you do about many areas of your industry. By nature such people are generalists. They don't have time to keep up with all the day-to-day developments in their business, and they often lack relevant details precisely because they've got their eyes on the big picture. *That in fact is exactly why they need you.* You can provide the details they need to make that picture clearer.

Top-management Economic Buyers are paid for the clarity of their crystal balls. Knowledge that increases their ability to predict the future, and thus decreases their perceived risk and uncertainty, is held in the *highest* regard: That kind of knowledge is more important to the Economic Buyer than anything of material value. The ideal situation for you, therefore, is to bring your Economic Buying Influences information that can serve as Windex for their clouded crystal balls.

This information may or may not be related to your immediate sales objective. Naturally, if the information you present demonstrates how to be in the forefront of an industry trend by buying *your* product now, so much the better. But you can still get the Economic Buyer on your side—and therefore increase the probability of approval for your sales objective—if you bring general, industry-wide information, whether or not it's part of your own presentation.

The importance of bringing Economic Buying Influences this kind of information was demonstrated by one of our clients, a major manufacturer of snack foods, a few years ago, when the company's national sales manager gave a joint presentation to the heads of several supermarket chains.

The occasion wasn't a product presentation. That is, the manager wasn't pushing *his* brand, or his company's lines in general, but simply presenting some overall information that could be broadly useful to the assembled Economic Buyers. Among the pieces of information he gave these supermarket executives, though, was the fact that the average profit margin for snack foods—no matter whose label they carried—was extremely high as compared to grocery items overall. The results of this information session were dramatic. Although our client made no claim that his products' specific profit margins were any better than those of his competitors, within a matter of months the company had significantly increased its shelf space in all of the affected stores. This was the Economic Buyers' way of saying, "Thanks for the information," and of increasing their own company profits in the bargain.

KNOWLEDGE THE ECONOMIC BUYING INFLUENCE *DOESN'T* WANT

The snack food manufacturer was successful in increasing penetration in the supermarket accounts because their sales force understood the Economic Buyers' real business needs. They understood that the knowledge they supplied had to relate to *long-term* increased profitability. People who forget this point often attempt to bring Economic Buyers the wrong kind of information, clouding rather than clarifying their crystal balls. The person who brings the Economic Buying Influence this kind of knowledge undermines his or her own position.

We've mentioned the "features and benefits" or "bells and whistles" bias that many sales representatives still bring to their work. This bias has a provisional usefulness when you're selling to User and certain Technical Buying Influences, but it's almost always a drawback when you're talking to an Economic Buyer. Knowledge about bits and bytes in computers, about torque and compression ratios in machinery, or about trace ingredients in food products isn't of immediate value to a person whose eye is on long-range planning, institutional stability, and return on investment. Don't waste your time, or your Economic Buyers' time, selling them these nuts-and-bolts features.

Think back to the parallel between the Economic Buying Influence and the captain of a ship. As a salesperson, you're like a marine instruments specialist trying to sell a new navigational system. Considering the captain's needs and interests, it would be a mistake to emphasize the size of the computerized system's memory, or to boast about how your product will do for this century what the sextant did for the seventeenth. The navigator (a combination User and Technical Buyer) may very well want to hear those details. The captain doesn't. He or she just wants you to answer one question: "Will this product help me plan my ship's course better?"

UNDERSTANDING THE CONCEPT

The distinction between the knowledge that the Economic Buyer wants and doesn't want can be stated in another way. In the second program that we developed at Miller Heiman, Conceptual Selling, we emphasize the importance of the customer's Concept as a critical factor in every decision to buy. As we use the term, the Concept is the customer's mental image of what she wants to have happen as a result of a sale. It's what the customer expects the product or service to achieve. The first and most important lesson of Conceptual Selling is that you have to understand the customer's Concept first, before you can sell any product in a Win-Win fashion. A product sale is successful, we say, only to the degree that it meets the requirements of the customer's Concept.

When you're dealing with Economic Buying Influences, this point is critical. Salespeople who do best with these key decision-makers always find out *first* what they want to achieve. Those who wonder why "Farley just isn't paying any attention to me" are usually trying to push in the product too early, before they understand Farley's problem and desired solution.

The difference between understanding the Concept and making a product sale can be understood readily if you consider two types of decisions that go into automating a plant or a series of plants. The decision to automate in the first place is a Concept decision. The Economic Buyer will be critical to making that decision, and if you want your company to be involved in its implementation, then you've got to begin by zeroing in on his Concept. You've got to find out what he thinks automation will accomplish.

But once the decision to automate has been made, you have to convince a whole range of other individuals that your particular product line is best equipped for the job. That's what we call "making the product sale," and this task is usually taken up chiefly with User and Technical Buying Influences. It always has to come *after* you understand the Concept. If you try to do it before, you risk promoting a solution that is irrelevant or even contradictory to what the various Buying Influences want to achieve.

Understanding the Concept and making the product sale are interrelated tasks, of course, but in most cases your discussion with Economic Buying Influences should focus on the former. When dealing with these long-range forecasters, you're better off presenting the *end* results and filling them in on how you'll provide those results—that is, your product specifics—only if they ask. Top managers seldom want to know "What is this feature called?" They want to know "What will this do for my company (or division or department)?"

Understanding the Economic Buyer's Concept is so important that we consider it one of the salesperson's chief responsibilities in dealing with these key Buying Influences. But there's another, related, responsibility that's just as important. You also have to establish your own *credibility*.

ESTABLISHING CREDIBILITY

This means not only your personal credibility, but your company's too. Credibility is the bedrock of sales success. In establishing it, we've found four techniques to be especially effective. These are like-rank selling, the advertisement of past successes, executive briefings, and bringing in the services of an expert or "guru."

LIKE-RANK SELLING

Although it's your responsibility as the orchestrator of your sales objectives to see that every Buying Influence base is adequately covered, you may not always be the best person to sell to each of these key individuals yourself. That's why we encourage our clients to practice team selling, and to set up meetings between buyers and sellers of *like rank*. Since executives and other business people are often most comfortable talking to their peers, your own boss (to use just one example) might find it a lot easier to establish credibility with your Economic Buying Influence than you would.

Your job is to be sure that each Buying Influence base is covered by the person *best qualified* to do so. Economic Buyers are seldom reluctant to exchange ideas with management peers. If you can arrange for your Economic Buyer to visit one of your company facilities where that's possible—or, even better, if you can bring one of your company executives to this key player—you'll be using like-rank selling effectively.

Putting executives together like this has the added advantage of showing the Economic Buyer that your company is committed, from senior management on down, to your proposal. This in turn has a significant spin-off effect: It provides a public demonstration of your personal value, thus establishing your credibility for future sales.

ADVERTISING PAST SUCCESSES

You can also arrange for your Economic Buying Influences to visit a customer installation where you have a successful track record, and where by definition you'll be immediately distinguished from the competition. By showing how your product or service has worked well for another client, you demonstrate both Concept and credibility, and also bring the Economic Buyers the one thing they most want: direct information about how to improve their *own* businesses.

THE EXECUTIVE BRIEFING

The executive briefing is used frequently in the fields of packaged goods and consumer products. Many of our Fortune 500 clients in these fields give such briefings once or twice a year to executives in their national accounts. At these periodic presentations, they review with their Economic Buyers the Results and Wins they've provided in the recent past, and suggest future joint ventures that will ensure that the customers will continue to Win. Even when there is no specific proposal on the table, the selling firm is thus still able to reinforce the satisfactions that its customers have enjoyed as a result of their previous associations.

BRINGING IN A "GURU"

A guru, in Strategic Selling terminology, is someone with expertise in an area that exerts influence on business trends. This expert may or may not be from your company, and may or may not be well versed in your particular business.

Economic Buyers achieve their positions of authority in part because they're receptive to new ideas. The advantage to you of arranging a meeting between a guru and your Economic Buyer is that it will introduce that person to new ideas. Not so incidentally, the credit will go to you, as well as to the guru, because of your part in making the expertise available.

In addition, employing a guru can allow you to bring the Economic Buying Influence knowledge that you have, but that *you* know will be more believable coming from an impartial expert. For example, having an R&D expert tell an Economic Buyer that your company is at the cutting edge of a certain technology may be a much more effective way of getting your message through than your saying, as a sales representative, "We've got the best stuff on the market."

The guru technique is used with some frequency—and with extraordinary effectiveness—in dealings between major firms. It's a way not so much of facilitating specific sales as of establishing a history of healthy interaction, in which key players at both the firm that supplies the guru and the firm that receives new knowledge see themselves as having Won.

We were called in as gurus ourselves some time ago, when one of our clients booked one of our Strategic Selling programs not for itself, but for one of *its* clients. Our new participants were very pleased with the program, and their appreciation extended not just to us, the gurus, for having presented it, but also to the company that had made it possible. So everybody Won.

These four techniques are only samples. You may come up with other techniques that are also effective in improving your position with Economic Buyers. Use anything that works, of course, as long as you're sure that you're delivering what the Economic Buyer always needs—knowledge to improve his or her forecasting ability—and that you're delivering it in a Win-Win manner.

It's true that you'll have to assume the immediate burden here, since typically the company delivering the knowledge picks up the tab. But you'll almost certainly be repaid in future business. Delivering knowledge to an Economic Buying Influence is not a gift. If the knowledge is relevant and useful, the technique is an investment.

Keeping in Touch

It's especially crucial to cover the Economic Buying Influence on an initial sale to a new account—and to do this early in the selling cycle. But that's not enough. Maintaining *regular* contact with all the potential Economic Buyers in every account is critically important to long-term selling strategy.

How regular is regular? Even among experienced sales professionals, there's a high degree of uncertainty about how frequently Economic Buyers should be contacted to maintain healthy business relationships. Thus one of the questions we are asked most often is "How often do I have to see the Economic Buyer after I make that first sale?" The question has a two-part answer, and it links up everything we've said about bringing the Economic Buyer what he or she needs, about reducing your own discomfort, and about preparation:

- Contact with the Economic Buying Influence must be *periodic*, not sporadic.
- Whenever you contact this person, you should have a *valid business reason* for doing so.

You don't have to contact the Economic Buyer on *every* repeat sale, but contact after the first order should still be *periodic* rather than haphazard. If you don't schedule meetings with your Economic Buyers on a regular basis, it's easy to fall back into the old discomfort trap and to let contact with these key players slide until your position in their accounts has eroded. As a general rule, you're risking such erosion unless you meet with your Economic Buying Influences every six months.

Since they know that they'll be seeing their Economic Buyers in another month, or three months, the best sales strategists are always on the lookout for valid business reasons to do so—that is, for contributions they can make to the way the customer is doing business. These contributions can be as major as showing the Economic Buyer that your company's new refining process can save her company 18 percent in materials cost—or as "minor" as bringing her an article on outsourcing, a new SEC regulation, or a productivity seminar. As long as they highlight future trends that might, directly or indirectly, have an impact on the company's business, such contributions will always be appreciated—*even if the Economic Buyer has already seen them.* The point is for you to demonstrate that you want this individual to Win. An Economic Buyer who understands that can be an invaluable ally in any sale.

Personal Workshop 6: Your Position with the Economic Buying Influence

Take out your Buying Influences Chart, your Win-Results Chart, your Alternate Positions list, your notebook, and your Red Flag and Strength stickers. You'll need about twenty minutes to test your position with the Economic Buyer for your chosen Single Sales Objective.

STEP 1: WHO IS THE ECONOMIC BUYING INFLUENCE FOR THIS SALES OBJECTIVE?

In defining exactly who the Economic Buyer is for your sales objective, remember that this *single* individual has *final* authority to *release the needed funds*. Look at the name you've placed in the Economic Buyer box of your Buying Influences Chart, and ask yourself whether or not you *know* for certain that this person controls the funds for *this* sale. If you're not certain, look over your Buying Influences Chart again and see if you can uncover a "hidden" Economic Buyer in one of the other key players. Think also about the rest of the account, to see if you've overlooked a "mere rubber stamp" high up in the buying organization who will actually give final approval to release the money.

Once you've come up with the name of the person who you believe controls the funds you need, even if you're certain that you've got the right person, test yourself by asking these further questions about your equivalent of Dan Farley:

- Is Farley at the right *level* in the buying organization to make such a buying decision? If such a decision were being made in *my* company, would the Economic Buyer approval come from the same level? (Remember to take into account the relative size of the two companies.)
- Have I considered the five *risk* factors that might cause the Economic Buyer role to float upward or downward from this level?
- Am I focusing on the Economic Buying Influence for this Single Sales Objective, rather than last month's or next year's?
- Is Farley's approval *final*? Can I honestly take his yes as a release of funds, or is it only a recommendation?
- Is there anybody else in the buying organization who can *veto* Farley's approval?

In asking these critical questions, remember that you have several sources of information to tap. Don't rely only on your *own* impressions of the sales situation. If possible, ask the Economic Buyer himself or herself, using direct or indirect questions. And double-check the answers by asking your Coach.

STEP 2: HOW WELL IS THE ECONOMIC BUYING INFLUENCE COVERED?

Keeping in mind that *any uncovered Buyer is a threat*, determine how well you've covered the Economic Buyer by asking yourself questions like these:

- Have I personally seen Dan Farley, or have I arranged for him to be contacted by someone better qualified to do so? (Until you've seen to it that the *best qualified* member of your selling team has contacted the Economic Buyer, you have to consider that Buying Influence base a Red Flag. If Farley has been contacted by someone in your organization, that is a Strength.)
- If Farley hasn't yet been contacted, why not? If he's geographically distant or being screened by a secretary, can I use good proxies or *like-rank selling* to get through?
- If I'm being *blocked* from getting to Farley, what's my best strategy for dealing with the blocker? In this specific sales situation, is the best strategy to go *along*, go *around*, or show the blocking Buyer how to *Win*?

STEP 3: HOW RECEPTIVE IS THE ECONOMIC BUYING INFLUENCE TO MY PROPOSAL?

We've said that each Response Mode dictates a different selling strategy. In this step of the workshop, test the assessment you made in Chapter 8 of your Economic Buyer's Response Mode, to assure yourself that, at this point in the selling cycle, you're approaching this individual with the appropriate strategy. Do that by asking yourself these questions:

- If Farley is in Growth Mode, does he understand that my proposal will help him *improve* the business process or processes that he wants improved?
- If he's in Trouble Mode, does he understand that my proposal will *fix* whatever's wrong? Is he convinced that I understand the *urgency* of his problem?

- If he's in Even Keel Mode, can I demonstrate to him that there's a *discrepancy* he hasn't perceived between his current reality and desired results? Can I have another Buying Influence alert him to Trouble on the horizon?
- If he's in Overconfident Mode, is it wise for me to try to sell him at this time—or should I lie low until he cycles into Trouble? Have I made the necessary *preparations* to solve his problem when it eventually arises?

STEP 4: AM I PLAYING WIN-WIN WITH THE ECONOMIC BUYING INFLUENCE?

You know you're playing Win-Win with your Economic Buying Influence when you can give positive answers to the following questions:

- Have I delivered, or can I deliver, to Dan Farley's company a Result that will create a positive impact on one or more of its business processes?
- Does this Result translate for Farley as a personal Win that will satisfy his self-interest? (Remember here that Wins are individual and intangible, and that you can often use Coaching to give you reliable information on how a given Buying Influence Wins.)
- Does he *understand* that I've been responsible, and will continue to be responsible, for delivering Win-Results to him? In other words, does he *know* that I want to serve his self-interest as well as my own?

If you can't give yourself concrete, positive answers to these questions, you need to reconsider your position. Look over your Buying Influences Chart and your Win-Results Chart again, concentrating on the Economic Buying Influence. Review the Win-Results Statement that you wrote for this person. Place Red Flags any place on your charts where the answers to the above questions weren't satisfactory. What questions do you need to ask your Coach or Coaches to help you eliminate these Red Flags?

Look also at the Strengths you have identified on the Buying Influences Chart. Are you able to use any of them as leverage against the Red Flags to further improve your position with this Economic Buyer?

STEP 5: DO I HAVE A VALID BUSINESS REASON FOR SEEING THE ECONOMIC BUYER?

No matter how solid your position with your Economic Buyer may look to you, it's always in jeopardy unless, every time you see this person, you have a valid business reason for doing so. Test whether or not you have such a reason by asking yourself these questions:

- What *knowledge* do I have that Farley can use to forecast future trends in his business? How will this knowledge help him clean his crystal ball?
- How is this knowledge Concept related rather than product related? How will the contribution that I can make to his business impact organizational stability and growth, and not just the nuts and bolts of daily operations?
- How does my contribution not only help the customer's business, but also establish the credibility of *my* company? Whether or not it leads to an acceptance of my immediate sales proposal, how does it distinguish me from the competition?

STEP 6: REVISE YOUR ALTERNATE POSITIONS LIST.

Throughout this workshop, you've been asking yourself questions designed to clarify your current position with your Economic Buying Influence. Use the answers to those questions now to improve that position. Take out your Alternate Positions list and add to it any strategy options that this workshop has suggested.

As you revise the list, work only on those Alternate Positions that relate to the Economic Buying Influence. Continue to be *specific,* and continue to *test* each entry against the rule of thumb that every good Alternate Position eliminates a Red Flag, leverages from a Strength, or does both.

For example, if in Step 2 of this workshop you noticed that Gary Steinberg was blocking you from getting to Farley, it's not sufficient to list "Get past Steinberg" as an Alternate Position. A more specific Alternate Position would read something like this: "Show Steinberg how he can make an impression on Farley by helping me bring him my productivity-increasing proposal."

Or, if in Step 4 you noticed that you still don't understand how Farley is going to Win in the sale, you can't just list "Get Farley to Win." A sound Alternate Position—one that employs a Strength to eliminate a Red Flag—would be "Ask Doris Green to explain how a 15 percent productivity-increase would translate into a Win for Farley."

A FINAL POSITION CHECK

Your continual revision of your Alternate Positions list is a way of remaining *prepared,* and thus of *reducing discomfort,* each time you meet your Economic Buying Influence. But you won't be able to carry this list around with you, and to review it in detail, every time you knock on this person's door. To reduce your discomfort before each individual meeting, you need a "short form" test, to gauge the most important features of your upcoming interaction. We've found that you can efficiently and quickly reduce your discomfort in the face of meeting an Economic Buyer if, just before you go in, you ask yourself four key questions:

1. *What do I need to FIND OUT?* That is, what *information* do I need to get from this Economic Buyer, or from someone else, to help me better address the required Results and personal Wins?
2. *What do I want the Economic Buyer to KNOW?* That is, what contribution can I make to this person's long-range business planning?
3. *What do I want the Economic Buyer to DO?* That is, how will that contribution provide Results that will have a positive impact on both the buying organization and my own?
4. *What do I want the Economic Buyer to FEEL?* That is, how will those Results translate into a personal Win that the Economic Buyer will attribute to me?

When you can answer these questions clearly, and when you know how you'll get the Economic Buyer to know, do, and feel what you want, you'll automatically feel more relaxed about facing this key Buying Influence, and will be able to go into your meetings with much greater confidence.

CHAPTER 12

THE COACH: DEVELOPING YOUR PRIME INFORMATION RESOURCE

Throughout our ongoing analysis of your current sales objective, we've stressed the importance of developing Coaches to improve your strategic position with the other Buying Influences. Beginning in Chapter 1 with the story of Greg, the computer salesman who utilized an outside consultant to reposition himself with an Economic Buying Influence, we've said that the use of effective Coaching can be the difference between a sale that *almost* makes it to the close, and one that not only closes in your favor but also generates Win-Win sales for you far into the future. We've also made the point that, unlike the other Buying Influences, a Coach won't be sitting out there in the buying organization, waiting to be identified. Coaches have to be "nominated" into their position, and then developed as resources for your particular sales objectives.

Because a good Coach is so essential to good strategy, and because the Coach is significantly different in some respects from the other Buying Influences, we consolidate here, in a single chapter, all the information you need to know in order to "nominate," develop, and use your Coaches wisely. We do this partly in deference to all those clients who, when we asked them what they'd like to hear more about, said "First, the Economic Buyer. Then, the Coach." A good Coach is often a key to locking in your position with all the other Buying Influences. Here we show you how to use that key.

A good Coach functions essentially as an information resource. He or she can not only enable you to check the accuracy of the information that you're getting but also provide information that you haven't been able to get elsewhere. Just as important, Coaches can help you tie together everything that you know, or are still trying to find out, about the Buying Influences for your Single Sales Objectives. More specifically:

1. As you begin your strategy, your Coach can help you find the *real* key players for your sales objective and help you determine each one's Degree of Influence.
2. Your Coach can help you identify areas of Strength in your position that you can use to eliminate Red Flags.
3. Your Coach can help you understand each Buying Influence's perception of reality—and thus gauge how each one is likely to react to your proposal in terms of the four Response Modes (Growth, Trouble, Even Keel, and Overconfident).
4. Your Coach can help you understand the Results each Buyer needs to Win—and how to deliver those Results so that your Buyers perceive themselves to be in a Win-Win relationship with you.

Your Coach will be able to help you in these areas, though, only if he or she fits a very particular "job description."

Wearing a cowboy hat doesn't necessarily mean you know one end of a horse from the other. Similarly, not everyone who looks like a Coach can necessarily meet the special qualifications of the Coaching role. Therefore, you need exact criteria to determine who can, and who probably cannot, function as this critical information resource.

THE THREE COACHING CRITERIA

We've explained that a good Coach can be found *anywhere*—in your organization, in the buying organization, or somewhere outside both. It's not geography or organizational placement that determines whether or not a person can fill the Coaching role for you, but rather how well the candidate fulfills three specific Coaching criteria:

- *Criterion 1: Your credibility.* A Coach is someone with whom you, the person orchestrating the sale, have personal credibility. That is, your Coach has got to believe in you, to be convinced that you can be *trusted.* And we mean trusted in a professional, selling capacity. Your mother might trust you not to filch cookies when she isn't looking, but that doesn't make her a suitable candidate for a Coach. Generally, when you have credibility with a potential Coach, it's because this person has Won with you professionally in the past. So the first thing to ask yourself, when you're considering candidates for the Coaching role, is this: "Do I have a track record of performance with this person?"
- *Criterion 2: The Coach's credibility.* A good Coach must have credibility with the Buying Influences for your particular sales objective. They—or at least some of them—

have to trust the person you're considering well enough to share with him or her the information you need. This trust can't be diffuse, and it can't be based merely on imagined prestige. That is, it's not enough to say that "the Manetti people trust Toni" because she's a high-level executive who "no doubt" commands respect. If Toni is really a potential Coach for your objective, she knows the relevant Buying Influences at Manetti personally, they have Won with her in the past, and she has not only their respect but their confidence. Since you need your Coach to clarify for you how the buying decision will be made, this criterion is fundamental. So the second question to ask is "Do the Buying Influences for my Single Sales Objective trust this person?"

- *Criterion 3: Desiring your success.* The crucial distinction between your Coach and the other Buying Influences is that by definition the Coach *wants you to make this sale.* For whatever reason, this person believes that, when your proposal is adopted, he or she will Win. As we explained in the discussion of Win-Results, it would be useful for you to know what that reason is, but that's not essential. What is essential is that your potential Coach see a direct correlation between your getting this piece of business and his or her self-interest. Therefore, the third question to ask is "Does this individual see a personal Win in my making this sale?"

Twelve years ago, in the first edition of this book, we suggested that, while an ideal Coach fulfills all three of these criteria, it's possible to work with people "who don't measure up on all three counts." "Just beware of people," we said, "who don't meet *any* of the criteria; they're definitely not Coaches. Concentrate on the people who come closest to passing this three-part test."

This is one of the very few areas in Strategic Selling where we've changed our advice. Further experience has shown us that, unless your Coaching candidate fulfills *all three* of the criteria we've outlined, you should be extremely cautious about considering this person a Coach. At the very least, you should identify each criterion that is unfulfilled as a Red Flag. Our clients continually tell us horror stories that reinforce the importance of this modified advice.

Suppose, for example, that you were considering Toni's suitability as a Coach in the following situations with the Manetti account:

- Everybody at Manetti trusts her, she's all fired up about your proposal, but she doesn't know you from a hole in the wall. That would be Criteria 2 and 3 fulfilled, but not 1.
- She's worked with you well in the past, she loves your proposal, but nobody at Manetti knows *her* from a hole in the wall. OK on 1 and 3, but zero on 2.
- She trusts you and they trust her, but she's so preoccupied with an operational glitch in another department that she sees talking to you about Manetti to be a giant distraction. That's Criteria 1 and 2, but nothing on 3.

In all of these cases, it would be reckless to go along with the popular expression and say "Two out of three ain't bad." Two out of three here could be terrible, because attempting to utilize Toni when she's not fully *qualified* could actually bring more damage than good to the situation.

That's not a death sentence, though. We're not suggesting that, when you find yourself in a two-out-of-three situation, you simply discard that person as a potential Coach. Because Complex Sales are dynamic, not static, and because your strategic involvement can itself bring about changes, you should consider every Toni that you encounter to be an undeveloped but still potentially good resource.

Think of potential Coaches as diamonds in the rough. When a diamond comes out of the ground, it's a lump of milky stone. What makes it worth a million is the faceting and polishing—in other words, the process of gem development. The same principle applies in turning Coaches into "gems." Look for Coaches who pass all three of the qualifying tests. For those that pass one or two, start the process of development. This means treating your potential Coach like any other Buying Influence—as someone who needs personal Wins that you might be able to deliver.

Avoiding "False Coaches"

In narrowing down the field of candidates so you can focus on the best possible potential Coaches, we've found it useful to identify at the outset certain categories of individuals who are often mistaken for Coaches—people who may look like Coaches, but who cannot really fulfill this critical role. Among these "false Coaches" are the following:

THE "FRIEND"

Probably the single most common error made in identifying potential Coaches is to confuse the Coach's liking the salesperson *personally* with his or her liking the *sales objective*. In the search for reliable Coaching, "He likes me" should *never* be taken as an equivalent of "He likes my proposal and wants me to make this sale."

You want your Coach to like you, of course. You're not

going to get reliable data easily from someone with whom you have no rapport. But personal rapport isn't enough. You want your Coach to like you for a particular reason—because this individual has *Won* with you in the past. A person who has Won with you already is likely to believe that he or she can Win with you again. Therefore, you'll have the necessary *credibility* with that person that constitutes our first Coaching criterion.

But that's still only one criterion. Don't forget the other two. No matter how close you are to Doris Green, and no matter how great a person she thinks you are, she's not a Coach unless she's trusted by the other Buying Influences, and unless she perceives a Win in *this* sales objective for herself. A Coach *must* like your current proposal.

THE INFORMATION GIVER

It's true that your Coach's primary duty is to provide you with information. But not just *any* information. To be a reliable Coach, the person has to get you information that's *unique* and *useful* to you in this particular sale.

- By "unique" we mean information that you can't readily get elsewhere.
- By "useful" we mean information that will help you improve your position with the other Buying Influences for this sale.

These two characteristics are interactive and equally essential. The person who gives you capital expenditure figures from the buying company's last stockholders' report may be giving you useful information—but it's hardly unique, since you easily could have (and should have) gotten it yourself. On the other hand, the person who tells you that your Economic Buying Influence has a star-shaped mole on his left shoulder is giving you unique information that's useless. The *unique* and *useful* information that you want your Coaches to provide will tell you how the buying organization *really* makes decisions, how each of the Buying Influences *really* Wins—and how the Results *your proposal* delivers can help each of them do so.

Ideally, your Coaches provide a map that guides you to the other Buying Influences. Beware of Coaches who offer you "rare" or "interesting" maps that don't show you where you want to go. There's no point in having the definitive map of New Jersey in your pocket if the people you're trying to work with live in Kansas.

THE INSIDE SALESPERSON

An inside salesperson, as we use the term, is someone in the buying organization who does some of your selling for you, and who usually recommends you over the competition. In other words, he takes on some of your responsibilities—almost always because he sees something in the sale for him. This means that he fulfills the third Coaching criterion: He sees your pending success as a personal Win.

But, again, that's only one criterion. By itself, it's not enough to make a person a good Coach. As important as inside salesmen are to many Complex Sales, not all of them make good Coaches. To tell which ones are, and which ones are not, going to be reliable information resources, we urge you to test inside salesmen against the first two Coaching criteria as well: (1) They have to trust *you* and (2) the Buying

Influences for this sale have to trust *them*. If they don't trust you, their desire for you to make the sale may prove unstable. And if they aren't trusted by the other Buying Influences, they may not get you accurate information.

There's an additional danger in seeking Coaching from inside salespeople. By definition an inside salesperson *sells*. That's not what a Coach does. Coaches belong on the sidelines, giving you direction. As the orchestrator of a sale, you should do your own selling. After all, how far would an NFL quarterback get if he asked his Coach to take the snap from center? How many gold medals would Kristi Yamaguchi get if she asked her Coach to perform her triple axels? In developing inside salespeople as Coaches, remember one cardinal rule: The more you let somebody else run the plays *for* you, the less control *you* have of the ball.

THE MENTOR

As you know, many executives today get their professional start under the wing of old-timers in their organizations (sometimes outside of their organizations) who take on an unofficial responsibility for showing the newcomers the ropes. The older person introduces the younger one to the "right" people, explains company protocol and procedure, and in general grooms the novice executive to carry on his or her personal brand of leadership.

It's true that you may find Coaches in your own organization. And it's true that a mentor such as the senior executive we're describing here can be a valuable asset. But you shouldn't confuse a mentor with a Coach.

By definition a mentor wants you to succeed in your *career*. He grooms you to follow in his footsteps so that your success in business as a whole will reflect well on him. A Coach's desire for your success, while just as solid, is far more focused than that: Your Coach by definition wants you to succeed *in this sale*. As fervently committed as a mentor may be to your success, she may have nothing to contribute to your current Single Sales Objective—to gathering and refining the information you need for this sale. Your Coach, on the other hand, may care relatively little about your long-range plans. But a Coach who sees a personal Win in your closing *this* piece of business can still be a reliable, sale-specific asset.

The Best Possible Coaching Situation

Although good Coaches can be found almost anywhere, there is one ideal source. The best of all possible Coaching situations is to turn the Economic Buyer for your sales objective into a Coach in his or her own organization. The benefits of doing this should be obvious:

- The Economic Buyer is likely to understand better than the other Buying Influences how the buying organization as a whole actually works—that is, how critical purchasing decisions are made. So this person can guide and introduce you to the other key players.
- If the Economic Buying Influence is convinced of the Concept advantages of your proposal, you'll have less trouble selling its product advantages to the other Buying Influences.
- The simple fact that the Economic Buyer is usually a top manager means that this person's counsel will carry weight with the other Buying Influences.

- Turning your Economic Buying Influence into a Coach significantly reduces the risk of the sale being vetoed late in the game.

For different but related reasons, it's always good to get to the Economic Buyer early and to develop a good Coach early. Turning the Economic Buyer into a Coach accomplishes both these tasks simultaneously.

If the Economic Buyer favors your proposal early in the game, one good way of turning this person into a Coach is to ask for Coaching about *another person*. "Dan," you can say, "I'd appreciate some Coaching on the best approach to take with Will Johnson." Such a question reinforces your position with the Economic Buying Influence *and* improves the Coaching possibilities.

ASKING FOR COACHING

When you've winnowed out the false Coaches and have found someone who you believe fulfills the three Coaching criteria, you should ask that person for Coaching. We mean this literally. The term "Coaching," because of its use in sports, has a very positive connotation in our culture. It decodes as "I'm competent and I'll do my own work; just give me some direction." Because of this positive connotation, most people are flattered to be asked, and welcome the opportunity, to provide Coaching. So use the word: "Coaching."

Don't say, "I need your help," or "Can you refer me to the right people for this sale?" The words "refer" and "help" and "recommendation" decode badly: They're heard as "I'm incompetent; I need you to carry the ball for me." By asking for Coaching rather than for a referral, moreover, you're likely to discover a happy paradox. The salesperson who asks for a referral or for help may not get either one. On the other hand, the person who asks for Coaching usually gets not only the information she needs, but the referral besides.

What's fundamental is the point we mentioned previously, when we defined the difference between an inside salesperson and a Coach. Your Coach's role is to provide information, direction, guidance—and in many cases access to the other Buying Influences. *But the Coach doesn't do your selling for you.* Be wary of giving any potential Coach the idea that that is what you're looking for.

Your Coaching Network

You should try to develop at least one Coach per major sales objective. But often one is not enough. Often, too, even a Coach who has proven invaluable on one sales objective will prove useless on a future one. So your long-term aim should be to develop a *network* of Coaches within each account whose expertise you can draw on when and as needed. The larger and more complex the account, the greater the need for a network of Coaches.

There are two basic reasons that you need to develop such a Coaching network. One is that every sale is *unique:* You need a different Coach or Coaches for each Single Sales Objective, and the more people you have to draw from, the better off you will be. The other reason is that there are so many ways to be *misinformed* that success is usually the result not of relying on one person's information, but of comparing a variety of data from many sources.

COACHES FOR THIS SALE

A friend of ours in computer sales discovered the importance of having a Coaching network recently, when he nearly blew a major software deal by relying initially on a single Coach, a buying organization middle manager whom he described as "my old buddy Mel." Mel had Coached him very well on a couple of former deals, and naturally our friend went to him for direction when he was about to propose a third.

On this third sale, though, Mel was lukewarm. He gave our friend advice that boiled down to "Hang in there—you're doing fine." Encouraging, sure—but not exactly the kind of information the salesman needed to develop incrementally greater certainty about his position. For about a month he kept going back to Mel, with negligible results, until he suddenly realized his problem. On the previous sales, Mel had been one of the User Buyers as well as the Coach; he'd seen that it was in his immediate self-interest to have our friend make those deals. On this sales proposal, however, our friend was trying to sell a software package that had nothing to do with Mel's department. Because Mel felt that he had nothing to gain from the transaction, his "assistance" was more cordial than illuminating.

"When I realized that," the salesman told us, "the light really went on. I saw that he was still my friend, but that he had no interest in this particular sale. I'd have to look elsewhere for a real Coach."

The way he did that illustrates the importance of networking. Once he saw that Mel was the wrong resource for *this* unique sales objective, our friend went to him and admitted his dilemma. "Look, Mel," he said, "I'm in a bind here. Is there anyone who can give me the kind of information on this sale that you gave me on the last two?" Our friend was still using Mel as a Coach, but in a totally different, and much more effective, manner. By getting his "old friend" to guide him toward another sale-specific Coach, he accomplished three valuable things:

1. He reinforced his former Win-Win relationship with Mel by letting Mel know that he valued and appreciated his advice.
2. He positioned himself with the right Coach for this sale—a woman who saw a Win in the sale for herself.
3. He widened the network of possible Coaches on whom he could draw in the future.

NETWORKING AS A CHECKING MECHANISM

The second reason you need to develop a variety of Coaches is that, even within each individual sale, there are still plenty of chances to be misinformed. The more people you have giving you information, therefore, the more opportunity you'll have to check each individual person's assessment against other people's views. In addition, the more Red Flags you'll be likely to turn into opportunities.

A Northwest area director in food service sales, a man we'll call Rod, uses a "total coverage" technique in setting up and nurturing his Coaching network. "I always try to use everybody I can as a Coach," he explains. "I deal mostly with people at the vice-presidential level, and almost everybody at that level has some information you can use. I get Jack Smith to give me a handle on Mary Jones's Wins, and then I get Mary to tell me about Jack's. That way I can double-check what each person is telling me, so I never end up working with misinformation."

Rod's technique has several times helped him become salesman of the year. It works because it incorporates several of the Strategic Selling principles we've described:

- In a sophisticated way, it covers—and re-covers—the bases to be sure that as many Red Flags as possible are turned into opportunities, and that as many Strengths as possible are leveraged against those Red Flags.
- It effectively focuses attention on the individual Buying Influences' probable Wins.
- Finally, it highlights the basic rule that every sales strategy has to be constantly tested and reassessed to remain effective.

The obvious problem you'll encounter in using networking as a testing mechanism, of course, is that you'll uncover not just *verifying* information, but *conflicting* information. Since no two Coaches are ever going to perceive a given selling situation in exactly the same way, you'll inevitably be involved in sales where one Coach tells you one thing about a key Buying Influence, and a second Coach tells you the opposite. Sorting your way through this difficulty means being able to assess each Coach's information independently against the reality *you* perceive.

We used this strategy recently to resolve the fundamental question of who was really the Economic Buying Influence for a pending sale. Our initial Coach for the deal, a Technical Buying Influence, said that a vice president of sales, a man we'll call Fox, would give final approval for the sale. "He's been here forever," the Technical Buyer said. "And he'll be here when we're all gone."

A User Buying Influence, however, gave us conflicting information. According to her, there was a corporate shake-up in the works and Fox was on his way out. She had given us good information in the past, but the Technical Buyer was organizationally closer to Fox. Which Coach were we to believe?

To decide the issue, we arranged a meeting with Fox in which we could look unobtrusively for signs of the uncertainty that the User Buyer had warned us about. "The guy is walking on eggshells," she had said. "You see if he looks like somebody who's going to be here in another month." The meeting proved her correct. Fox was uneasy, hesitant to see us, and very reluctant to commit himself to anything, much less give his approval for one of our processes.

Once we saw that, we decided that, even though he had been the Economic Buying Influence for other purchases of our programs, he wasn't acting like an Economic Buyer now. So we began to look elsewhere for final approval, and none too soon, as it turned out: A month later, Fox took early retirement. By that time, we had effectively repositioned ourselves with the real Economic Buyer. Thanks to our second Coach, and to our reality-testing session, we had avoided investing any more valuable time in trying to make our case to "yesterday's decision-maker."

One final note on your Coaching network. Unless you sell only one product, at a fixed rate, to a single customer, developing more than one Coach per sale is only the beginning in the effective use of a network. Since you very likely work with different products or services, different dollar amounts, and a variety of customers, you need to develop a network that permeates your entire industry and thus touches every possible sales situation.

To some degree, an industry-wide Coaching network is the logical outcome of developing multiple account networks. If you're like most of our clients, the bulk of your business is probably concentrated in a handful of industries. When that's the case, the utility of a good Coach—like that of a guru—can often "spread," so that a single well-positioned individual can give you reliable help in several accounts. In addition, such networks inevitably overlap, which makes it possible for you to develop cross-account, or territorial, Coaching opportunities.

The bottom line here is clear enough. The more reliable Coaches you nurture and develop over time, the more quickly you'll be able to find the right Coach for each aspect of each new sales objective.

THE FINAL TEST: YOUR FEELINGS

Even after you've verified that each person you're utilizing as a Coach fulfills the three Coaching criteria, even after you've sorted through the "false Coaches" we've described, and even after you have checked your Coaches' conflicting information against your own perceptions of the selling situation, you may still be uncertain about a potential Coach's ability to guide you in a given sale. When this happens, you can fall back on what we've found to be a reliable court of last appeal. When all other means have been exhausted, you should ask yourself how you feel about using a given person as a Coach.

This relates back to our discussion of the Euphoria-Panic Continuum in Chapter 3. We said there that, although you can often be misled by your head, your gut reactions to a given sales situation are generally reliable. If you feel "uneasy" or "a little funny" about a sale, there's a good chance that there's something wrong with your position—even if you don't know what it is.

The point applies to your assessment of Coaches as well,

and to your need to test each one against those with conflicting information. Trust those uneasy feelings. If everything a certain Coach is telling you about a Buying Influence's Wins or about an account situation *sounds* right, but something still *feels* wrong, look at that Coach again. If you're uneasy with the guidance that you're getting, the chances are you're not talking to a real Coach.

Personal Workshop 7: Testing Your Coach

By this point in your strategic analysis, you should already have identified at least one Coach. The purpose of this Personal Workshop is to have you *test* that individual to see whether or not he or she can in fact provide good Coaching. So pull out your Buying Influences Chart, your Alternate Positions list, the Win-Results Chart, and your Strengths and Red Flags. Since your Coach is a principal key to your other Buyers, the chances are that much of the information you've written in on these various charts came directly or indirectly from this person. You're going to test it now for reliability.

STEP 1: DO YOU HAVE CREDIBILITY WITH YOUR COACH?

Begin by measuring your Coach against the first of the three Coaching criteria. If you have two or more Coaches identified—as in our sample Buying Influences Chart—assess them separately, one by one. There's nothing subtle or esoteric about this step. To test whether or not you have credibility with Sandy Kelly, for example, ask yourself these questions:

- How has Sandy *Won* with me in the past?
- If she hasn't Won with me personally, has she at least Won with my *company*?
- Am I certain that I have Sandy's *trust*?

As always, be specific in your answers. If you can say, "I sold Sandy that promotional deal when she was with Smith Industries, and it got her a vice presidency," then you can be fairly certain that you've earned her trust. But if you can't say something like this—if you can't identify a *concrete,* and preferably *recent,* Win that you've brought her—look at her again. Unless she believes that you can be trusted to deliver Wins for her, *you* may not be able to trust *her*.

STEP 2: DOES THIS COACH HAVE CREDIBILITY WITH THE BUYING INFLUENCES?

Now look for evidence that Sandy can provide you with reliable information on the various Buying Influences for *this* sale. To get that information, they have got to trust her. If they don't, her efforts on your behalf will at best be useless, and at worst could lead you to undermine your own position.

Past history is your best yardstick here. If Sandy told you about a marketing decision at Contour Industries two months before it became public, she looks like a good bet for a Coach: Somebody at Contour obviously trusts her enough to give her an inside track. But if your last experience with her was that she misidentified an Economic Buying Influence there, you might think twice about using her now.

Testing the credibility of your Coach with the Buying Influences is particularly important if he doesn't come from the buying organization himself. Coaches you draw from your own firm, or from the club and convention network, may or may not be able to guide you effectively. They *may* make excellent Coaches—but you can't assume that to be the case until you test them.

Even if the Coach you've tentatively chosen to help you get into Contour is part of that organization, though, you *still* have to test his or her credibility. As you know, not everyone sitting at a nine-foot desk actually knows what's going on. Don't rely on titles and offices to test your Coach on this second criterion. It doesn't matter what her corporate position is if you can't be certain that what she tells you is accurate.

Use your Coaching network too to test one Coach against another. What is Doris Green saying about Sandy? What does Sandy say about Doris? Which one of them, judging from your own perceptions, is giving you a better fix on the Contour reality? Is there a third person you might go to in order to clarify any conflicting information?

STEP 3: DOES YOUR COACH WANT YOU TO MAKE THIS SALE?

Since your Coach's role is to guide you in the sale, this person must be not only able but *eager* to give you proper direction. The only way to guarantee this eagerness is to demonstrate to your Coach that there's something in the sale, personally, for him or her. Your Coach always has to perceive the sale as a Win. So put Sandy to the test again by asking yourself this question:

How will this person's self-interest be served by my making this sale?

You need a clear, concrete answer to that question—something like this: "The sale will enhance her reputation in the company by making her look like a problem solver." If you know how Sandy will Win when you Win, then you know she fulfills the third Coaching criterion. If you don't have such an answer, you can't be certain that you have a reliable Coach.

If that's the case—if you can't identify a supposed Coach's reason for wanting you in there—then you need to reconsider your position with him or her. Coaches can be the keys you want only if they perceive that they will Win with you in this sale.

One way of determining whether or not a possible Coach sees himself or herself as playing Win-Win with you is to examine critically the information you've already gotten. Do that by asking yourself these questions:

1. Has this Coach helped me to find the real key players for my sales objective—and to understand the exact *role* each of them is playing?
2. Has this Coach helped me to identify areas of uncertainty (Red Flags) in my position—and given me sound, workable advice for eliminating them?
3. Has this Coach given me reliable information regarding the *receptivity* of each of my Buyers to my specific sales proposal?
4. Has this Coach supplied me with *unique* and *useful* data on the Win-Results I need to deliver to each of the Buying Influences to manage the sale into a Win-Win outcome?

You should get positive answers to most, if not all, of these questions. If you don't, your "Coach" isn't serving as the resource you need.

STEP 4: ASSESS YOUR CURRENT POSITION WITH YOUR COACH.

If your Coach isn't providing you with appropriate data for this sale, you should investigate why not. If you've discovered through this exercise that Sandy Kelly isn't working out to your satisfaction, take this discovery as a Red Flag for opportunity and go on. Find out why.

- If it's because you lack credibility with her, is there something you can do to create or restore it? Can you remind her of a past Win she may have forgotten?
- If it's because she lacks credibility with the Buying Influences, can she at least guide you to someone in that organization who *does* have credibility? Or would your best option here simply be to get rid of Sandy and look elsewhere for a Coach?
- If it's because she sees no Win in this sale for her, what can you do to change that? What information can *you* give *her* that shows her self-interest will be served by the sale? Or, if she sees no Win in the sale for her, is she correct? Would a better option be to acknowledge that she has nothing to gain from the sale—and go on to choose or develop another Coach?

Remember that there's more than one Coach in the corporate sea. Sometimes your most suitable option is the difficult one of "firing" one Coach and getting someone else—someone who can better guide you in the sale.

STEP 5: REVISE YOUR ALTERNATE POSITIONS LIST.

Now use the information you've uncovered in this workshop to revise your Alternate Positions list. Look at the Red Flags that still remain on your Buying Influences and Win-Results Charts. Concentrate first on options that can eliminate or reduce the impact of those Red Flags. Are there any newly discovered Strengths that you can use as leverage against them? Pay special attention to the information your Coach can still provide you. Frame the questions you need to ask your Coach, and write them down as new items on your Alternate Positions list.

For example, if you still don't know exactly what's in this sale for Dan Farley, one Alternate Position could be "Get Doris Green to explain how Farley can Win." If Steinberg's inventory problem is still unclear to you, you might write down, "Ask Sandy Kelly why Steinberg is so worried about his department."

After you've listed options in which your Coach can be of assistance, list options that might improve your position with this critical player. Consider the questions that you asked about your Coach in Step 4 of this workshop. Do the answers to those questions suggest further Alternate Positions?

Continue to assess each possible Alternate Position against the two-part rule of thumb that has been the hallmark of all your revisions. Make sure that every strategy option you consider eliminates or reduces the impact or a Red Flag, leverages from a Strength, or does both.

A Final Word: Reassessment

We'll close this chapter on Coaching by emphasizing a point that's particularly suggested by the Personal Workshop you've just completed, but is implicit in all aspects of Strategic Selling. The point is that, to be effective as a sales strategist over time, you must continually *reassess* your position.

One reason that your Coach is indispensable to your strategy is that he or she can help you, on a regular basis, to perform this necessary reassessment. The way you use your Coach reflects to a great degree the way you manage your sale. If you treat this unique Buying Influence as merely an inside salesperson or a "buddy," you'll almost certainly develop poor Coaches and use the potentially good ones in inefficient ways. But if you *test* your Coaches' information and then use it to apply the Key Elements of strategy to your sale, you'll find your position in that sale continually and predictably improving.

You must do this over and over. A sound strategic analysis is only as good as its last reassessment. In using your Coaches wisely to guide you through each reassessment, you'll find that this critical Buying Influence can be a key not only to the other Buyers, but to a predictable Win-Win record over time.

CHAPTER 13

WHAT ABOUT THE COMPETITION?

Two thousand years ago, in a treatise on business practices, the Roman orator Cicero described two merchants who are trying to beat each other to a nearby town to determine which one can set up shop there first. Competition, it would seem, is as old as selling, and this fact hasn't changed very much in the past twenty centuries. Throughout history, every salesperson who has ever eyed a market opportunity has been painfully aware that others were looking at it too.

The competitive situations that people are facing today, however, are much more intense and trickier than they've ever been before. This has made a concern about what the other guy is doing a major item on most sales professionals' worry lists. Our clients make this clear to us all the time. Even the most successful of them often wonder aloud why we don't spend more time addressing this critical issue. Nearly all of them seem to be looking for a method that will get them to the finish line first in the race for revenues. In every Strategic

Selling program that we deliver, someone asks the question "What about the competition?"

It's a good question. The reason we haven't answered it up to now is that, in our view, competition is grossly overrated as a "make or break" factor, and we didn't want to be seen as endorsing the notion that the secret to sales success is "beating the other guy." (That is actually a result, not a cause, of success.) But so many people continued to raise the issue that eventually we realized we had to address their concerns.

This chapter, with its accompanying workshop, is our response. It begins by explaining why competition is so fierce today, shows why strategies that "obsess" about the competition are doomed to failure, and defines a uniquely customer-driven approach to the problem that successfully builds on your Strengths to eliminate Red Flags. Let's begin with the current competitive frenzy.

Why Is Competition So Tough Today?

There are four basic reasons that maintaining a competitive edge has become so difficult. In brief, these relate to lack of *differentiation,* increasing *savviness* in the marketplace, the rise in different *types* of competition, and last but certainly not least, a widespread *obsession* about what the "other guy" is doing.

The Bold Line Fades

In talking with our clients, one thing we hear frequently is that the bold and dark line that every good salesperson would like to have between her products and the competition's products is getting fuzzier. Lack of differentiation between competing products or services is becoming an endemic rather than accidental condition. Whether you think of this as a copycat phenomenon or as evidence that good ideas have a way of catching on, the outcome is the same: There are very few products or services out there today that are perceived as providing a unique advantage in *themselves*.

Even in those cases where a bold dark line does exist, before you can blink an eye it has been here and gone. The rate of technological change, enhanced by competitive pressures to innovate, has made even the best features and benefits temporary as well as tenuous. The competition is so savvy and nimble about responding that, even when you develop a slight product edge, you certainly can't count on maintaining it for very long. Therefore, if you rely on product differentiation to keep you ahead, you'll be locked in a quarter-to-quarter game of marketplace leapfrog.

THE SAVVINESS FACTOR

Your competitors aren't the only ones who are getting faster and smarter. Your customers are smarter, too—better informed about available products and services, less compliant when confronting product "experts," and more insistent about demanding customized solutions. There was a time when as the salesperson you were the expert, and in many cases you could walk into a customer's office and expect that he would be suitably dazzled by your "bells and whistles" spiel. Those days are gone. Today, most of your customers have done their homework. They already know what bells and whistles you can offer. And they know that your competitors are offering much the same things.

As a result, they can often use price as a lever. Since it's so hard to secure or maintain real product differentiation, the customer can confidently and honestly say to all vendors, "We don't see a nickel's worth of difference among the lot of you, so we're giving the business to the one with the lowest price tag." So you and your competitors are forced into a dogfight over bones, grumbling as you struggle to embrace a Lose-Win position.

NEW TYPES OF COMPETITION

The traditional image of the competitor, since Cicero's day, is another salesperson (or a salesperson's firm) who is trying to secure the same piece of business that you are. Actually, that is only one type of competition. In Strategic Selling, we take a broader view. We define competition as *any alternative solution* to the one you and your company are proposing. Buying from somebody else is one alternative solution—the one that most of us mean when we say "competition." But consider the following scenarios:

TYPES OF COMPETITION

Competition is defined as any alternative solution.

- **Buy from someone else**
- **Use internal resources**
- **Use budget for something else**
- **Do nothing**

 SS57

- **Using internal sources.** The company you're approaching decides that it's more efficient to provide its own solution to the problem you're addressing. Today, most large companies have the resources to accomplish nearly anything they want to without outside assistance. Often, they don't, because purchasing and outsourcing are considered more cost-effective. But the possibility of internal solutions is always there. If you're selling to a firm that has the option to put its own ship in order, then that capacity is a serious, though hidden, "competitor."
- **Using the budget for something else.** Similarly, a company that is thinking about your proposal may decide that the necessary funds should go elsewhere. A colleague of ours once tried to sell a new lighting system to a hotel chain. She lost out not to another lighting supplier, but to a fire-prevention supplier. The chain's executives had decided that, no matter how attractive new lighting might be, fixing their antiquated sprinkler system was a higher priority. Our friend hadn't even considered fire-prevention to be part of her competition, but it was that, not a rival lighting firm, that lost her the account.
- **Doing nothing.** Although few people in business would identify inertia as a competitive pressure, sometimes it's the most serious one of all. When a customer decides that it's not worth it to spend the time, money, resources, or personnel to accomplish something new, that's a direct attack on any solution you may be proposing—as well as to equivalent changes offered by other companies.

In all three of these cases, the lesson is the same. Going head to head with a rival company can be tough, but that is only part of the competitive picture. What you're competing for today isn't your customer's signature on your order form rather than on someone else's. You're really competing for the customer's decision to allocate resources to your solution rather than to any number of alternatives.

OBSESSING ABOUT THE COMPETITION

Few people in sales recognize this fact, and that points to a fourth major factor in why competition is so tough. It's tough because we *make* it tough. Rather than remembering the reality that no one is invincible, we construct an image of the competition as a combination of Albert Einstein and The Terminator—infinitely smarter and ready to eat us for lunch. The field of possible alternatives becomes The Competition, larger than life and virtually indestructible.

A friend of ours was a fair-to-middling wrestler in high school. One year he had to wrestle a student from a neighboring school who, for the previous two years, had been state champion. "Whatever you do," our friend's coach told him before the meet, "don't let him get you in a headlock. He's pinned sixteen guys with that move, so watch out for it." Very bad advice. Our friend was so busy worrying about the state champ's patented clincher that, as if it were preordained, he fell for it.

"I was doing great with him for two periods," he remembered, "until he got me in that trick move, and suddenly everything I knew about wrestling went out the window. I thought 'He's got me now,' and sure enough, he did. In two seconds I went from an inexperienced but capable wrestler to just another victim of Tommy Terrific." That's a classic example of tying yourself up in your own knots—of allowing yourself to focus so much on the "invulnerable" competition that whatever you do to protect yourself still falls short.

WHY FOCUSING ON THE COMPETITION DOESN'T WORK

We're not saying you should forge ahead as if the competition's strengths didn't exist. Of course you have to consider the advantages to your customer of alternate solutions—including the solution of buying from a competing firm. The issue is one of balance and of relative focus. Our friend's problem wasn't just that he paid attention to the other guy's strengths. It was that he concentrated so exclusively on them that he had no room left over to develop his own. Probably the state champ was a better wrestler. But it's also true that our friend made it easy for him to win.

Salespeople make an analogous mistake all the time. Don Keough, the former president of our client Coca-Cola, once made the point well when he observed, "We have long held that one of the commandments for losing in business is to concentrate on the competitor rather than the customer." The reason is that a competitive strategy focusing on the competition is, naturally and inevitably, a *reactive* one. The best it can say to your customers is "We are better." Commonly, a reactive strategy gives an even worse message. Its hidden message is not "better than" but "me too."

There can be major repercussions in sending that message. Among the most negative are the following:

- *It allows the competition to write the rules of the game.* When you compare yourself to the high and mighty "them," you tacitly say to the customer, "*They* are the standard. It's their pace, their achievements, their agenda, that we've got to match." Whether you phrase this admission as a "better than" or "me too" argument, the subtext is "We're trying harder—because we *have* to."

- *It advertises your weaknesses, not your Strengths.* Every solid strategy leverages from your Strengths. If you spend all your energy trying to offset *another* person's Strengths, you run the risk of beating yourself to the punch. In effective selling, you show the Buying Influences what you can do. A reactive strategy shows them only what you can *undo*. Unless what they want is a bodyguard, that decodes as a weakness.
- *It invites price slashing.* When you ask a customer to line you up against the competition, one of the things she will certainly compare is your prices. That's OK only if your major selling point is low price *and* if you don't mind dropping it even lower in a price war. A price war, indeed, is nothing but *mutual* reactivity. It's an ultimately profitless me-too spitting contest in which the only winner is a customer who is willing to take advantage of you.
- *It makes you look stupid.* Maybe "unimaginative" or "uncreative" would be a less offensive term, but the idea is the same. In a reactive strategy, it's like you're sitting around a table with your competition and a customer, and you speak only to respond to what the competition says. When your strategy is a reflex response to somebody else's thinking, you're telling the customer "I have no ideas of my own."
- *It deflects attention from the customer's concerns.* A competition-driven strategy cannot be responsive to real customer concerns, for a simple reason. Such a strategy is a response to *your* needs—your anxieties, your projections, your fears about losing business you don't even have yet. If that's what's driving you, you cannot devise real solutions. Even worse, your customer will know that you can't.

Any one of these outcomes could seriously threaten your strategic position. Taken together, they comprise a recipe for disaster—for letting your customers know that your thoughts are elsewhere, and for handing your competitors a club and telling them "Beat me."

THE PROACTIVE ALTERNATIVE: RESTORING DIFFERENTIATION

The alternative is to think far less about what the competition is doing, has done, or might do, and more about what selling is about in the first place—the providing of customized solutions to individuals' problems. What's wrong with all competition-driven strategies is that they sidetrack you from your professional mission. A strategy that puts you back on track must be *proactive,* not reactive; must focus on the *customer,* not the product; and must enable the customer to recognize a significant *contribution.*

WHY "PROACTIVE" IS MORE EFFICIENT

When you use a proactive competitive strategy, *you* set the agenda and the standards. Rather than looking over your shoulder or sideways at the competition, you spend your time analyzing the situation to be sure that you are as effectively positioned as you can be. This means doing all the things that you have been practicing in this book: identifying and covering the Buying Influences, determining their Response Modes, making sure that you are delivering Win-Results, leveraging from Strength and eliminating Red Flags, getting good Coaching, and so on.

These things may not sound like parts of a "competitive" strategy, and if by that you mean a strategy that revolves around the competition, you're right. It's not a strategy that is *determined* by the competition. But it is an effective strategy for making Complex Sales, and for that very reason it is *highly* competitive. It allows you to stand out dramatically from other so-called "strategists" because while they are squandering resources fighting with each other, you are able to devote all your energies to the job at hand. A defensive approach inevitably leads to diffuseness. A proactive approach keeps you focused on the target, so it is a more efficient use of your skills and resources.

FOCUS ON THE CUSTOMER

You can capitalize on this efficiency, however, only if you focus on the customer. The worst competitive strategy is to focus on the competition, but probably the second worst is to become so enchanted with your own product or service that you imagine you can beat the other guy just by trumpeting its virtues. We explained in Chapter 11 why that doesn't happen. It's that you have to understand a customer's Concept first—that is, his or her idea of what doing business with you will accomplish—before you can hope to make headway with benefits or specs.

If you try to beat out the competition by stressing how much better your product is than theirs, you are falling into the old comparison trap and shifting the focus, again, back to them. In addition you're running the risk of praising a product in which a given Buying Influence may have no interest. Competing by pushing product—no matter how honestly you do it—is like walking into a room and singing your favorite song, without asking anyone there about their musical tastes. Maybe they'll love the song as much as you do.

Maybe not. Why put yourself in a position that's so fraught with uncertainty? If you're competing for an audience's attention, it makes sense to ask first what songs they'd like to hear. If you don't do that, you'll lose out to somebody who does ask.

MAKING A CONTRIBUTION

To compete effectively, you've got to be different from your competitors. More important, you've got to be *perceived* as being different—and different in a way that *makes a difference* to the customer. This goes back to what we said in Chapter 8 about discrepancy. To sell effectively, you must be perceived as eliminating your customer's discrepancy, as providing something that brings him a change for the better.

That "something" might relate directly to your product or service, or to a specific sale, but it might not. It might have to do with broader aspects of your business relationship as a whole. When that's the case, you have a unique competitive opportunity, if you can demonstrate to the customer that the "something" you bring to the table (a) has value for his or her company and (b) cannot be obtained anywhere else. In our company's Large Account Management Process, we call this broader something a *contribution*, and we show that it is among your greatest competitive weapons.

As the bold dark line of differentiation becomes increasingly fuzzy, differentiating yourself on the basis of product alone becomes harder and harder. That is why the concept of contribution is so important, and why the most successful people in business today spend so much time and money researching their clients' business needs, so they can contribute something of value to their results.

Think back to what we said in Chapter 11 about the value of bringing the Economic Buying Influence knowledge—knowledge that will help him or her run his business better. That's the kind of contribution that we mean, and that every sales professional should be seeking. When you consistently provide such contributions, you inevitably solidify your relationship with key Buying Influences. This in turn reduces the importance of price—and turns *you* into the standard that the competition has to match.

A Good Offense

"The best defense is a good offense." That old football saying provides a fairly good summary of this chapter's argument. Defending yourself against the other team might be an essential part of field strategy, but in itself it will not win you the game. To win, you have to score, and that means offense.

Another sports analogy might make the point clearer. In analyzing competitive sports, you can readily distinguish between "face" sports like football and boxing, where the opponents battle it out face-to-face with each other, and "side" sports like swimming and track, where they move side by side, trying to be the first to reach a common goal. We can summarize what we've been saying by referring to that distinction. Traditional competitive behavior may be seen as a "face" strategy, where your efforts and your resources are focused on the competition. The proactive behavior we are urging is more of a "side" strategy, where you and your competitors are both "racing" toward the same goal.

The analogy works because waiting at that goal is a cluster of those critical Buying Influences that every "race" must reach. If you think of yourself as focusing on the goal, training hard (through strategic analysis), and running the best race you know how to, you'll have a good idea of what we believe competition is about. The point is to look straight ahead and offer the customer your best performance, not to be distracted by what's going on in the next lane. As any competitive runner will tell you, one sure way to stumble is to look to your side.

In the real world, unfortunately, potentially good salespeople do something that's even worse than that. Instead of treating their competitive sales as "side" processes, they insist on mentally transforming them into head-butting contests—frenzied and often bloody "in your face" games in which the customer is relegated to the role of a spectator in the bleachers. Sometimes this is a temporary plus for him or her, because after you and your major competitor have finished duking it out, the customer can simply waltz down and pick up the pieces, that is, award the winner's ribbon to the lowest-priced battler.

How do you wake up from this nightmare? Be proactive. We're not saying to ignore the competition. But put them into perspective, as the "side" effect they are. Selling doesn't take place on a three-way street. It takes place between you and your Buying Influences, and nobody else. The only competitive strategy that can bring you success is a strategy in which you keep your eye on the customer.

THE EXPERTS SPEAK: FOUR "NON-METHODS"

Now that we've outlined our uniquely customer-oriented approach to competition, let's look at some of the other methods you may have encountered to increase your revenues by outfoxing the competition. As the term "outfoxing" suggests, most such methods violate our basic premise that you should be aware of, but not obsessed by, what your competitors are doing. In addition, as you'll see, even though the "sales experts" who recommend them call them methods, they bear very little resemblance to true methodologies. Let's look at four of the most popular ones.

SCHMOOZING FOR A LOSING

One expert advises that, in pitting yourself against a tough competitor, it's smart to get to know that competitor personally. You should go out of your way to meet the rival company's salespeople at exhibitions and trade shows, to play golf with them, to get into their heads on a one-to-one basis. Knowing your opposite numbers personally, he suggests, will help you deal more effectively with them in the field. It will defuse the mystery of why they're a threat to your business, and it will enable you to use "inside information" in countering that threat.

There's nothing wrong with knowing your competitors personally. In fact, any information you can gather about the sales situation, from whatever source, can be a benefit to you in solidifying your position. The problem with this approach is that it's misdirected. It can easily turn the Strength of personal knowledge into the Red Flag of unidirectional thinking. When you spend all that energy getting to know your competitors personally, you're very likely to end up with a selling approach that is inordinately focused on the information that they give you. Not only will that information be suspect (consider the source), but focusing on it may lead you to neglect other information that would be far more valuable in drafting an effective position.

For example, recall what we said about "the other guy" being only the most obvious source of competitive pressure. You could spend weekend after weekend schmoozing your opposite number George the Gadget Seller, only to discover, some months down the line, that the major customer that both of your companies are targeting has decided to replace its gadget system with widgets—leaving the two of you equally out in the cold. The moral: Picking the brains of the people who sell against you is even less valuable, eventually, than picking your own. The head that you need to get into is your *customer's*.

"I'M WORTH IT"

This same expert says that you can overcome the single most common competitive issue, price, by talking instead about "added value" and "price performance." Admit that you're higher priced than a similar supplier, but stress the fact that your "total package" makes you worth it. In other words, you can overcome the hurdle of price by redefining it as a plus—as an perfectly legitimate index of superior quality.

This approach sounds sophisticated, but it's really just a rehashed version of the old features-and-benefits routine: "Pay us 15 percent more because we have the bell of faster delivery, the whistle of a state-of-the-art design." That may be fine when you're talking to a customer who wants that particular bell or whistle, but what if you're not? Even worse, what if you don't know whether you are or not?

For all its potential utility, the problem with this "price performance" gambit is that it generally comes too late in the selling cycle. Salespeople drag it out, like a rusty but reliable old cannon, when the sale is almost completed, or when it's in jeopardy, and they expect it to serve as the final, decisive argument. But if you need an argument like that, you aren't well positioned in the first place. If you have to jiggle with semantics to prove to your customers that you're "worth it," the chances are good that they don't perceive you that way, and that mere talking about "added value" will not make a difference.

Don't misunderstand us. It's a great idea to talk about, and to emphasize, your added value. But do it first, not last. When you do it first—when you strive from your first meeting with a Buying Influence to show how your company can make a contribution to her company's profitability—then price seldom emerges as a decisive factor. The only real way to "overcome" the price issue is to demonstrate to your customers how your solution will impact their business concerns—how it will help those in Growth mode to improve something, and those in Trouble to put out their fires and move on. When you do that, you're truly being proactive.

"YOU REALLY OUGHTA WANNA"

Another solution to the competitive pricing issue is to look objectively for the areas in which you lead the competition, and to attempt to show how those areas ought to matter to the customer. In the words of one expert, you should try to "change the criteria" by which your customers assess products and make decisions. If you're strong in support programs, for example, you should concentrate on convincing the customer that support is what matters. Work on changing his wish list so it reflects what you sell.

This potentially terrific idea has three drawbacks. First, it tries to slip in the product sale before you have fully understood the customer's buying Concept; we have already seen how that can backfire. Second, it imposes your needs and expectations on the Buying Influences; in the words of a recent self-help book, it conveys the unwelcome message "You really oughta wanna do it my way." Third, by the time you get into a criteria changing discussion, it's usually too late. The time to be working with the customer on his or her buying criteria is very early in the game, before those criteria are clear in his or her mind, and while your capabilities and expertise can still make a difference.

In fact, one of the most important contributions you can make to any customer's business is to help him or her develop solid buying criteria. When you do that, you not only provide valuable guidance. You also differentiate yourself from every competitor who doesn't provide such assistance—giving you an advantage over even the cheapest alternative.

But the intention is important here. "Getting the customer to change" is manipulative and self-serving. "Helping him to design solutions" is a very different thing. Doing that accomplishes more than distinguishing you from the competition. It establishes you and the customer as joint-venture partners. As we've been stressing throughout the book, that is a far more valuable achievement than closing any order.

FIRST CHOICE FOR SECOND PLACE

In using this method, you begin not by avoiding the competition but by acknowledging it head-on. You admit to your customers that they have a solid, even enviable, business relationship with one of your competitors, and you make it clear that you respect that relationship—that your intention is not to undermine something that is bringing them value. Then you explain why you want to be their "first choice for second place" as the preferred supplier. If you're second in line for enough business, the expert who proposes this method believes, then it's only a matter of time before you'll become first in one or more of them.

Again, there's some value to this approach. If you cut through the apparent gimmickry of "going for the silver," what this method really says is that you'd like the opportunity to demonstrate that you have capabilities that can be of value to the customer. You respect the relationships that they have with other suppliers, and you don't want to threaten them, but you'd like to do your best to help them when and if they need help. If there is a problem with another supplier, you'd like to be in a position to make that contribution.

This is essentially a technique to establish a beachhead. If there actually is room on the beach, then that's fine: it may be a fairly effective long-term strategy. If you adopt this approach, however, be willing to wait. Respond to whatever questions or requests the customer may have for you, but don't succumb to the temptation to throw a wrench in the works by creating, or imagining, a nonexistent problem. That would violate the very principle that you're setting out here, which is that you would like to provide assistance *when it's needed.*

If a customer or prospect is perfectly content with another vendor, repeated "offers of assistance" will be at best wasted effort. At worst they will signal the customer that, your soft soap notwithstanding, what you're really interested in doing is destroying his relationship. The only place that strategy will ensure you is last.

THE "FAKE SINCERITY" PLOY

Finally, consider the expert who suggests that you might get your customer to prefer you over the competition by insinuating that they have problems they're not admitting. You should combine this less-than-straightforward tactic, he says, with a seemingly humble admission that you're not perfect—that your company has had problems, but you're now on top of them. According to this advice, the customer will draw the conclusion that if you have problems, your competitor probably does too, and he should give his business to the people who are honest enough to acknowledge them.

We don't have much good to say about this one. It's game playing, pure and simple, and it makes the double error of disrespecting both the competition and the customer. It plays dirty pool with the competition by starting a self-serving rumor, and it treats the customer like a pawn in the game, a dupe whose function is to help you deflect business from the other guy. All of it reminds us of the old Hollywood agent's advice to his actor client: "We're in Tinseltown. If you can fake sincerity, you've got it made."

Maybe in Tinseltown, but not in the world of selling. Not if you want to build a reputation for credibility—which, as we've said, is the one thing you *cannot* do without. The trouble with this approach is not just its blatant insincerity. It's that, in practical terms, it generally backfires. Instead of reassuring the customer, it puts her on her guard. It gets her wondering why, if you're all that competent, you would go out of your way to advertise your own shortcomings. If that isn't playing from weakness, we don't know what is.

FOUR TRICKY CASES

Our clients continually challenge us by presenting tricky cases, where overcoming competitive threats seems the key to the sale. We'll end this chapter by discussing four of them.

1. THE COMPETITION IS ENTRENCHED.

What do you do when the competition has been the sole supplier for ages? There's no single solution to this problem, but whatever solution you adopt, it is likely to require innovative thinking and a great deal of patience. If it were easy to unseat an entrenched supplier, you'd see it done every day, and there wouldn't be a lot of point in stressing long-term relationships. The keys, therefore, are research and hard work.

As a first step, it's likely that you will need to meet more people in the customer's organization than you know now. The more Buying Influences you position yourself with, the more you'll find out about areas in their business that may not be adequately addressed by the competition, no matter how firmly entrenched they are. The point again isn't to "steal" business, but to explore opportunities where you, better than anybody else, can make a contribution to your customers' business performance. If they're happy with their current supplier, those opportunities may take a while to develop. By establishing low-pressure relationships with numerous Buying Influences, you'll be positioning yourself to capitalize on them when they do.

2. YOU'RE FIRMLY ENTRENCHED YOURSELF.

Here's the reverse scenario. How do you defend yourself against a new competitor who is targeting you when you're the sole supplier? The first step here is to understand what your current strategy is. It's not enough to pat yourself on the back and say you've been reliable for ten years. You've got to ask yourself why you've been in there so long. What is it about your relationship with the customer that has made them uninterested or unwilling to look elsewhere? Who in the buying organization feels so good about you that the competition hasn't been able to get in the door?

Most important, perhaps, is there anything that has changed recently in the customer's organization to make them open to a possible change of vendors? Recall the automatic Red Flags that we mentioned in Chapter 6. When you feel that you are being threatened by a new competitor, you should examine your position particularly for these Red Flags. Ask especially whether there are any Buying Influences new to the job, any uncontacted Buying Influences, or any reorganization in the works. If the answers are yes—or if you don't know the answers—it's time to be especially alert to threats.

You're never totally safe in a sole supplier situation. When trouble looms, your strategy should be to go back and review the contributions that you've made in the past, and then either reemphasize them or show how they can be modified to meet your customer's changing business needs. What you need to do is to reassure the Buying Influences that their decision to stay with you for ten years has been a good one, and that it's still a good one today. This is a never-ending process. The minute it stops, you're offering the competition a foothold.

3. YOU'RE THE HIGHER-PRICED SUPPLIER.

In this situation the trick is to remember that expensive and higher-priced don't necessarily mean the same thing to the person who is buying. If I say that something is expensive, what I mean is that it may not be worth what I'm paying for it. That may or may not be the case with a high-priced product. Your challenge, when your product or service is priced higher than that of the competition, is to help the customer see that it's not really more expensive.

This isn't a semantic game or a contradiction. It's not the

sticker price but the customer's *perception of value* that determines whether something is priced correctly or not. If the customer sees higher value in your higher-priced product, then it's not expensive—it's priced correctly. On the other hand, if she doesn't see that value, you cannot make her see it simply by slashing the price. All that does is to acknowledge that the product is worth less than she has been paying for it—not exactly a move to inspire confidence.

In addition, cutting your price sends the customer the message "I know that buying this is a Lose for you, so let me make it a Lose for me too, so you'll feel better." We've already seen where that "generous" logic leads. The bottom line? Your job as a seller isn't to offer your customers "cheaper" products. It's to demonstrate, whenever and wherever possible, that the contribution you are bringing makes the purchase cost-effective.

4. THE CUSTOMER JUST WANTS YOU TO BID.

Sometimes, customers seem totally uninterested in developing relationships. They put out for bids, and demand that you play it by the numbers. When our clients ask us what to do in this situation, we quote an old saying: "If you don't have it wired, don't bid." Often, the response to that comment is nervous glances. Then somebody usually says, "Not bidding tells the customer that you're not interested in his business. Doing that will close us off not just from this business, but from all future opportunities with this customer."

It sounds right, but it's dead wrong. What has happened when you're asked just to bid is that somebody else—maybe a consultant, maybe one of your competitors—has already been in the door, helping the customer to set bid specifications.

When you merely answer the bid request, you're tacitly accepting that person's agenda, playing by his or her rules. In this situation, when you've had no prior contact with any of the Buying Influences and you don't have an inside view of the customer's problems, you're setting yourself up for a Lose no matter what you bid.

In addition to that, bidding is not selling. Bidding can be done by a computer, while selling requires a human being interacting with other human beings. Because of that, our general recommendation is that you avoid the blind-bid game altogether. In cases where it seems unavoidable, you should at least be having discussions with your management before you bid, to determine whether there is any value in entering an arena like this before you really know what's going on.

One positive alternative to submitting a bid is to send a polite letter explaining why you don't answer blind bids and explaining why it isn't appropriate for you to respond that way. The letter should make it clear to the customer that you would very much like not only their business, but an opportunity to talk to them about their needs, to see if you have products and services that would be of value to them. Eventually, if you're selling effectively, you've got to end up in a person-to-person relationship to make any Win-Win sale. Our advice is to start that process early.

PERSONAL WORKSHOP 8: COMPETITION

Now you'll have the chance to apply the lessons of this chapter to your own competitive situation, in a Personal Workshop that further clarifies your Single Sales Objective. You can do this on a new notebook page, labeled "Competition."

STEP 1: IDENTIFY YOUR COMPETITION.

Begin by identifying all the likely alternatives to the proposal you're offering the customer for this Single Sales Objective. Remember that a rival firm that is targeting this business is only one of those alternatives. Your customer could also choose to provide an internal solution, use the money or resources elsewhere, or do nothing. To help you clarify these options, ask:

- What could make the money for this proposal go away?
- Does the customer have internal options available that might prove more cost-effective, less difficult, or in some other way more attractive than our proposal?
- Is the customer facing other problems to which the needed funds might be diverted?
- How have they handled similar projects in the past?

Remember that for any one of these questions, you might have one or more answers. There could be three companies, for example, that are targeting this same piece of business. The customer could have a dozen alternative uses for the money. Your goal here is to identify all of them.

STEP 2: ASSESS YOUR MAJOR COMPETING FIRM OR FIRMS.

If you're not absolutely certain that you've identified all of your customer's available alternatives, mark that down as a Red Flag, and look for Coaching. Then test the information you have for further Red Flags, and for Strengths, by asking yourself these questions about your major competing firms:

- How does our Single Sales Objective differ from the competing firm's objective? Are the two of us really targeting the same piece of business, or is there some overlap between the objectives we're trying to achieve?
- Who is Coaching this competing firm? Who is their Economic Buyer? Who are their chief sponsors and anti-sponsors?
- What has this firm sold this customer in the past? Did they deliver as promised?
- What product or service advantages does the competitor have for this Single Sales Objective? What are their weaknesses?
- Is there a significant price difference between what we are offering and their alternative? What about service or support differences?

Ask too about the customer's *attitudes* toward competing firms. Do they have a history of preferring sole suppliers, or would they rather have multiple sources? Place a Red Flag next to any question for which the answer is unclear, and a Strength sticker next to those that indicate you are better positioned than the competing firm.

STEP 3: ASSESS THE CUSTOMER'S OTHER ALTERNATIVES.

Now assess the other alternatives for which this customer might use the necessary money and resources. Ask:

- If the customer decides to fix or improve the situation internally, will that really be a more cost-effective or trouble-free solution? If so, can we become involved in this internal solution?

- If the customer decides to divert funds to another project, are there sales opportunities for us in that project?
- If the customer decides to do nothing, what do we need to do to maintain our presence there until they have a more immediate need for our help?

Again, identify areas of Red Flags and Strengths in your answers. Notice, too, that in this step and in the previous one, your Red Flags can be considered your competition's Strengths, and your Strengths can be considered their Red Flags.

STEP 4: DEFINE YOUR CONTRIBUTION TO THEIR BUSINESS.

Looking not just at your product or service strengths, but at the entire context of your relationship with this customer, define the *contribution* that you make to their business that allows them to differentiate you from the competition. This contribution should be something that makes you stand out from the other alternatives, that puts you in a special, "joint venture" category.

Write this contribution—or these contributions—down. If you can't come up with at least one significant difference that matters to the customer, mark this down as a significant Red Flag in your strategy—and get Coaching. If you do have such a contribution, it's a Strength.

STEP 5: REVISE YOUR ALTERNATE POSITIONS LIST.

Finally, add to your Alternate Positions list any new actions suggested by this workshop. As always, be specific, and test each possible action against the strategist's rule of thumb: Be sure it leverages a Strength, eliminates the impact of a Red Flag, or does both. We recommend that you focus here not just on product or service Strengths, but on long-term contributions. And try as well *not* to concentrate on the other guy. Remember that the best way to outrace a fast-track competitor is not to step into his lane, but to run smarter.

PART 4

STRATEGY AND TERRITORY: FOCUSING ON YOUR WIN-WIN CUSTOMERS

CHAPTER 14

KEY ELEMENT 5: IDEAL CUSTOMER

All of us who make our living in sales are under constant pressure to sell: pressure from managers, from colleagues, from family and friends—maybe most of all from ourselves. Because of this pressure, we are often tempted to take on marginal or potentially troublesome business that we really ought to stay away from. Few of us can resist that temptation all the time. So, at one time or another, most of us have sold business that we later ended up regretting.

Throughout this book we've stressed that getting an individual order is never enough. We've said that the real craft of selling becomes evident only when every order leads to a Win-Win outcome—an outcome that brings you satisfied customers, long-term relationships, repeat business, and solid referrals. So far, so good. Pretty much everybody in business would agree that this is how you would like all your sales to conclude.

But we go one step further. We say that, if you're involved

in a selling situation where it's obvious that you're not going to get a Win-Win outcome, you should bite the bullet and consider *turning that business away*. No matter how good they may look in terms of immediate commissions, the fact is that some sales objectives are not worth pursuing.

According to a lot of people in sales—especially those who came up through the ranks under traditional sales "trainers"—this kind of thinking is a little off the wall. "Any sale is a good sale," they tell themselves. Or "All dollars are alike." Or "A bad customer's money is just as green as a good one's."

We might give these old saws more credence if we ever heard them from either our own or our clients' sales leaders. We don't. In fact the people who spout them are invariably sales amateurs—either newcomers who don't know the ropes or people desperate for commissions. The real sales leaders—and this is true whether you're talking about individual salespeople or companies—understand a plain fact of economic life: No single product is for everybody at any given point in time.

They understand too that all dollars are not alike, and that if you're going to be successful in the Complex Sale over time, you are virtually obliged to turn some business down. If you don't, you will inevitably clog your calendar with dead-end business—with sales objectives that, even if you bring them to a close, will later have you muttering "I wish I hadn't done that."

In our experience, these poor-quality sales objectives can account for as much as 35 percent of the potential business in most sales representatives' territories. If you think that figure is inflated, consider that it's based on our conversations with hundreds of regional and national account managers. These professional overseers of their representatives' sales objectives tell us that they're regularly forced to throw out a sizable proportion of their people's suggested prospects because they have a slim-to-nothing chance of ending up at Win-Win.

In this and the following chapter, we carry the lessons of the Win-Win principle to a logical conclusion, by showing you a method for separating the wheat from the chaff *before* you wear yourself out. In using this method, you will define, for your own business situation, a hypothetical Ideal Customer. Then you will use that Ideal Customer as a practical standard against which to measure your actual customers. This will enable you to cut down on that 35 percent of lousy prospects that you don't want cluttering up your territory in the first place and to concentrate on the customers who can get you to Win-Win.

DIGGING FOR A MATCH

The reason that up to 35 percent of the prospective business in most salespeople's territories is poor is that they lack a dynamic, field-tested process for analyzing their customers' real needs. In all too many companies, the responsibility for doing this is handled by the marketing department, and the bizarre assumption is made that the sales representative actually knows *less* about what customers want or need than that department does.

The situation is complicated further by the fact that many marketing people have no clear idea of how to *meet* their customers' needs, once they determine them, and they pass that added confusion on to the sales force. Even worse, they pass on a traditional ambivalence about the real function of selling that can leave the salespeople uncertain about what their actual job is.

You've probably encountered this ambivalence. Most

people in sales have. On the one hand, we're told that our mission is to sell as much of our product as we can to anybody who will buy it, at any time. This "cram the product" approach is, of course, the traditional philosophy of the slick-talking huckster—the person who is able to sell snow to Siberians. On the other hand, we're told that we should be selling to need—that we should always be "digging for a match" between our product or service and the customer's real requirements. This is the more modern, marketing-based approach to sales.

You cannot have it both ways. Cramming product and digging for a match are mutually exclusive approaches to the selling process. We trust that we've left no doubt as to which one we recommend. If you're to be successful in Strategic Selling, you'll have to leave the old-time huckster philosophy where it belongs—in the past—and learn how to dig for a real fit between what you have and what your customers need. Finding that fit is the heart of every honest—and successful—marketing approach to the Complex Sale.

You need to do this on an account-by-account basis, so that you can supplement the data provided to you by your marketing people. What they do might be called macromarketing. By focusing on large economic trends, it seeks to uncover the preferences of broad audiences. We're suggesting that you do a kind of micromarketing on your accounts. Use your company's marketing data as a base and go on from there. Only by assessing your individual customers' needs, and weighing them against broader market designs, can you adopt effective "matching" strategies for all your accounts.

YOUR OWN NEEDS MATTER TOO

These strategies must satisfy *your* needs as well as those of your customers. The term "match" implies reciprocity, and indeed the whole point of a Win-Win approach is to generate outcomes in which both you *and* your customers Win. A significant element in the development of an Ideal Customer Profile, therefore, is to concentrate on customers who not only want what you have, but also have what you want.

And we don't mean just money. As we've said, getting the order isn't enough. Nor is pocketing a commission, no matter how hefty it is, enough to make a sale a Win-Win sale. We can illustrate this point with a story told to us recently by the sales vice president of a large moving-and-storage company.

The company, which handled a large number of corporate accounts, advertised "special treatment" for executives whose household goods had to be transferred from one end of the country to the other. About a year ago, the vice president told us, the company went after a potentially huge new account: a nationwide chain of discount stores whose managers were transferred so often they thought they were nomads. In terms of volume, landing this one account would have boosted the moving company's revenues by about 12 percent a year. But, as good as that sounded, the discount chain turned out to be far from ideal in other ways.

"Because of the seasonal nature of our business," the vice president explained, "we prefer to handle accounts that will let us move their people off-season rather than in the summer, when we're short of vans. Also, we like long-distance moves rather than short hops, large households rather than apartments, and ideally about a month's lead time."

These "requirements" of an Ideal Customer made sense to us. Obviously, the moving company understood what types of accounts brought it the best profit margins, and preferred to focus on them rather than to go indiscriminately after everybody.

"The discount chain didn't fit that bill?" we asked him.

"Couldn't have been worse," he said disgustedly. "They gave us plenty of volume, sure, but it was nothing but grief. Their standard pattern was to give us three days' notice and then expect us to move a management trainee across state—and usually in July. After that first summer, I realized that our people were doing twice as much work for half the revenue. So we let the business go."

The lesson should be clear. It's not enough to sell to a customer who likes your product or service—as the discount chain liked the moving service. You also have to make sure that as many of your customers as possible come as close as possible to meeting *your* needs as a seller. You don't develop Win-Win scenarios on a one-way street.

Narrowing the Territory Early

In every salesperson's environment, unless you're in a *very* mature territory and industry, there are almost limitless possibilities for contacting prospects and making sales. If you don't begin to focus on the real Win-Win possibilities as early as possible in your selling cycle, you'll almost certainly find yourself in the common, but unhappy, position of juggling more bad business than you know what to do with.

In Part 5, when we discuss the Sales Funnel, we'll show you how to manage your time more efficiently, so that you spend the optimum amount of time every week working on each of your potential and established accounts. But that won't do you any good if you've recklessly taken on so many of these accounts that the most you can spare any one of them is an extra ten minutes.

Therefore, to get the most out of your limited selling time, your first steps are to sort through the "Universe" of potential customers, to assess which ones are most likely to pay off in *good* business, and to make a determination as to which ones have to go. Unless you start by judiciously restricting your Universe, the best time-management in the world will get you nowhere.

This "judicious restriction" is the focus of the following chapter.

CHAPTER 15

YOUR IDEAL CUSTOMER PROFILE: DEMOGRAPHICS AND PSYCHOGRAPHICS

When we use the term Ideal Customer, we're not referring to an actual, real-life customer. You'll never find the mythical "perfect" customer. The Ideal Customer is a *standard* against which to measure your actual customers, so that you can focus on the good ones, get rid of the truly bad ones, and anticipate problems with those who fall in the middle. In this chapter you'll develop that standard for yourself by analyzing your current best customers to see exactly what criteria make them best. Then you'll use those criteria to define a composite picture of the *hypothetical* perfect customer. This will be your Ideal Customer Profile.

In drawing up this profile, you need to consider two categories of possible customer characteristics. The first is called *demographics,* the second *psychographics.*

DEMOGRAPHICS AND PSYCHOGRAPHICS

Since most marketing departments work exclusively with demographic data, you may already be familiar with the term *demographics*. To the sociologist and statistician, "demographics" refers to the size and composition of selected human populations. In marketing—and in our selling processes—the term is modified slightly, so that it refers to the size and composition of individual *customer* populations. Examples of demographics as we use the term would include the following:

- Size of the target audience
- Number of end users of your product or service
- Age and condition of the customer's present equipment
- Distance of the customer's location or locations from your firm's shipping points
- Proximity to your service and support centers
- Compatibility of your product or service to the customer's existing facilities

Notice that all of these examples share one feature: The characteristics they describe are measurable and objective.

Unlike "demographics," *psychographics* is not yet a widely used term. Some advertising agencies and marketing departments are familiar with it, but it's hardly a household name, and your marketing people, unless they're cutting-edge, may not have heard of it before. Yet understanding psychographics is critical to sales success.

Psychographics are the *values and attitudes* shared by the individual Buying Influences within an organization and held collectively, as it were, by the organization itself. In today's business world, the sharing of such values is a common phenomenon. Especially at the managerial level, most successful people lock on in some degree to the official or unofficial "attitudes" of the firms that employ them. Examples of psychographics would include:

- Importance placed by the company on reputation in the marketplace
- Ethical standards—whether or not they appear in a company "code"
- Attitudes toward people, including customers, suppliers, employees, and other "stakeholders"
- Openness to innovation
- Relative importance placed on quality rather than quantity

Psychographics aren't as accessible to measurement as are demographics because they're not usually objective. But they're equally important to you as a sales professional because they define the company cultures into which you're trying to sell.

COMPANY CULTURES

As observers of the corporate scene have been pointing out for decades, today's most successful corporations owe their success at least in part to the fact that their employees, from the CEO on down, are conscious and eager participants in organizational cultures. Their people, no matter how individual and diverse they may be in their private lives, also share certain assumptions and values that allow them to conform to an internal pattern in the work environment.

We don't mean that people in today's top companies behave like the "organization man" of the 1950s, adhering mindlessly to a gray-flannel, pinstriped model. On the contrary. The most successful companies usually generate company cultures that emphasize innovation rather than tradition, quality of service rather than the old-fashioned "bottom line" mentality. A few examples from our clients:

- *Sterling Healthcare,* which manages hospitals and counseling centers across the country, places a premium on the individuality of its services. Its salespeople take pride in providing not boilerplate facilities, but highly personalized, customer-driven solutions.
- The *Coca-Cola* culture is marked by a dedication to making Coke a first-class, global leader in every respect. Whether they're choosing an advertising campaign or buying art for corporate headquarters, supervising quality control or handling customer inquiries, Coke managers try to make "number one" the watchword of every decision.
- Finally, at *Hewlett-Packard,* there's a company-wide recognized insistence on building the most technically advanced products in the electronic instruments and computer field. People who work at this firm are committed, across the board, to making the name Hewlett-Packard synonymous with quality, value, and state of the art. Innovation in research has therefore become a central aspect of the H-P internal culture.

These few examples point to the fact that, in today's corporate environment, most of the people you sell to are likely to share many of the social and business attitudes of others in their respective companies.

Social scientists would say that business people within a firm share a set of "normative values," that is, values that define the basic acceptable range of the social group's behaviors and beliefs. Since corporations are certainly social groups, it makes sense that they will generate such normative values, and that the people who become most successful in a given company will be those who most readily accept, or adapt to, these common values.

To revert to Strategic Selling terminology, we can say that a company's normative values are one of its most significant *psychographic* characteristics. And these values apply not only to the corporate entity as a whole, but to all of the individual people—the Buying Influences—who make buying decisions for that entity.

This observation has enormous implications for anyone who sells. What the existence of corporate psychographics means to you is that, in positioning yourself with your various customers, you can gain an immense competitive advantage by analyzing not just the "hard facts"—the demographics—of each account, but its key players' values and attitudes—the psychographics—as well.

The Importance of *Your* Psychographics

Because psychographics define companies as well as individuals, and because both sellers and buyers display psychographic characteristics, you can take a major first step in "judiciously restricting" the Universe of your potential customers by determining which of them most closely approximates the psychographic profile of *your* firm. Built into your product and services are *your* company's values and attitudes, and the customers who come closest to matching your Ideal Customer standards will be those who already hold those values and attitudes—or who can be educated into doing so.

For example, let's say you sell a product whose principal

advantage over the competition is its quality and value over time. If you're selling to a firm that sees price alone as the critical factor in selecting vendors, you'll probably be in for trouble. But if you're selling to one that concentrates on "price performance"—a firm that's willing to pay a bit extra to get a more exact match to its needs—then your competitor's low bid probably won't be enough to carry the day.

A friend of ours at a national food services company understands this principle very well. "We sell quality," he told us recently, "and I refuse to try for accounts where the appreciation of quality is not a fundamental perception. They've got to share that attitude or there just won't be a match with what we offer them." This three-time salesman of the year boasts a success rate of well over 50 percent with his major presentations and, as he admitted to us, "I haven't been low bid in the last ten years."

What's implicit here is something that we've stressed throughout this book. The *real* reason people buy isn't simply that your product or service matches their objective business needs. People buy not only to get Results, but to get personal Wins as well. They buy because they perceive that your sale will satisfy personal values and attitudes—and thus satisfy their own self-interest.

It all comes back to Winning. In Chapters 9 and 10, where we urged you to set up Win-Win scenarios with all of your Buying Influences, we said that the best way to do that was to deliver them Win-Results. The same thing is true on the *account-wide,* or *corporate,* level. The best way to Win with a given account over time is to understand that company's psychographic profile, because that profile is an important key to how each of its individual Buying Influences Wins.

If you're like most people in sales, up to now you've probably been concentrating only on demographics. Here we present a Personal Workshop that gives you the opportunity to utilize both demographics *and* psychographics in defining, sorting, and strategizing your potential opportunities.

Personal Workshop 9: Ideal Customer

In this workshop you will create your own personal Ideal Customer Profile, based on your current and past accounts, and then use that profile to test the real prospects of a Win-Win sale with all of your current sales objectives.

STEP 1: DRAW YOUR IDEAL CUSTOMER CHART.

Turn your notebook lengthwise and begin by drawing up a worksheet that will generate your Ideal Customer Profile. At the top of the page write the heading "Ideal Customer." Divide the page into five equal columns and label them with the following subheadings, from left to right: "Best Customers," "Characteristics of Best," "Ideal Customer Profile," "Characteristics of Worst," and "Worst Customers." When it's finished, the chart should look like the example shown on page 329.

STEP 2: IDENTIFY YOUR BEST CUSTOMERS.

List, in the left-hand column, your best current and past customers. Just customers, not prospects. Limit yourself to accounts where you've already done some business.

By "best" here we mean whatever *you* mean. You set the criteria. The accounts we want you to concentrate on are

IDEAL CUSTOMER				
Best Customers	**Characteristics of Best**	**Ideal Customer Profile**	**Characteristics of Worst**	**Worst Customers**

those that have given you the maximum number of Wins and minimal trouble. You're the best person to decide what criteria to use in identifying those accounts. Keep your own gut feelings in mind. Usually, you find that you *feel* great about your "Best Customers"—regardless of the amount of revenue they have generated.

List as many as you want of these Best Customers, but follow this guideline for establishing a cutoff point: First, write down your single Best Customer; then, write down number two; and so on down the line, until you come to a name that's *significantly different* in your eyes from the last one you wrote down. Stop there. If there's a quantum difference in quality between number three and number four, for example, make number three the last entry on this list.

STEP 3: IDENTIFY YOUR WORST CUSTOMERS.

Now go to the right-hand column of your Ideal Customer chart and list your worst past and current customers. Again, *you* set the criteria. Concentrate on those accounts where either you or the customer, or both of you, have lost, even though you've closed the order. Again, trust your gut feelings. Again, stop when you reach a quantum difference between the last name you wrote down and the next one that comes to mind. And again, identify these "Worst Customers" regardless of the dollars they've spent.

STEP 4: LIST BEST CUSTOMER CHARACTERISTICS.

In the second column from the left, list those characteristics that are common to, or unique to, the Best Customers you've just identified. You may include both demographic and psychographic characteristics here, but you should pay special attention to the latter. To give you some examples, our program participants often list psychographics like these:

- Trusts my company's performance
- Innovative, progressive management
- Is loyal to the vendors selected
- Committed to quality control
- Willing to pay for "value-added" aspects of my product
- Highest business ethics and integrity
- Wants a Win-Win relationship on every sale

Use these examples as a guide, but list the characteristics *you* personally find most attractive among your own Best Customers.

One caution. Don't list things like "Has money to buy," "Needs my product," or "Is creditworthy." We assume that *all* your customers, not just your best ones, meet these minimum business requirements. Focus on characteristics—either objective or psychographic—that distinguish your Best Customers from the rest.

STEP 5: LIST WORST CUSTOMER CHARACTERISTICS.

Now, in the second column from the right, do the same thing for your Worst Customers. List as many characteristics as you can that distinguish the customers in the right-hand column of your chart from the rest of the accounts you deal with. Examples from our corporate clients:

- Inflexible on price
- Slow in making buying decisions
- No loyalty to my company or to me
- Authoritarian management system
- Secretive and unwilling to cooperate
- Want me to Lose so they can Win

Again, your goal is to come up with a useful list of negative characteristics that are common to all, or at least most, of your Worst Customers. And again, *you* set the criteria.

STEP 6: CREATE YOUR IDEAL CUSTOMER PROFILE.

Now, in the central column of your Ideal Customer chart, you can define the standard against which your customers should be measured.

This step of the workshop is a process of distillation. Study the lists you've just made of Best Customer characteristics and Worst Customer characteristics, and distill out of the items there a new list of characteristics that you consider *most significant*. This process may take a little time. Don't rush it.

In assessing the items on your "Characteristics of Best" list, transfer only the most significant ones into the center column. In assessing the items on the "Characteristics of Worst" list, transfer *opposites* of the significant items listed. For example, if you've identified "leading edge in its industry" as a significant Best Customer characteristic, you simply list that characteristic in the center column. If a characteristic common to your Worst Customers is that they're "unable to make decisions," write in the center column something like this: "Has a process for making buying decisions quickly."

Once you've transferred all the relevant characteristics to the center column, study the items there carefully and zero in on the *five most significant* ones. Then turn to a clean page of your notebook and write "Ideal Customer Profile" at the top. Write down only the five most significant characteristics under that heading. This final distillation is your Ideal Customer Profile.

STEP 7: TEST YOUR CURRENT ACCOUNTS.

You now have a tool with which to measure two things: the compatibility of each of your accounts with the characteristics you personally find most desirable in a customer, and the problems that are most likely to arise in accounts that do *not* meet those characteristics. In other words, you have a tool for *sorting* your prospects and *anticipating* problems. You can do these two things now, beginning by evaluating the account to which you're trying to sell the Single Sales Objective that you've been working with since Chapter 3.

To do this, measure that account against each of your five Ideal Customer Profile characteristics in turn. Go down the list and, for each characteristic, ask yourself this question:

How well does this particular customer match with this ideal characteristic?

Then rate the customer on each item, using the same –5 to +5 rating scale that we introduced in the chapter on Buying Response Modes. If there's a very strong or near-perfect match to the first characteristic you listed, give your customer a +5 rating for that characteristic. If there's no match at all for the second characteristic, give the customer a –5 rating on that one. And so on. When you're done going down the list, you'll have five numbers, positive and negative. Taken together, they are a measurement of this customer against your Ideal Customer standard.

Once you've performed this exercise for your test case account, you can use it to rate your other accounts and prospects as well. For each of these actual customers or potential customers, generate a new set of five numbers based on that customer's matches, or mismatches, to your list of ideal characteristics.

Each set of numbers will, of course, be different. But each set, like the set you just generated for your test case account, will give you a reliable picture of how close that customer is to your standard. The higher the positive numbers, and the more of them there are, the greater the likelihood that you can consistently reach Win-Win outcomes with this account. On the other hand, the more negative numbers you have, the greater the chances that you'll have problems, at least in those areas where the profile match is poor.

These figures, though, are only rough guides. Each sale is unique, and we wouldn't presume to advise you either to drop a mathematically "bad" account or to become overly confident about selling a mathematically "good" one. What we do know is that, other things being equal, the above figures reliably indicate the *probability* of a given account's leading consistently to Win-Win outcomes.

STEP 8: REVISE YOUR ALTERNATE POSITIONS LIST.

Once you know how close a given account is to your Ideal Customer Profile, you're in a position to make a decision about how to improve your strategy for that account. Assuming there's a less than perfect match between a given account and your Ideal Customer Profile (this will almost always be the case), you can now do one of the following things:

- Decide to *sort* a given sales objective from that account out of your territorial workload because you realize it has a low probability of generating a good order.
- *Anticipate* the problems that will arise with that objective, based on its imperfect match, and devise strategies to deal with and overcome them.

You can make this choice now by considering each of your current customers in turn, starting with the customer or prospect to which you're trying to sell the Single Sales

Objective that you're analyzing in this book. Assess the ratings that you just gave each customer, and then decide what Alternate Positions you might adopt to increase the likelihood of a Win-Win outcome.

As we said in the previous workshop, you'll be able to do a fuller analysis on the customer for your chosen sales objective than on your other customers because you have more information about it. But your analysis of that customer can still serve as a *model* for all future Ideal Customer analyses.

Subjective judgment is obviously involved here, and in using it, you should consider everything you've learned about your accounts, and about your Single Sales Objective, thus far. The ratings you've just developed are a rough guide. *We don't advise anyone to use the Ideal Customer Profile as a cop-out for avoiding difficult business.* Instead, it should serve to establish the basic criteria that you need for Win-Win outcomes.

You should use those criteria as a baseline judgment, not a final one. For example, if your Ideal Customer Profile indicates that the Goliath account has several –4 or –5 matches, it would seem reasonable to think about dropping it. But if the potential revenues from that account are enormous, if the marketing people at your company are pushing you toward products that Goliath particularly needs, or if the "future investment" possibilities there are huge, then it might still be worth your time to continue working the account.

On the other hand, if you have a very strong profile for a given company, but that company has dealt exclusively with your major competitor for ten years and shows no signs of shifting loyalties, you may just be wasting your time in trying to make its people see the "perfect match" between what you have and what they need.

Remember that the Ideal Customer Profile is used to predict and deal with problems as well as to sort out potential bad business. This means that you should look at the *individual* characteristics on the list, not just the profile as a whole. For example, if you've decided to keep Goliath in your territory chiefly because of its huge commission potential, you might improve your position there by analyzing each profile characteristic in turn, to help you work more effectively on those areas where the match is imperfect. If Goliath scored low on your Ideal Customer rating largely because it's slow in responding to proposals, you might add "Adjust my selling schedule to accommodate Goliath cycle" to your Alternate Positions list. If Goliath has no apparent interest in quality and always takes low bid, you may want to add "Try to show them that our product will be the least expensive solution for them in the long run."

The key point here is that the closer an individual account comes to your Ideal Customer Profile, the easier the sale; the further away from the profile, the more troubles you'll probably encounter. The main virtue of the profile, as both a sorting and a predictive device, is in enabling you to identify potential problems and weigh them realistically against potential gains.

A Balanced "Admissions Policy"

You're aiming for balance. It almost never makes good strategic sense to target accounts whose Ideal Customer Profiles indicate they share *none* of your company's values and attitudes. On the other hand, no salesperson has the luxury of selling *only* those accounts that perfectly match an Ideal Customer Profile. The best way to reduce uncertainties in your sales and ensure Win-Win outcomes is to follow a policy that lies judiciously between taking anybody who knocks on your door and accepting only the "best."

You might want to think of the sorting and predicting we've been describing as a kind of screening process, similar to that which is employed by college admissions committees. Those committees, although they often have very exact and exacting requirements for their potential students to meet, also employ a great deal of give-and-take in making final decisions. Most admissions boards today tend to look not only for a "balanced" student body, but also for reasonably balanced personalities in the individual students they select.

That means that a student who didn't score high on the Scholastic Aptitude Test may still get in to her first-choice college if there's evidence that she can offer the college community something special in terms of, say, sports ability, a unique background, industriousness, or social adaptability. On the other hand, a student with great scores on this standardized test may not be admitted if he seems to be focused exclusively on French or chemistry, or if he's emotionally or socially limited in other ways—that is, if the committee feels the school will be likely to Lose by having this person as a member of its community.

Your goal, as always, is to Win—and to ensure that all your Buying Influences, in all your accounts, Win as well. The best way to do that, we've found, is to use your Ideal Customer Profile as a baseline test and then weigh the information it gives you against everything else you know about the account.

REVIEWING YOUR POSITION

That "everything else" has a great deal to do with the four basic elements of strategy that we outlined, and that you practiced, in Part 2 of the book. We recommend that you review those elements now, in the new light that has been provided by the Ideal Customer concept. We suggest you take out all the material you've developed so far. Lay it out in front of you. Then ask yourself the following questions:

- *Buying Influences.* Looking at your Buying Influences Chart, ask if the difficulties you've had in getting to your Buying Influences are related to their company's imperfect match to your Ideal Customer Profile. What specific demographic and psychographic mismatches have made selling them uncertain?
- *Red Flags/Leverage from Strength.* Look at the Red Flags on your Buying Influences Chart and on your Win-Results Chart. Is there a correlation between them and the Ideal Customer Profile items that show a poor match to the customer for your sales objective? The "best match" items on the profile should be considered areas of Strength. Can you use any of them to leverage against the Red Flags?
- *Response Modes.* Which of the items on your Ideal Customer Profile explain a willingness on the part of your Buying Influences to accept change? Which items explain a reluctance?
- *Win-Results.* Compare the Win-Results Chart with the Ideal Customer Profile. Do the demographic items on the profile translate into objective business Results? Do the psychographic items translate into Wins for the individual Buying Influences in the account? Do those individuals *know* that you value their account and are trying to play Win-Win with them?

As we've stressed repeatedly, the Key Elements of strategy become fully effective only when they're used *interactively,* as a system. Asking yourself these questions is a way of helping you see how the first five of these elements fit together.

With the addition of one more element, the picture will be complete. That element follows logically from what you've just learned. The Ideal Customer Profile enables you to sort through the virtually limitless field of potential sales opportunities, to create a personal territory that is actually manageable. To manage it efficiently, though, you need a territory management tool that we call the Sales Funnel. We'll introduce that final Key Element now.

PART 5

STRATEGY AND TERRITORY: MANAGING YOUR SELLING TIME

CHAPTER 16

OF TIME, TERRITORY, AND MONEY

When you handle several accounts or prospects at the same time, it's easy to become strategically confused unless you break the business you're targeting in each account into smaller chunks—what we have been calling Single Sales Objectives. This is especially important in the Complex Sales arena, where no two objectives in the same account may have exactly the same combination of Buying Influences. That's why we have recommended, throughout this book, that you practice each new principle of strategy by applying it in a Personal Workshop to the same objective—the "test case" that you selected in Chapter 3.

We offer the same recommendation for when you're out in the field: Always set strategies for one sales objective at a time. We realize, however, that this is easier to say than to do. Out in the field, it's often difficult to be single-minded. You have a territory to manage, and that territory is probably pulling you in twenty different directions at once because the test-case objective you've chosen to work with in this book is only one of many different business opportunities.

In the previous section, we discussed the Ideal Customer Profile, which can help you get a handle on this multiplicity by limiting your territory to accounts that are really worth your time. In this section, we take the next logical step, by introducing a sixth Key Element, the Sales Funnel. It's integral to our Strategic Selling approach because it enables you to get the most out of every account in your territory by managing your most precious resource, selling time, more effectively.

Your Most Precious Resource

Everyone we know in sales has at one time or another complained, "What I need is a forty-eight-hour day." This is a complaint of people in many walks of life, but it's especially aggravating to us sales professionals because, in addition to the actual *selling* time we have to put in (which most of us enjoy), we also have to put in time on many nonselling tasks, and these tasks take up the *bulk* of every sales professional's time.

If you doubt for a minute that most of what you do is nonselling, just think of how many hours a week you spend on the following tasks:

- Selling internally to your own company
- Making out expense reports
- Doing other paperwork
- Attending meetings
- Handling customer complaints
- Expediting orders

- Training customers to use your product or service
- Traveling

Don't misunderstand us. We don't mean that these tasks are unimportant. You know that they're essential to your long-term success. But they aren't selling. When we talk about selling time, we mean something very specific. We mean the time you actually spend face-to-face (or phone to phone) with your customers. In our Strategic Selling programs, we use the following definition:

Selling time is any time spent talking to a Buying Influence about Growth or Trouble, or asking questions of a Buying Influence to uncover a Growth or Trouble discrepancy.

When our participants understand this definition of selling time, they usually tell us that they're lucky to get five or ten hours a week to devote to this all-important activity. Most top salespeople, in fact, spend only about *5 to 15 percent* of their total work weeks actively engaged in face time with their customers. Among the thousands of sales representatives and managers we've counseled, we have yet to meet even one person who spends more than a quarter of his or her time talking to Buying Influences about Growth or Trouble.

Nobody likes this state of affairs, but it's a fact of every salesperson's life. As much as we would like to spend more time with our customers and less behind a desk or a steering wheel, selling time is still always in short supply. If it isn't managed well, the salesperson typically falls victim to a deadly pattern of fluctuating income—the pattern we call the Roller Coaster Effect.

THE ROLLER COASTER EFFECT

If you've been in sales for more than a few months, you're probably already familiar with the Roller Coaster Effect. This metaphor for the profession's typically uneven income pattern is represented in the chart below.

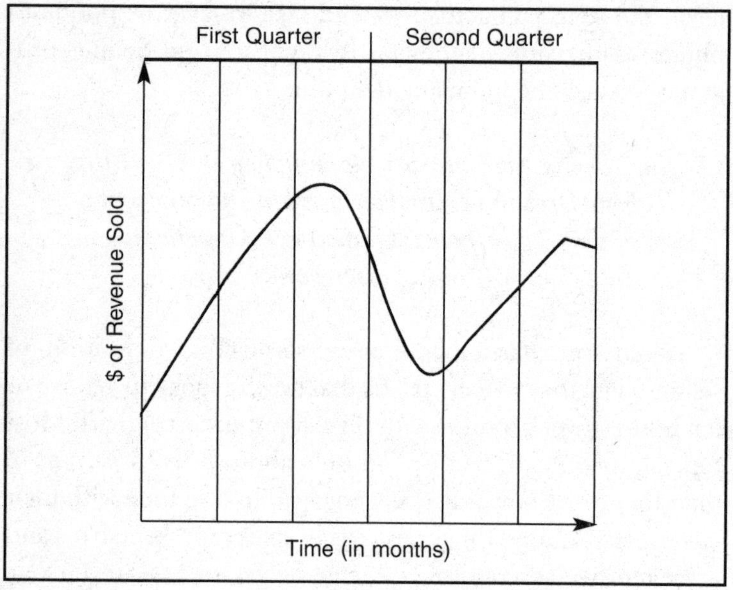

As you can see, the chart plots the relationship between each monthly accounting period and the amount of revenue sold—that is, between time and money. Assuming that you spend roughly the same amount of time selling in each period, the implication here is disturbingly obvious: Steady work won't necessarily give you a steady income. Or, to be blunt about it, time doesn't always equal money.

If you recognize this chart as being an approximation of your own time and money pattern, you've got a lot of company. Unevenness of income is so common in sales that many lifetime managers and sales representatives consider it a kind of natural law. As a regional manager once confessed to us, shrugging his shoulders in resignation, "That's the way the selling highway rolls. You've just got to hang in there and wait it through."

Wrong. No matter how natural and inescapable it may seem, the Roller Coaster Effect is *not* inevitable. And you *do* have an alternative to "hanging in there" until things improve.

Granted, under a market system *some* cyclical fluctuations in your income are inevitable. There are seasonal variations, annual budgets, interest rates, and a whole range of broad economic trends that impinge on every sales professional's work. Even governments have only limited success in adjusting them, and they seem pretty much beyond the ordinary citizen's control. However, our experience shows that the worst fluctuations of the Roller Coaster Effect are caused not by these economic forces, but by the salesperson's own poor management of selling time. That's something that you *can* control.

What the Sales Funnel Does

The Sales Funnel helps you to manage your precious selling time more effectively, so that you can avoid the deepest valleys of your personal selling cycles and translate that time into steady, predictable, income. In this section you'll learn how to use this time-management tool to focus your work so that you can accomplish the following essential tasks:

- *Define* exactly where you are in the selling process by sorting your sales objectives into four different categories, or "levels," of the Funnel

- *Track* each sales objective's progress as it moves "down the Funnel" from first contact to signed order
- *Set priorities* for working on the objectives in each level of the Funnel to ensure that you don't neglect any one of the four
- *Allocate time* to the objectives in each level of the Funnel so that you consistently perform four essential kinds of selling work
- *Forecast* future income based on how rapidly and smoothly your objectives are moving toward the close

When you use the Sales Funnel to accomplish these related tasks, you not only utilize time more efficiently. You also achieve the broader perspective needed for success in all your sales objectives over time. So let's see how this final Key Element works.

CHAPTER 17

KEY ELEMENT 6: THE SALES FUNNEL

The funnel metaphor that we use in our sixth Key Element of strategy may already be familiar to you. Many salespeople talk about putting prospects "into the pipeline," "into the hopper," or "into the top of the funnel" and then waiting for completed orders to come out at the other end.

We depart from this conventional usage in stressing that you cannot wait for orders. You've got to *work* the Funnel, routinely and aggressively, so that orders (and thus your income) are predictable. We're also different in that we segment the Sales Funnel conceptually into four distinct levels of account activity, each one corresponding to a different type of selling work. The first thing you need to know to use our final Key Element effectively is how to *sort* your sales objectives into these four levels.

THE FOUR PARTS OF THE "REFINED" FUNNEL

The Sales Funnel concept is represented by the chart on page 351. You can see that you are already familiar with some of its features. "Prospect," "qualify," and "close" are standard sales terminology, while "cover the bases" and "Universe" are Strategic Selling terms that have been introduced earlier in the book. What's new are our names for the three levels of the Funnel "proper": Above the Funnel, In the Funnel, and Best Few. Before we revised and expanded Strategic Selling, we spoke about the Funnel as being composed of only these three levels. In the current, refined version, we recognize that "narrowing the Universe" is a necessary preliminary step to working any objective down the Funnel. For this reason, we have added it to the Funnel diagram, as an integral part of the Funnel system. This gives the refined Funnel four levels.

You'll notice that each of these levels is associated with a particular kind of selling work. This is a central feature of the Funnel: Each part of the Funnel is by definition associated with one, and *only* one, kind of work. As a sales professional, you must be able to do all four. You have to be able to:

- Prospect
- Qualify
- Cover the bases
- Close the order

But, since you have many possible orders working at the same time, and since they're all at different stages of completion, you're not going to be doing the same kind of work on all of them at the same time. You'll be prospecting or qualifying on some pieces of business while you're closing others and covering the bases in yet others. You'll achieve the predictable

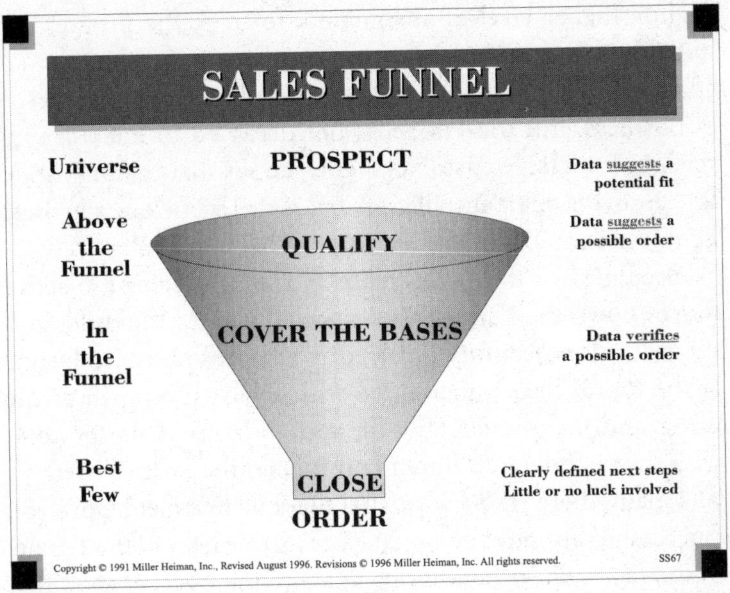

and sound income you want only if you consistently do the *right kind of work* on each possible order *at the right time.*

That's the reason you need to sort your work tasks. The Sales Funnel is, first and foremost, a tool to help you do that.

PRELIMINARY TIPS

Before describing the four parts of the Funnel in detail, we want to give you some preliminary tips about this tool as a whole.

First, the Sales Funnel helps you sort and track the progress of individual possible orders or Single Sales Objectives, *not* accounts. Some of our clients use it at a slightly higher level of abstraction, to track the progress of individual product lines or categories of business in an account. That's fine, too: it's still focused on individual pieces of business. But the Funnel is not designed to track overall revenue from large customers. You can say that "getting Apex to approve a pilot installation by May 15" belongs in Best Few. It makes no sense to say "Apex" belongs in Best Few.

Second, two things decrease as a Single Sales Objective moves down the Funnel: the expected *time* to the order and the level of *uncertainty* involved. Each sales objective begins at the top of the Funnel, often with a long time span to the order and many uncertainties, and ends up at the bottom, with the uncertainties under control and the order closed.

Finally, there are *prerequisites* that must be met before you can reasonably move an objective from one level of the Funnel to the next. These conditions relate to the *kinds of work* that you have to do at each level. One prerequisite for repainting an old table is that you scrape the old paint off and sand it first. You *can* paint it without doing that, but you probably won't be pleased with the results. Nor will you be pleased with a sales order that you rush to the finish.

The prerequisites for moving your sales objectives down the Funnel are indicated at the right hand side of the diagram. We'll explain them more fully now.

UNIVERSE

Since we've just devoted two chapters to the Ideal Customer concept, we won't go over all that information again. Here's the main point. There are nearly limitless selling opportunities out there. Maybe not as many as there are stars in the physical universe, but certainly more than you can handle at any one time. To bring realism, and therefore greater success, into your selling, you must begin by "judiciously restricting" those opportunities, focusing only on those that can get you Win-Win outcomes.

Therefore, the *prerequisite* for placing a business opportunity in your particular Universe—the world of your potential sales objectives—is that there's a suggestion of a reasonable fit to your Ideal Customer Profile. For example:

- You read a news report about a firm's expansion that could be facilitated by your product or service.
- A prospect attends a trade conference and takes home your marketing material.
- A firm's existing contract with a competitor is about to expire.

The *kind of work* you must do at this level is what is usually called *prospecting*. Too often that means following up every lead, no matter how unlikely, or cranking up blitz campaigns for the entire East Coast. When we say "prospect," we use it to mean "search for a fit." At the top of the Funnel, you assess prospects against your Ideal Customer Profile, and narrow the field down to those opportunities that measure up. In other words, you search for evidence that suggests a broad match between your company and each potential customer.

ABOVE THE FUNNEL

At the next level, you perform a similar task, but on a narrower, more focused basis. The *prerequisite* for identifying a possible objective as being Above the Funnel is that you have data that suggests a fit not just between your two companies but also between your product or service line and the prospect's immediate needs. Examples of this suggestive data:

- When you follow up on the news report, a possible Buying Influence confirms a potential need for your product or service.
- Your company receives a "bingo card," or some other request for information, from the potential customer who visited the trade show.
- The firm whose contract is expiring expresses an interest in your solutions.

These are only a few samples, but you get the idea. You don't need to be too exclusionary at this point. As long as there's even an outside chance of an order, place the prospect's name Above the Funnel.

The *kind of work* that needs to be done on a prospect that's Above the Funnel is to *qualify,* or *verify* your suggestive data. You do that by contacting the Buying Influences, including your Coach or Coaches. Verification of your data may take many forms. It may mean simply that a given Buying Influence shows interest in an initial phone call or presentation. It may mean that this person starts Coaching you on the other Buying Influences. Or it may mean that you get a direct request for a demonstration.

But one element of the verification process is essential. You must contact *at least one* Buying Influence and identify a Growth or Trouble discrepancy that your product or service can address. This is your *minimum* selling task on a piece of business Above the Funnel.

IN THE FUNNEL

The *prerequisite* for placing a sales objective In the Funnel is that you have verified the possibility of an order: You've contacted at least that one Buying Influence and spoken to him or her about Growth or Trouble.

The *kind of work* that you need to perform in this part of the Funnel is to *cover the bases*. This entails using all the Key Elements of strategy that we've already discussed. In covering the bases, you perform the following tasks:

- Identify all the Buying Influences for your sales objective, understand their Degrees of Influence, and ensure that each one is contacted by the person best qualified to do so.
- Understand the Response Mode of every Buying Influence, address their senses of urgency, and concentrate on eliminating the perceived discrepancies of every Buying Influence in Growth or Trouble.
- Identify the Results each Buying Influence needs to Win, and make sure that each one understands that your proposal will serve his or her self-interest.
- Continually reassess the sales picture—including any competitive threats—so that you reduce the impact of Red Flags and leverage from your Strengths.

We said that *time and uncertainty decrease* as you move a sales objective down the Funnel. Your purpose in covering the bases is to ensure that this happens.

BEST FEW

The *prerequisite* for placing a sales objective into the Best Few category is that you've all but eliminated *luck* and *uncertainty* as factors in the final buying decision.

We realize that this is a subjective judgment, and for that reason we acknowledge that the dividing line between In the Funnel and Best Few isn't quite as sharp as the line between Above the Funnel and In the Funnel. But it's *not* simply a matter of guesswork. You can test whether or not a possible order is really ready to go into Best Few by remembering the following specifics:

- In Best Few, there are *few discrete* tasks left to be performed and you know exactly what they are. In other words, the *kind of work* to be done involves "end tasks" such as overcoming last-minute objections, getting final confirmation, order signing, and so on.
- On a Best Few objective, you've *covered the bases* so well that you've moved entirely beyond trial and error or guessing. You know all your Buying Influences and their Response Modes, you've addressed their Win-Results, you've dealt with the risk of a last-minute competitive threat, and you've laid out a plan to eliminate any remaining Red Flags.
- Finally, in Best Few, there's at least a 90 percent probability that you'll close the order in *one half* or less the time of your *normal selling cycle*.

This last point needs clarification, since it introduces an unfamiliar term—"normal selling cycle"—that is crucial to the effective use of the Sales Funnel.

Your Normal Selling Cycle

When we talk about your normal selling cycle, we mean the amount of time that it typically takes you to move an order from the top to the bottom of your Sales Funnel—in other words, the amount of time between initial prospecting and the signed agreement to buy.

We're aware that selling cycles vary dramatically from industry to industry, and from product to product within the same industry or even the same company. Selling cycles are influenced by many factors, including the cost of the product, the identities of the Buying Influences, and the complexity of buying decisions. We know people in sales who have sold special promotions to retail chains in a matter of one or two weeks, and other people who have spent seven or eight years handling an aircraft sale to a foreign government. There's no such thing as a universally "normal" selling cycle.

What we're concerned with here is *your* normal selling cycle, for your business and your service or product line. Although your orders won't all move at the same rate, most of them will probably follow an average cycle. That average is what we mean by "normal."

Take a moment now to determine your own normal selling cycle. Think over the sales you've made in the last year or two, and consider how long each one took from first contact to final signature. In determining your personal average, throw out the renewals you did in your sleep, and those oddball orders that you moved to the signing two days after meeting the first Buying Influence. Throw out also the drawn-out orders that reflected extraordinary business conditions or peculiarly difficult Buying Influences or buying processes. Take the average of what's left.

For example, if most of your sales take somewhere between three and nine months to close, then your normal selling cycle is about six months. If it generally takes you somewhere between ten and twenty weeks to move from first contact to the close, then your normal selling cycle is fifteen weeks.

The reason that this is important has to do with *tracking*. That's our term for mentally moving a piece of business from one level of the Funnel down into the next one—for example, from In the Funnel to Best Few. You have to do this at the appropriate time for each individual piece of business. If you mentally move a sales objective down too early or too late, you can easily end up doing the *wrong kind of work* on that sales objective—and therefore putting even "solid" orders in jeopardy. Here's an example:

Barry, a friend of ours who sells word-processing equipment to small businesses, tried to sell a system two years ago to a company that at that time couldn't afford it. The company's officers obviously wanted the system and Barry had done a great job of covering the bases with all the Buying Influences. The only hitch was the budget. "We'll put it in for the next fiscal year," they told him. "But we've definitely got a deal."

When they told him that, in January, they *did* have a deal. That is, they really did intend to buy from Barry, as soon as the resources became available. The trouble was that the new budget wasn't due to be approved until July. As Barry found out, a lot can happen in six months.

Normally, he would have closed a deal like this in about five or six months. But since things had gone so well up to January, he considered the order in hand. In other words, he mentally moved the order *out* of the In the Funnel position and into Best Few. And he figured that the only work he had to do between January and July was to wait for the new budget to go through.

That was a big mistake. When he went back to the customer in July, he found that he had already lost the sale to a competitor—one who had stayed on top of the situation right up to the last minute.

If Barry had kept the "one half of normal selling cycle" rule in mind, he wouldn't have made this error. Realizing that six months was more than half his normal selling cycle, he would have kept the order In the Funnel, and kept covering the bases with his Buying Influences, right on into the summer. If he had done that, he might not have been blindsided by the competition.

A word to the wise: In tracking your sales objectives, always remember the prerequisites and the kinds of work that are relevant to each level of the Funnel. The Sales Funnel becomes operationally effective only when you satisfy the prerequisites before moving any piece of business down, and when you do the right kind of work at the right time for every sales objective that you're tracking. You'll practice these principles now, in a Personal Workshop.

PERSONAL WORKSHOP 10: THE SALES FUNNEL

In this Personal Workshop you're going to sort your own current sales objectives, to see how near each of them is to being completed and to determine what specific tasks you still have to perform to move them further down your Funnel. You'll need your notebook, pencils, and Alternate Positions list. The exercise should take about thirty minutes.

STEP 1: LIST YOUR SINGLE SALES OBJECTIVES.

Open your notebook so that you have two clean pages facing you. Remembering that the Sales Funnel sorts and tracks sales objectives or possible orders, *not* accounts, list the individual sales objectives on which you're currently working. *Be specific.* In Chapter 3 we said that a Single Sales Objective:

- Is *measurable*. It gives numerical answers to the questions who, what, and when.
- Focuses on a *single outcome* that you're trying to bring about in an account.
- Can be defined in a *simple* rather than a compound sentence.

You may have only a few objectives to list, or dozens. Just be sure to list working orders or potential working orders, not accounts. You can't track "Handle the Tintax account" in the Sales Funnel. What you need to list is "Sell Tintax one gross of our #39 package by June 15."

Technically speaking, totally untested prospects shouldn't figure in here, because at that preliminary stage, it's still too early for you to have identified *specific* pieces of business that might come from an account—much less a timetable for securing them. In other words, for new prospects you haven't yet identified Single Sales Objectives. That's all right. For the sake of completeness, we'd like you to list here all the pieces of business and potential pieces of business that you consider part of your sales agenda.

STEP 2: SORT THESE OBJECTIVES.

At the top of a new notebook page write the heading "Sales Funnel." Divide the page into four columns, and at the top of each one place a subheading describing one of the four parts of the Funnel.

You should do this in a special sequence. Make the subheading of the left-hand column "Best Few," that of the second column "Universe," that of the third column "Above the Funnel," and that of the right-hand column "In the Funnel." We're aware that this probably isn't the sequence you would have chosen on your own. We'll explain in the next chapter why it's crucial to your success. When you're done, the worksheet should look like the example on page below.

Best Few	**Universe**	**Above the Funnel**	**In the Funnel**

Now sort your sales objectives into the four columns, depending on the kind of work still to be done to move each one closer to completion. Be sure to include the objective that you've been using as a test case in this book. You should end up with sales objectives in *each* column.

STEP 3: TEST YOUR SORTING.

To ensure that the Sales Funnel scenario you've just constructed is realistic, test each entry by asking yourself specific questions:

- For each entry in the "Best Few" column, ask: "Have I covered all the bases here? Am I 90 percent certain that I can close this piece of business in less than half my normal selling cycle? Do I know what specific tasks I need to perform to ensure I can close the deal?"
- For each entry in the "Universe" column, ask: "From what I know about this prospect's business focus, is there at least a possibility that there's a match between their way of doing business and our Ideal Customer Profile?"
- For each entry in the "Above the Funnel" column, ask: "Do I have concrete data suggesting that there's a possible fit between this prospect's current business needs and my product or service?"
- For each entry in the "In the Funnel" column, ask: "Have I confirmed the data that suggests a possible fit? Have I contacted at least one Buying Influence and spoken to that person about a Growth or Trouble discrepancy?"

If you get a resounding yes to all of these questions, go on to the next step. If not, make the necessary sorting revisions and then go on.

STEP 4: ANALYZE YOUR INFORMATION.

Now look at your entire sales picture as you've sorted it. What you have is a snapshot of your *current* overall sales situation.

Using that snapshot, and using everything else you know about your accounts, look for patterns of movement and position across the four levels of the Funnel. You want to look especially for indications that your Funnel is either drying up or getting jammed up—that is, indications that you don't have enough business moving down, or that you have too many Single Sales Objectives stuck at one level.

Ideally, each of the parts of the Funnel should have *some* objectives in it at all times. They ought to be moving toward the close at a predictable, steady rate. If you find that this is not the case—and especially if you find that a given objective has been stuck in the Funnel for more than your normal selling cycle—then you have to consider modifying your strategy by taking Alternate Positions.

STEP 5: REVISE YOUR ALTERNATE POSITIONS LIST.

The final step in any Sales Funnel analysis is to search for ways you can move your various sales objectives more steadily and more predictably toward the close. Assess how your objectives are moving down the Funnel now. Start with the Single Sales Objective you've been working on all along, and ask yourself this question:

> *What specific tasks can I perform right now to move this particular sales objective further down the Sales Funnel?*

The answers to this question should always relate to the specific *kind of work* that's required at the level of the Funnel where your sales objective is currently located. For example, if that objective is now Above the Funnel, appropriate

Alternate Positions will involve qualifying work that seeks to verify a suggested fit. If the objective is In the Funnel, reliable Alternate Positions will involve covering the bases. If it's in Best Few, good Alternate Positions will involve performing the closing tasks that secure the order.

Write down the answers to this question on your Alternate Positions list. Remember that, in addition to relating to the appropriate kind of work, every Alternate Position you list must also eliminate a Red Flag, leverage from a Strength, or do both.

Since the Sales Funnel is designed to help you plan strategies for all your sales objectives, eventually you'll submit all of them to the same kind of analysis you're doing here. You can't do that yet, because you don't have enough information about those other objectives—you haven't yet put them through a strategic analysis. Once you finish this book, you can begin to gather that information, to set strategies for all your objectives, and to perform further Funnel analyses, based on this model. As you use the Sales Funnel concept again and again over time, it will become an invaluable tool in helping you set strategies for your entire territory, including *all* your sluggish or stuck objectives.

Whatever your current account situation is, we're now going to introduce two concepts that, when used interactively over time, are guaranteed to bring it further improvements.

CHAPTER 18

PRIORITIES AND ALLOCATION: WORKING THE FUNNEL

Your ultimate goal in using the Sales Funnel concept is to be able to move your various sales objectives down the Funnel at a steady and predictable rate, so that your income is also steady and predictable. You do that by working on two interrelated tasks:

- Setting appropriate *priorities* for the four kinds of selling work that need to get done
- *Allocating* your limited selling time so that these four kinds of work always *do* get done, on a consistent basis

Setting work priorities and allocating time are *not* synonymous. Although they're frequently lumped together, the people who use the Sales Funnel concept most effectively understand that they're distinct operations. For one thing, they have to happen in a certain order. You need to determine what your priorities are before you can allocate time to them. So we'll discuss priorities first.

SETTING YOUR WORK PRIORITIES

By "setting your work priorities" we mean determining which of the four kinds of Funnel work you should do first, which you should do second and third, and which you should do last.

Obviously we're speaking here not about the work sequence in which an individual sales objective is processed; all orders start with prospecting and qualifying, go on to covering the bases, and finish by closing. We're speaking about the sequence you should follow in addressing your *total* sales picture. Determining work priorities means deciding—for any given day or given week—which *types* of sales objectives you should work on first, which you should address next, and which you should leave until all the others are done.

If you're like most of the people we work with, your natural inclination is to work the Funnel from the bottom up. That is, you perform the four kinds of work in this sequence:

1. Work on closing tasks for objectives in Best Few.
2. Cover the bases for business In the Funnel.
3. Qualify prospects that are Above the Funnel.
4. Look for entirely new business by prospecting in the Universe.

Psychologically, it seems sensible to follow this sequence. Since uncertainty gets smaller as you move down the Funnel, working the Funnel "in reverse" is a "comfort zone" pattern. There's less immediate anxiety in starting with the most certain objectives (Best Few), then handling those with medium certainty (In the Funnel), and putting off until the last minute those with low certainty (Above the Funnel and Universe).

Virtually *all* people in sales do this. In fact, in all our years in business, we've met only two kinds of sales professionals—those who hate to prospect and those who lie and say they like it. The payoff for narrowing the Universe and for working Above the Funnel objectives is so far down the road that almost everybody treats these tasks like the kid's proverbial spinach—something you get to only when you've got no more options.

The trouble is, this sequence often *closes off* your options. It may not be true in nutrition, but it's clearly true in sales: If you leave your spinach until last, you are going to go hungry. Why? Because the traditional, timeworn sequence of approaching selling tasks is a fundamental cause of the dreaded Roller Coaster Effect.

ROLLER COASTER EFFECT: THE CAUSE

In order to ensure a steady and predictable income profile, you have to have sales objectives moving steadily and predictably from Universe to Best Few. The priority sequence we've just described ensures that this will *not* happen. The reason is simple logic. When you consistently put off your prospecting and qualifying work, it becomes the kind of work that never gets done. So by the time you finish closing all your Best Few and In the Funnel sales objectives, the top of the Funnel has, not so mysteriously, run dry. Unless you "feed" it consistently, this is automatic.

The "dry Funnel syndrome" and the Roller Coaster Effect are really only two metaphors for describing the same unwelcome reality. There are two ways of dealing with this reality: the right way and the wrong way.

The wrong way is to wait until the last minute and then panic. We're not being facetious. This is the "method" for dealing with uneven income that's adopted by nine out of ten people in sales. They ignore their Above the Funnel objectives week after week until everything else has closed. Then, seeing trouble on the way, they rush around prospecting and qualifying madly, throwing anything and everything into the Funnel in the vain hope that they can forestall the inevitable.

This method fails for two reasons. First, if you wait until the last minute to prospect, you simply don't leave enough lead time for a new prospect to "mature" before it can generate the income you want. Most of the time you can't rush your normal selling cycle: If you've put a new prospect Above the Funnel three months later than you should have, that's how long you're going to have to wait to have it bring results.

Second, prospecting for new business when you're in a panic state is psychologically ineffective. Remember what we said about being on the panic end of the Euphoria-Panic Continuum. When you're worried about your position, you tend to do everything at once—and nothing produces results. You can't prospect or qualify intelligently when you're desperate for new leads. You certainly can't project confidence to one of those leads when you're feeling "I need this business *now!*"

ROLLER COASTER EFFECT: THE SOLUTION

The *right* way of dealing with the Roller Coaster Effect is to arrange your work priorities in such a way that you never experience a dry quarter or a dry Funnel in the first place. Here's the priority sequence that will ensure that:

1. Do closing work on your Best Few objectives.
2. Prospect by narrowing the Universe.

3. Qualify your Above the Funnel objectives.
4. Work the objectives In the Funnel.

As untraditional as this sequence is, it is the *only* one that can ensure predictable income over time.

You'll notice that we follow tradition here in advising you to work on your Best Few sales objectives first. That's common sense. Not only do these objectives provide the best chance of a quick return on investment, but also you have more time invested in them, they pay the bills, and they're most vulnerable to capture by the competition, precisely because they're so near to completion. Neglecting a Best Few order means risking the worst of all possible worlds: having somebody else pocket the commission for your work.

Where we depart from tradition is in insisting that the next priority should go to objectives "at the top." The only way of being certain that your Funnel won't eventually dry up is to devote some time consistently to Universe and Above the Funnel work. It's because putting this kind of work off is so easy that we advise you to do it second and third in the sequence, not last and next-to-last.

This doesn't mean you should let your In the Funnel objectives take care of themselves. They won't. You've got to keep covering the bases on all your working sales objectives. But salespeople often spend more time than they should doing this kind of work, simply because it's more *comfortable* than prospecting and qualifying. It's a lot more fun to take your old pal Harry Barnes to lunch one more time than to strike out for virgin territory and risk rejection. But you've got to discipline yourself to do that—or you'll risk much more than rejection.

To help our clients remember the sequence that we've found effective, we give them a simple rule of thumb:

Every time you close something, prospect or qualify something else.

A colleague of ours with an editorial consulting service told us recently that, when we first mentioned this rule to him a couple of years ago, he finally understood what he'd been "doing wrong for ten years." When we asked him to explain, he said this: "Ever since I started in this business, I've assumed that the feast or famine cycle was inevitable. Since you explained about keeping the Funnel filled, I've been following a new system. I take one morning a week, every week, to scout around for new clients—even if I've got more work than I can handle. It's saved my financial life. I'm now in the incredible position of having to turn down business—and I haven't had a dry month in two years."

The lesson is obvious. Since *everything* starts at the top of the Funnel, the one way to avoid a dry Funnel is to make your prospecting and qualifying *regular* priorities.

Allocating Time: A Dynamic Process

Once you've established the priorities for the four kinds of work your sales objectives need, you should then determine how much time each kind of work needs and allocate it accordingly.

Time allocation isn't a static process. It differs in this sense from the priority system we've just explained. That priority system *is* static. To get optimum results, you have to follow the same sequence of work all the time. Time allocation, on the other hand, is *dynamic*. The *amount of time* that you should give to each level of the Funnel must be continually adjusted, depending on several factors. Among the most important are the following:

1. NUMBER AND TYPE OF TASKS TO BE PERFORMED.

The first and most important factor is the *number and type* of selling tasks that must be done in order to move your objectives steadily down the Funnel. The Sales Funnel is a snapshot of your total territory at a single moment in time. As objectives move down, that picture changes—and you have to adjust your allocation of time in response to this change. Knowing how much time to allocate to each part of the Funnel right now, therefore, means attending to the distribution right now of all the discrete selling tasks you must perform.

Say your Funnel today contains forty separate Single Sales Objectives. If that Funnel is perfectly "balanced," with ten pieces of business at each of its four levels, then the task of allocation is fairly straightforward: You should spend roughly one quarter of your week working at each level. But if next week or next month, 50 percent of that total has moved into Best Few, then you will need to adjust your time allocation, spending more like half of your week tackling closing tasks.

2. DIFFICULTY AND AMOUNT OF WORK REQUIRED.

Since every Complex Sale is different, no two sales objectives require exactly the same amount of work. You have to adjust your time allocation to accommodate those sales objectives that demand more (or less) than your customary amount of selling work.

Say you have a total of ten possible orders in your Sales Funnel, and only one of them is in Best Few. By strict mathematics, you should devote not more than 10 percent of your time to closing that one order. But if it's an extremely complicated order—if the closing work involves numerous individual tasks to be performed and you know that failing to perform any one of them can imperil the sale—then you're justified in spending more time on this one objective. Similarly, if 80 percent of your orders are Above the Funnel but all you need to do to move most of them to In the Funnel is make a quick phone call, there's no point in spending 80 percent of your time in qualifying. The Sales Funnel is designed to help you allocate your time most *efficiently*. You must make the adjustments that will ensure that, based on the needs of your accounts.

3. AMOUNT OF REVENUE INVOLVED.

No matter where an objective is in the Sales Funnel, you'll probably want to give it special attention if it's going to mean major income down the line. Remember the editorial consultant we just mentioned. Throughout most of last year, although he had numerous objectives in his Funnel all the time, and although the distribution of his work was constantly changing, he consistently spent well over half his total working time tracking a *single* order from Above the Funnel to Best Few. He did this for an excellent reason: That single piece of business, when it closed, accounted for more than half his income that year.

The bottom line here is . . . the bottom line. It always

makes sense to adjust your allocation of time to favor those orders with big payoffs. Assuming, of course, that you don't neglect the rest of the Funnel.

4. ACCOUNT POTENTIAL.

Some years back, we got a feeler from one of the Fortune 500 companies that said it was interested in our processes. We happily put its name Above the Funnel and went about trying to move it down. We've gotten nowhere with it, and maybe we never will. But we still go back to that firm on a *regular* basis, taking time away from more immediately lucrative projects, because we know that, if it ever pans out, it will be worth every minute we've invested.

We don't recommend this as a *standard* course of action. Normally, if a potential order has been Above the Funnel for two or three years and we're not able to budge it, we let it go. We see this account, however, as an investment in the future. We're willing to allot some time to it on a regular basis because the potential payoff is so high.

5. ACCOMMODATION OF BUYING CYCLES.

You know that individual companies, and individual industries, work on buying cycles that may have nothing at all to do with the way you like to sell, or with the scheduling that you would prefer to adopt. But since it's virtually impossible to sell outside of a customer's buying cycles, you cannot ignore them.

This is especially true in government contracts. One excellent sales representative we know, whose major customers are state university systems, has learned to adjust her own personal workweek allotments to the government schedules that dictate when her clients will buy. Her Buying Influences have their own fiscal cycles; their own systems of bidding, examination, and rebidding; their own scheduling procedures. Our friend is successful partly because she understands the inflexibility of their decision-making process and is willing to adjust her own preferred schedule to theirs.

Considering what we said in Chapter 7 about your customers' *perception of reality,* this is only common sense. No matter how eccentric you may consider your Buying Influences' purchasing cycles, they're an unavoidable factor in how you arrange your time.

6. PRODUCT-MIX QUOTAS.

On the other side of the coin, you may also have to adjust your time allocation to meet the quota requirements of *your* company. You may have to spend more time than you would like in pushing a low-commission product because your marketing people see it as a priority. Product-mix quotas are part of a continual push-pull between the factory and the field, and although few of us in the field really like them, we can't ignore them. Especially not if we're going after the bonuses that meeting these special quotas often generates.

One of our clients manufactures scientific instruments ranging from circuit-board test equipment that can cost several hundred thousand dollars to simple oscilloscopes that start at twenty-five hundred. We know hundreds of sales representatives in that company, and we have yet to meet one who would prefer to spend selling time pushing the oscilloscopes. But all of them do it anyway. It's an unavoidable part of their sales responsibility.

You'll probably be able to identify further factors influencing your allocation of time. But these five are enough to make our point. The allocation of your time—like everything else in your strategy—must be *constantly reassessed* if it is to remain effective. The goal of this constant reassessment is to keep your potential business moving steadily and predictably down the Sales Funnel. The time allocation that does that is the right one for you.

PERSONAL WORKSHOP 11: PRIORITIES/TIME ALLOCATION

Now look at the Sales Funnel chart you constructed in the last chapter, and incorporate the information we've presented in this chapter.

STEP 1: IDENTIFY YOUR WORK PRIORITIES.

If you look now at your Sales Funnel chart, you'll understand why we asked you to place the Best Few column to the left, the Universe and Above the Funnel columns in the middle, and the In the Funnel column to the right. This left-to-right order is the *single optimum sequence* in which you should approach the four kinds of Funnel work.

STEP 2: ANALYZE THE DISTRIBUTION OF THE TASKS YOU NEED TO DO.

Notice how the various sales objectives you listed in the last Personal Workshop are arranged in this chart. Count the number of objectives listed in each of the columns and, at the bottom of each column, write that number down. Compare the number of objectives in each column with the total number of objectives to determine what percentage of your total work load is now in each of the four parts of the Funnel. Write the relevant percentages down at the bottom of each column. This will give you an *approximation* of the time you should now be allocating to each part of the Funnel, based on the number and type of tasks to be done.

STEP 3: WEIGH OTHER TIME ALLOCATION FACTORS.

Now you should adjust the percentages you have just identified by considering the five other factors that frequently affect the appropriate allocation of time. Ask yourself these questions:

- Do I need to give more time to sales objectives that are particularly complicated or difficult?
- Should I shift some of the indicated time allotments to give more time to objectives with a high dollar value?
- Do I need to divert time to an order with low dollar value that can be an opening to an account with huge potential?
- Do I have to accommodate my own time allocation to my various customers' buying cycles?
- Do I need to revise this basic allocation to account for current product-mix quotas?

The answers to these questions should help you to reassess the time allocation that's suggested by the distribution of your objectives.

STEP 4: COMPARE REAL AND IDEAL TIME ALLOCATIONS.

You now have a reliable picture of how you *should* be allocating time to your various sales objectives: a picture, in other words, of the ideal. But it's not always possible to be perfectly systematic in working the Funnel, and we know that some of the things you're actually doing with your accounts right now won't fit into this ideal picture. So we urge you to compare your current reality—including the work priorities you presently follow and how you allocate your time—to the ideal you've just constructed. Do this on an individual basis, for every sales objective now in your Funnel. One by one, ask yourself the following questions:

- Have I been doing the appropriate *kind of work* on this objective, based on its position in the Funnel?
- Have I been working on it in the proper *sequence*—that is, first if it's in Best Few, second if it's in Universe, third if it's Above the Funnel, and last if it's In the Funnel?
- Have I been allocating the appropriate *amount of time* to it, considering the quantity and quality of the work needed to get the business?

STEP 5: REVISE YOUR ALTERNATE POSITIONS LIST.

Finally, you can use the answers to the above questions to revise your Alternate Positions list. Eventually you'll be using the lessons of the Sales Funnel to set appropriate strategies for all of your account objectives. You can begin that process now by looking at where your test-case objective is in your current Sales Funnel, and what you can do to move it further toward the close.

- If it's in Universe, ask yourself whether the account you're targeting is really a match to your Ideal Customer Profile.
- If it's Above the Funnel, ask yourself how you can verify the data you have suggesting a possible fit between your product or service and the buying organization's current needs.
- If it's In the Funnel, ask yourself whether or not you've adequately covered all the bases required for the successful completion of your deal.
- If it's in Best Few, ask yourself what individual end tasks are yet to be done before you have a signed agreement.

Remembering that every sound Alternate Position eliminates a Red Flag, leverages a Strength, or does both, use the information you uncover here to make the necessary adjustments on your Alternate Positions list.

Save this list, and save the Sales Funnel chart you've been developing. The initial Sales Funnel analysis you've just completed will become fully operational only when you return to it in the future, and use it again, dynamically, to create a new picture.

Using the Sales Funnel over Time

This is an essential feature of the Sales Funnel concept—one that you'll begin to appreciate only after you've done several Funnel analyses. Used on a regular basis, the Sales Funnel gives you a broad-spectrum picture of your account situation *over time*. The more often you use it, and the more frequently you compare the snapshot at different points in time, the more effectively it will help you to clarify your constantly changing account situation.

For example, let's say that the Funnel you just put together showed a heavy cluster of possible business Above the Funnel. Suppose you do another Funnel analysis in a month and discover that only one or two of these sales objectives have moved down to In the Funnel. By comparing the two Funnel analyses, you'll be able to highlight a problem: your difficulty in verifying initial, suggestive data.

Or say that the Funnel you just did shows an even spacing of prospective business up and down the Funnel, but that one you do a month from now shows a bunching in Best Few, and an Above the Funnel and Universe that are almost dry. That will tell you two things: You have to pay more attention to prospecting and qualifying, and you have to find out what's holding back those Best Few objectives from being closed.

Lack of movement down the Funnel might also indicate that you categorized a certain piece of business incorrectly in a previous Funnel analysis. For example, a sales objective that you categorized a few months ago as Best Few might really have belonged In the Funnel, because it still had uncovered bases. As a general rule, whenever you find a given sales objective in the Best Few category for two or three Funnel checks in a row, the chances are good that it wasn't Best Few in the first place. Through regular comparison of your Funnels, you'll gradually learn to anticipate and avoid such mistakes.

Because such comparisons are so useful, we urge you to save not only the Sales Funnel chart you've just done, but every one you do in the future. By comparing these snapshots of your account situation, you'll eventually be able to construct a kind of motion picture describing the development, from one sales period to another and from one year to another, of your evolving sales situation.

Funnel Analysis: How Often?

How often should you do a Funnel analysis? This question, which is asked constantly in our programs, has no single answer. The frequency with which you should do a new Sales Funnel analysis depends on the amount and rate of *change* in your particular sales situation. Some people will profit from doing a new analysis of their accounts every week, and others can profitably hold off for a month.

Generally speaking, the longer your normal selling cycle, the longer you can reasonably wait between Sales Funnel analyses. Just don't wait too long. We advise our clients to do a new analysis a minimum of once a month. Since you're just beginning to use the concept, we recommend that you do such an analysis, for now, once every two weeks.

The people who use the Sales Funnel concept most effectively start out by doing such an analysis so regularly that it soon becomes second nature to them. That's an ideal to aim for. Once you internalize the use of the Sales Funnel concept, you'll know instinctively when it's time to take another snapshot. And you'll be able to do such analyses more and more quickly.

The point to remember is that use of the Sales Funnel concept must be *periodic* rather than sporadic. You can use the concept profitably even if you do only one analysis a month—provided you're rigorous in adhering to that once-a-month design.

READING THE FUTURE

Used periodically, the Sales Funnel concept provides the salesperson with an accurate picture not only of current reality, but of future prospects as well. We began our discussion of the Sales Funnel by promising that it would give you a means of *predicting* your future income—and thus of avoiding the unpleasant uncertainties of the Roller Coaster Effect. Many of our clients tell us that this is the single most attractive feature of the concept. "I don't use it just to *track* my business," one regional manager told us. "I use it to *forecast* the future."

The Funnel allows you to do that because, by definition, uncertainty decreases as you move toward the close. Or, to put it positively, *probability increases*. We've said that you put an order in the Best Few category only when there is a 90 percent likelihood—or probability—that it will close in half the time of your normal selling cycle. We can also assign rough probabilities to the other levels of the Funnel.

When an objective is in Universe, that is, when it's still on the verge of being qualified, the probability of its closing in half your selling cycle is minimal—perhaps no more than 4 or 5 percent. When it's in Above the Funnel, you've begun to qualify it, and the probability rises to 10 or 15 percent. An objective that has progressed to In the Funnel may have a 20 to 80 percent probability. Taking these figures as rough guidelines, it's easy to see how the Sales Funnel gives you a fix on the future.

Several of our clients see this ability to read the future as the Sales Funnel's greatest advantage over other forecasting tools. Hewlett-Packard, the computer and electronics instrument firm to which we've delivered hundreds of our programs, incorporates the Sales Funnel model into its own forecasting system. So does Sentient Systems, Inc., which has fused the Funnel with its own customer database management process. And many of our clients successfully transform the individual Sales Funnel concept into one with regional and national implications: They use their sales representatives' individual Funnel analyses to feed into "branch Funnel analyses," and then into regional and national Funnel projections.

When it's used consistently, the Sales Funnel enables you to look both forward *and* backward, freeing you to use your limited selling time more efficiently to ensure a steady flow of profitable business. It lets you look at what's happened in the past, to see what's coming in the future, and to allocate your time today in the most strategically effective manner.

PART 6

FROM ANALYSIS TO ACTION

CHAPTER 19

YOUR ACTION PLAN

You now have all the principles you'll ever need to set solid strategies not only for the sales objective you've been working on in this book, but for all your future objectives as well. Taken together, those principles constitute a methodology that can give you an edge over your competition in every sale you tackle. For that to happen most effectively, though, you should use them as parts of a dynamic planning vehicle called an *Action Plan*.

An Action Plan is a list of concrete, practical actions that you can perform before each sales call to improve your position regarding your immediate objective. It provides a bridge that leads from pre-call analysis, or strategy, to the tactical selling that you do while you're *in* the call. As the final step in your strategy, it enables you to know before you're face-to-face that you'll be meeting the right person in the right place at the right time.

Don't be misled by the word "final." An Action Plan is the

last thing you should do before each call, but it's not an end in itself, and it's not static. It's a dynamic vehicle that must change from call to call as part of an ongoing process of assessment, feedback, and reassessment—a process that makes you continually responsive to change.

In this chapter, you'll make the bridge between theory and practice for your own chosen sales objective, in terms of (a) your current position with your Buying Influences, and (b) what you expect to accomplish the next time you're face-to-face with them. At the same time, the Action Plan you create here will be a model for all your future plans.

An Essential Ground Rule

In drafting a list of practical actions to improve your position, the emphasis is on *practical*. You want to be sure that each action you adopt can *in fact* move you closer to attaining your objective. In our Strategic Selling programs, one simple Ground Rule helps our participants keep practicality in mind:

Each action that you list as part of your Action Plan should capitalize on a Strength, eliminate or reduce the impact of a Red Flag, or do both.

We've been stressing the Red Flags/Strengths principle throughout the book. We rephrase it here as a rule to provide a baseline check on wishful thinking—a means of testing the *real* potential for actions to move you closer to your chosen sales objective.

It's worthwhile repeating, too, that, even though Red Flags are danger signals, they should never be seen as problems or as negative. In sales, anticipating danger is the most positive thing you can do. Finding Red Flags is therefore the best assurance you have that your Action Plans are working against real weaknesses and building upon real Strengths. *Not* finding them would be a real problem.

PUTTING THE THEORY INTO ACTION

In creating your list of practical actions—your own model Action Plan—begin with the Alternate Positions list that you've been developing throughout the book. With that list in front of you, look at your current position with regard to each of our Strategic Selling concepts. As you do so, list in your notebook any actions you might take, before the next sales call, to improve that position. Focus on these areas:

- Your Single Sales Objective
- The Buying Influences involved in that objective
- The Response Mode of each Buying Influence
- The Win-Results of each Buying Influence
- The level and nature of your competition

Test each area briefly, asking yourself questions to uncover remaining Red Flags, and then consider which actions can turn them into opportunities. Here are some guidelines for doing so.

YOUR SALES OBJECTIVE

To succeed in any sales endeavor, you have to understand clearly what you're trying to accomplish in the account that isn't happening right now. A sound sales objective is always *specific*, *measurable*, and *realistic*; in addition, it always has a clearly defined *time frame*—that is, you know when you expect to accomplish it. If you don't define the objective precisely, and if you don't have a good reason for believing you can accomplish it by a certain date, you'll end up like today's computer novices who spend hours and hours running in circles on the Internet because they don't know where they're going or how to get there.

So look at the sales objective you defined for yourself in Chapter 3. Does it meet the conditions we're setting out here? If not, you should consider redefining it.

For example, suppose you've identified your current sales objective as "Sell Goliath Industries a pilot program by May 1." It's now late March, and negotiations have stalled. Everybody at Goliath seems interested in your proposal but, according to Joe Garcia, the manufacturing manager, "It's just a bad time of year for us to commit." Faced with that situation, you may have to redefine or reschedule what you're trying to accomplish. A redefining action for your Action Plan might be something like this: "Arrange meeting at Goliath next week to have Garcia explain their buying process."

Notice that the phrasing of this hypothetical action is *precise*, is geared to improving your current position *now,* and answers very *specific* questions. It tells you:

- *Who* will be involved in the sales call or other meeting. In the case described here, only you and one Buying Influence are involved. Remember, though, that a single call may involve more than one Buying Influence—and that it may or may not involve you, personally, as the person best qualified to perform every action.
- *Where* and *when* the meeting will take place. Remember

that actions may be implemented in your own organization or on neutral ground as well as at the customer's place of business. And remember that the ideal time to implement an action is as soon as it's convenient for you and your Buying Influences.

- *What* specific information you expect the call to give you. Until you're actually positioned to make the close—and often even in a closing call—each action should help you to either confirm or invalidate suspected information, or to secure information that you don't have.

Of course, in addition to specifying the who, when, where, and what of the sales call, each action you include in your Action Plan must also follow the Ground Rule. In this example that basic condition is met because the suggested action is designed to reduce the impact of one of the automatic Red Flags that we described in Chapter 6—lack of information.

BUYING INFLUENCES

We've emphasized that understanding the identities of all the key players for your sales objective is the foundation of every good strategy, and we've given you a method for locating those players by defining the *four* Buying Influence *roles* that are always present in every Complex Sale. It's essential, before any given sales call, that you assess your position with each of these key figures.

Using as starting points your Buying Influences Chart and Alternate Positions list, you should now list actions that will capitalize on Strengths and address Red Flags in this critical area. These actions should ensure that all of the people playing each of the four Buying Influence roles for your sale are covered adequately—by the person *best qualified* to do so.

You'll begin, of course, by making sure that you know the identity of each of these people. You should have at least one name in each of the four boxes of your Buying Influences Chart. If you don't, you should address actions to deal with that automatic Red Flag. *What* Coaching data do you need to fill in the empty space? *Who* can get you that data? *When* and *where* can you meet that person? The answers to these questions should suggest specific actions designed to capitalize on Strengths and remove Red Flags.

Suppose the boxes are all filled in but the key players are not all *covered*. Maybe you can't get in to see your Economic Buying Influence because according to her secretary "She never sees salespeople." Here you might want to arrange for an executive of like rank to see her. One action furthering that plan would be to make an appointment with someone in your own organization—ideally, someone who has already given you good Coaching—to determine who is best qualified to get past the secretarial screen. Notice that, while this action prepares you for a future sales call, it's implemented not on your customer's territory but on your own. The *where* in this case might be your own boss's office.

Or suppose that the Economic Buying Influence is strongly in favor of your proposal, but you can't overcome the resistance of a Technical Buyer who has an unidentified "problem" with it. Here you might consider using Coaching downward, from the Economic Buyer to middle management. One possible action: "Meet Thursday with Farley to determine why Steinberg feels he's Losing."

Alternatively, you could use one person you've already identified as a Coach, Doris Green, to help you better understand Steinberg's resistance. This action would have the added advantage of utilizing the Degree of Influence concept: Since you've identified Green as having a High influence, she might be the appropriate lever to turn the Medium-influence Steinberg around. Notice, too, that both of these suggested actions observe the Ground Rule: They capitalize on the Strengths of your supporters to leverage against the Technical Buyer's negativity.

Remember, finally, that whenever you meet an Economic Buyer, you need a valid business reason for doing so—valid in *his or her* eyes, not just your own. Farley will be more disposed to give you the information you need if you first bring him information *he* finds useful. Suggested actions: Remind Farley of an upcoming conference on national productivity decline, set up an executive briefing on your past Win-Win sales, or bring him a journal article on problem solving. As always, you should know where and when each of these possible actions is to be implemented.

RESPONSE MODES

Only if you first understand all your key individuals' *current* perception of the situation can you be alert to their receptivity to the change you are offering them. The point here is that there are only *two* Response Modes, Growth and Trouble, in which a Buying Influence will be open to change. These are the only modes in which Buyers perceive a *discrepancy* between their current business reality and the Results that they need to Win. By definition, having a Buyer in one of these two modes is a Strength (if there's a positive rating), and having one in Even Keel or Overconfident Mode is a Red Flag (no matter what the rating).

With your Buying Influences Chart and Alternate

Positions list still in front of you, list actions that would highlight your Buying Influences' perceived discrepancy between reality and Results—and that would also demonstrate to those in Growth or Trouble that your proposal can eliminate the discrepancy.

In the sample Buying Influences Chart that we presented in Chapter 8, for example, we identified Dan Farley (Economic Buyer) and Doris Green (User, Coach) as in Growth Mode, and Gary Steinberg (Technical) and Sandy Kelly (Coach) as in Trouble. So the best immediate actions here would probably focus on these four people, rather than on Will Johnson (Technical), who's in Overconfident Mode, or on Harry Barnes (User, Technical), who's in Even Keel.

Suggested actions: First, "Lunch with Green and Farley Friday to reinforce Growth potential of proposal"—an action that observes the Ground Rule by capitalizing on a proposal Strength. Then, to overcome Steinberg's negativity, "Tour of Steinberg's department next Tuesday with Kelly so Kelly can show how proposal will solve Steinberg's problem"—an action that reduces the impact of a Red Flag. Remember again, you don't have to sell everybody by yourself. In this situation, Kelly may be better qualified than you to sell Steinberg because the two of them share a perception of Trouble.

One caution. The four Response Modes must be viewed as *situation* perceptions, not personality types. This means that they can change at any time.

WIN-RESULTS

The fundamental goal of every sales strategy should be to ensure Win-Results for all your Buying Influences, as well as

Wins for yourself. The key point here is that Winning, the underlying reason that anyone buys, isn't measurable or quantifiable: *Wins* reinforce *emotional* values and attitudes. Objective business Results are the means by which Buyers obtain Wins, but they're only a beginning. If you focus only on Results, your Buyers will Lose—and so will you.

Are you sure that your sales proposal can provide each of your Buying Influences a corporate Result that will provide him or her with a personal Win? Look at your Win-Results Chart. Do you have a clear Win-Results Statement written for each and every one of your Buying Influences? If not, that's a Red Flag.

On the sample Win-Results Chart we set up in Chapter 10, for example, we failed to identify a Win for either Farley or Steinberg. We placed Red Flags there to make our lack of data visible. If you were managing this sale, your Action Plan would have to include specifics for setting up meetings to eliminate those Red Flags. Coaching from people who know Farley and Steinberg better than you do would help you determine the who, when, and where of those meetings. A sample action: "Appointment Friday with Sandy Kelly; have her explain Farley's Wins."

Three warnings: First, although it may seem unnecessary for you to know everybody's Wins on every sale—and although you can in fact close deals without knowing this—delivering Results alone is still a hazardous strategy. Since you're in the account for the long run, the sooner you know how each of your key players Wins, the more effectively you'll be able to meet each person's needs in future sales. Ignoring a Buyer's Wins will eventually undermine your position with the entire account.

Second, getting everybody to Win to the same *extent* may not be possible on every Complex Sale. But your goal should remain to provide the highest degree of Winning and the lowest degree of Losing for everyone concerned. Sometimes the best you can do is to minimize the Losses. In our view, this is still playing Win-Win.

Third, don't forget your *own* Wins. You wouldn't think sales professionals would have to be reminded of this, but sometimes they do: We've already mentioned how salespeople can give away the store in the hope that their Buying Influences will one day pay them back. We urge you to drop from your list any action that might put you in this Lose-Win scenario. There's little point in closing business that you'll resent later—and even less in doing business that you resent *today*.

COMPETITION

Finally, consider adopting actions that can minimize the importance of your competition for this Single Sales Objective. Remember that competition, as we've defined it, isn't just the multinational giant who's trying to "steal your sale." Competition is *any* alternative to the solution you're offering the customer, including the customer's decision to use the available resources elsewhere, to provide an in-house solution—or to do nothing.

In devising actions to offset these unattractive alternatives, concentrate on the principle of Leverage from Strength. Instead of asking defensively "How can I avoid being beaten up here?" think positively and proactively. Ask what added value you can bring to this customer's business that will make doing business with you the most attractive solution.

In seeking that added value, look beyond the product. Maybe what you have to offer is the special knowledge of one of your own key executives. Maybe it's a track record for spotless service excellence. Maybe it's a willingness to help the customer design new criteria. Whatever it is, the actions you select should establish your difference. They should establish the uniqueness, not just the cheapness, of your solution by saying to the Buying Influences, "We don't push commodities. We want a relationship that will contribute to the way you do business."

THE "FINAL" LIST

How many actions should be included in an Action Plan? We recommend a short list because an Action Plan is a *dynamic* instrument designed to help you improve your *current* position. Once you've implemented the actions on a sales call, that position by definition will have changed. Once it's changed, you'll have to reassess your strategy and devise the *next* Action Plan. In a world like ours that's spinning a mile a millisecond, there's no point in saddling yourself with a twenty-point action agenda that stretches six months into the future. You could be halfway through that list when it becomes obsolete.

For the test-case objective you're targeting in this book, you should be in good shape if you can narrow your list to just *four* or *five* solid actions. As long as each one moves you visibly and demonstrably closer to your sales objective, you'll have accomplished everything you need to accomplish right now. As you practice the principles of Strategic Selling, and as you design Action Plans for future objectives, you'll be able to identify appropriate actions with increasing speed and accuracy—often without actually writing them down. Naturally, the actions you choose in the future will be unique to their own situations. But the selection *process* you're performing here is the *model* for all those future efforts.

Often, you can get your "final" list down to this optimum number of four or five by measuring each possible inclusion against three criteria. The best four or five actions will be:

- *Logical:* They'll build naturally on the work you've already done toward your sales objective.
- *Urgent:* They'll have a high priority, in terms of your getting to the close.
- *Do-able:* They'll be actions that, given your current position, you can realistically accomplish in the next one or two sales calls.

These criteria for choosing the best actions, of course, are meant to amplify rather than replace the Red Flags/Strengths Ground Rule. Every one of your best four or five actions will by definition still observe that rule.

A Wider Perspective

If you're having trouble defining valid actions, you may want to use the Key Elements of Ideal Customer and Sales Funnel to help you. They may not always be as relevant to setting up individual sales calls as the five test areas we've just discussed. But they do provide a wider perspective on your total account picture that can act as an extra check on the validity of your actions.

For example, suppose your chosen sales objective, like the Goliath example we mentioned earlier, is a stuck order. If reviewing the areas we highlight in this chapter is not helping you to unstick it, you might want to look at where it is in your

Sales Funnel, to determine whether or not you're giving it the right *kind of work.* You may discover that you've moved it down the Funnel too rapidly, and that you're trying to put a close on a customer who's not yet ready for it. In that case, an appropriate action might be to reconsider your position and "re-cover" the bases.

Or you might want to test the overall viability of a sales objective against your Ideal Customer Profile. If none of the actions you're considering seems likely to improve your position significantly, maybe you're working on a dead-end account. Check the account's alignment against your profile. In a small but significant number of situations, the best action may be to let a difficult piece of business go.

THE ACID TEST

Here's one final test to measure the validity of your actions. In Chapter 3, when we presented the Euphoria-Panic Continuum, we mentioned that your own gut reactions often provide confirmation of your real position faster and more reliably than cerebral analysis does. Judging how you *feel* about your position can also be an acid test for the four or five "best" actions you've selected. So refer to the Euphoria-Panic Continuum one more time and use it as a final check of your plan.

For each action that you're now considering implementing in your Action Plan, ask yourself whether or not it makes you feel more *comfortable* about the overall sales situation. If the actions on your list are reducing your feelings of stress, uneasiness, or uncertainty, then they probably really are your best actions. If they aren't doing that, you should retest the plan, zero in on what's making you uncomfortable, and find out why. And make sure you do it before the next call.

From Strategy to Tactics—and Back Again

The Action Plan you've just devised, in addition to providing you a model for future use, has also prepared you to make a given call on one or more Buying Influences. Since the selling process is dynamic, once you make that call the plan will be rendered obsolete precisely because it has done its job. And it will be time to consider new actions.

As we mentioned early in the book, strategy and tactics are different, but they aren't disconnected. They work together, like one hand washing the other. Every Action Plan you create will enable you to enter an individual sales call so well prepared that, once you're face-to-face with your Buying Influence, you can use your tactical skills to your best advantage. At the same time, each call will give you added information about your sales objective that you didn't have at your disposal before you went in.

You won't let that information lie there. You'll *use* it to reassess your position, reconsider your Strengths and Red Flags, and plan your next set of actions. All tactical encounters are opportunities for reassessing your position. Your evolving Action Plans are the engines of that reassessment.

CHAPTER 20

STRATEGY WHEN YOU HAVE NO TIME

Drafting an Action Plan like the one you've done in the last chapter typically takes about an hour to do properly. If you had the time, you could perform this kind of in-depth planning on all your accounts, for all your sales objectives, before every sales call. Your sales figures would undoubtedly justify the expenditure of time.

But you don't have the time. Even though creating a complete Action Plan becomes easier and quicker the more you do it, and even though such detailed plans can help you understand everything from the most modest to the most extravagant of your sales objectives, the reality is that your time is a finite resource. Given all the other things you have to do to be successful, you simply cannot spend that sixty minutes on every one of your potential pieces of business.

This doesn't mean that you should decide by chance which

sales objectives deserve the full treatment. And it certainly doesn't mean that you should enter *any* sales call without the benefit of *some* strategic planning. In determining how to give the appropriate amount of advance planning to each sales call, we recommend that you consider a two-part solution.

First: Determine which accounts and which sales objectives really call for a "long form" Action Plan —and give them the hour that they deserve. Second: Adopt a "short form" action analysis for those sales objectives and those upcoming sales calls where conditions just don't allow for the extended treatment.

Long-Form Analysis: When It's Needed

At many of the companies who have adopted our Strategic Selling process, "long form" analyses are required by management for all objectives where certain conditions are met. The conditions vary from client to client, but generally they have to do with some combination of immediate dollars involved and long-term potential. At some companies, salespeople must give their managers a complete analysis for all objectives worth over one hundred thousand dollars. At others, the critical figure is fifty thousand dollars. At others, there is no official cutoff point, but managers may still require complete analyses whenever the account being targeted promises potentially huge returns.

Because of the variety of situations that any sales organization may encounter, there are no hard-and-fast rules for when you "must" put in that full hour. There are, however, a number of generally reliable indicators. Consider, for example, the following common sales scenarios:

1. You've just "inherited" an important account from another salesperson.
2. You're handling a big-dollar account, or one in which there will be severe negative impact if you fail to get the order.
3. You're in a tough battle with the competition.
4. You don't know who the competition is.
5. You're handling an account that represents an important new market or new industry.
6. Your sales objective is stuck in the Sales Funnel, the expected closing date has passed, and you don't know what to do next.
7. You're about to review the status of a difficult account with your sales manager.
8. You lack a piece of information that's essential to the sale and you don't know how to get it.

In cases like these, we advise you never to opt for a short-form analysis. Whenever the sales objective you're considering involves big money, can significantly alter your long-term sales picture, or is filled with uncertainties, we urge you to find the time for that "full sixty." To put it negatively but cogently, if you try to approach difficult sales situations like these without a detailed Action Plan, you'll be fooling yourself—and offering a good opening to the competition.

When to Use Short-Form Analysis

On the other hand, when the objective you're aiming for doesn't involve a huge dollar amount, when the risks involved aren't particularly high, when you're not working against a high degree of uncertainty, or when there are only a few Buying Influences involved, a short-form approach can be of significant value.

When a complete Action Plan isn't essential, or when you simply don't have time to construct one, we suggest that you employ one of two modifications of the sixty-minute model. Which one to use depends on the individual situation.

MODIFIED ANALYSIS 1: THE TEN-MINUTE "QUICK AND DIRTY" ANALYSIS

Suppose you recently inherited an account with a modest but reliable sales volume. Your current sales objective is to get that account to approve a pilot program for a new product line within the next six months. You've met the Economic Buying Influence and a couple of User Buying Influences, and are scheduled to meet the Economic Buyer again this afternoon at four. You wanted to draft an Action Plan for this meeting, but your other accounts took up all your time. It's now twenty to four. What kind of strategic planning can you do?

A brief analysis, like all the analyses you've been doing in this book, involves asking yourself questions designed to uncover areas of uncertainty and suggest ways to improve your position with the Buying Influences. When you have only ten or fifteen minutes, you obviously have to narrow the questions down to the most essential ones. We suggest the following four:

- Do I know who all my *Buying Influences* are? That is, do I know the identities and buying roles of all the key individuals for this sales objective? If not, do I *at least* know who is acting as the Economic Buying Influence for this sale?
- Do I know all these individuals' *Win-Results*? Do I know how each of them will Win personally by getting a business Result that my proposal can deliver?
- Am I capitalizing on *Strengths* and working to eliminate or reduce the impact of *Red Flags*?
- Do I have at least one reliable *Coach* for this sale?

If you can answer all of these questions positively, you're probably in a fairly sound strategic position. In the sales call that follows this quick analysis, you can build on what you already know to continue addressing Win-Results, leveraging from Strength, and eliminating Red Flags.

If you can't answer these questions affirmatively, you know that you have to use that sales call to begin getting the answers. The benefit of asking these four questions *before* you go in to see a Buying Influence is that, even if you draw a blank, you'll know *where* you're missing information, and what kind of data you need to get from that person. Often the most valuable thing you can accomplish in any sales call is simply to secure or confirm such essential information.

How you get someone to give you this information—that is, how you ask questions designed to better your understanding of the sale—is a matter of tactics, not strategy. Tactics are essential to good selling, of course, and we cover them extensively in our Conceptual Selling program and book. Strategic Selling is designed to give you the fullest possible understanding of the sales situation *before* you see the Buyer. A "quick and dirty" method for increasing that understanding is to find out how well you can answer the four suggested questions.

MODIFIED ANALYSIS 2: THE "CRISIS IN THE ELEVATOR" ANALYSIS

Sometimes, of course, you don't even have the ten minutes you need to investigate these four questions properly. So here's an even briefer analytical model.

Maybe it's a small account where you didn't really think that strategic analysis was necessary. Maybe it's a "routine" renewal in an account where "nothing ever changes." Maybe it's a new account for you, and your manager has just dropped a note on your desk that says, "Just found out Lacey, at CPI, is leaving for Australia in the morning. He's expecting you at four this afternoon." For whatever reason (and the above reasons, as you know, are only the tip of the iceberg), you find yourself in an elevator bound for the seventeenth floor, with no more than a fuzzy idea of who the customer is, and fifty-two seconds to go until zero hour.

No need to panic. Even if you've never done any conscious strategic planning for this account and this sales objective before, you still know *something* about it—even if it's only office scuttlebutt about the customer or the names of a couple of key players. What you need to do in that fifty-two seconds is to identify just what you *do* know so that, when you meet the Buying Influence, you'll at least have made your current position—shaky as it might be—more visible, and therefore more manageable.

As in any analysis, making your position visible means asking yourself appropriate questions. The less time available for analysis, the more fundamental the questions. Here are the most fundamental ones of all:

Do I know who my Buying Influences are? If not, do I at least know who is the Economic Buying Influence for this sales objective?

Answering these questions, especially in fifty-two seconds, isn't going to give you a detailed picture of any account. But identifying the account's key decision makers, and reminding yourself of the roles they're playing for your specific sales objective, concentrates on what we've repeatedly said is the foundation of good strategy. If you don't know who the key players are, and how they fit into your sale, you really know nothing at all.

Admittedly, not knowing who your User Buyers are, for example, isn't a very good position. But it's a much better position than *not knowing* that you don't know. If you *realize* that you know nothing, you should also realize that you have to use the upcoming sales call to begin filling in the blanks.

The bottom line here is that *any* strategic analysis performed in advance of a sales call is going to be to your advantage—even if all it gives you is a knowledge of your own missing data. The only absolutely untenable position is to go into a sales call cold, with no information and no strategic principles to guide you. What Socrates said about life is just as true about sales: The beginning of wisdom is recognizing the depth of your ignorance.

To quote a less august authority, listen to the words of a

branch sales manager we know who attributes a recent record quarter to our system: "Going into a call without asking who your Buying Influences are is like walking into a room with a blindfold on. Before taking your program, I used to do that all the time—and over and over I ended up banging my shins. Asking that one basic question is like taking the blindfold off. I don't always know exactly where I am in every sale, but at least I know where the furniture is."

Strategy First—Again

We don't advise anyone to use the "elevator" or the "quick and dirty" analysis as a *substitute* for a more detailed analysis. The ten-minute model functions best as a quick review of an account situation with which you're already familiar. The crisis model is just that—a default model appropriate only for emergencies. Sometimes neither of these models will be appropriate, and you'll have to make the time for a full-fledged Action Plan analysis. The model you should adopt in each case depends on how much preparation is necessary to make you feel comfortable before the next call.

It all comes back to strategy, and to the observation that we made in Chapter 2: Strategy and tactics are both essential to long-term sales success, but strategy must always come *first.* No matter which model you decide is appropriate for a given sales objective and a given account, you'll still profit from Strategic Selling only if you do your strategic analysis *before* the selling event. The moment that you sit down in Farley's office is no time to be wondering whether or not he really *is* the Economic Buyer. Address your strategic questions first, and you'll be free in the selling event to do what you do best—sell.

If you always put strategy first, you'll be assured that no matter how small a *quantity* of time you have available, in every case it will still be *quality* time.

CHAPTER 21

STRATEGIC SELLING: A LIFETIME APPROACH

Sales-improvement programs usually end with a snappy little speech about "positive mental attitude" and "hard work," at the end of which the trainer wishes the assembled sales representatives "good luck" out in the trenches. We don't end our programs that way, and we won't end this book that way, because when you look at your selling strategically, it's not about luck.

Strategic Selling is successful precisely because it reduces the uncertainties associated with luck, trial and error, and blind chance. It has worked effectively for twenty years—and in dozens of different industries—because it's founded on logic and on a sound understanding of all the Key Elements of the Complex Sale. By applying our methodology consistently, you make your *own* luck.

The reason that Strategic Selling professionals are able to make their own luck is that they understand two critical keys to sales success.

The first is *method*. Strategic Selling professionals approach their sales with a planned system of selling steps that are logical, visible, and repeatable. These salespeople understand that, in selling as in any other human activity, it's *the way the professional does things* that sets him or her apart from the competition.

The second key is something that we've stressed again and again in our Personal Workshops. It's the importance of *constant reassessment*. Since change is the only constant in your Complex Sales, and since you can be undermined by change only if you fail to adapt to it, you'll get the most out of Strategic Selling if you treat it as a *dynamic* system—one that's always in the process of refinement.

There's a logical conclusion to be drawn from this observation: The more you *use* Strategic Selling, the better it works for you. Not only that, but the *easier* the system becomes to use.

When we described the use of the Sales Funnel, we observed that repetition makes Funnel analysis a progressively simpler task, so that eventually it becomes almost second nature. Once you've worked through a Sales Funnel analysis several times, the techniques and concepts involved become *internalized*, and you're able to perform further analyses in a quicker and more efficient manner.

The same thing can be said about Strategic Selling as a whole. Not only do the six Key Elements individually become easier to use with practice, but the system itself becomes *self-reinforcing* over time. We've observed this consistently in follow-up surveys we do of our program participants: The most successful ones owe their success to the constant use of our strategic principles, in all their accounts, all the time. In the words of a Midwest branch manager who attributes his latest sales-manager-of-the-year award to our programs, "The more I practice, the luckier I get."

We hope you'll take this observation as so many of our participants take it, as a watchword for future success. Strategic Selling is a *lifetime* approach to the Complex Sale. The analysis that you performed on your test-case sales objective in this book is a model. As you continue to apply and refine this model in future sales efforts, increasingly you'll be able to say, "It's the way I go about it that makes me number one."

"Luck," a savvy slogan writer once observed, is "where preparation meets opportunity." Strategic Selling, it has been frequently proven, can prepare any dedicated professional to meet sales opportunities more effectively. If, by using the principles and techniques presented in this book, you and your Buying Influences continue to Win in all your sales objective—then we at Miller Heiman will have Won as well.

AFTER TWENTY YEARS: RESPONDING TO OUR CLIENTS' MOST CHALLENGING QUESTIONS

Over the twenty years that we have been introducing sales professionals to Strategic Selling, we have had the privilege of hearing them pose literally hundreds of provocative questions and conceptual challenges. These examples of "client participation" have given us tremendous satisfaction, for they have forced us again and again to follow our own advice and to subject our thinking about selling to constant review.

Most of the clarifications to which our clients have thus prodded us we have already woven into the fabric of this expanded text. A handful of their questions, though, seemed so provocative and so important that they called for special treatment of their own. We therefore end the book by addressing them directly. The following "fabulous fifteen" client questions illustrate both the insight and the sophistication of our fellow salespeople as they wrestle with the many complexities of our profession. We offer our responses here to further the dialogue in the fascinating conversation that we call selling.

1. Where Do I Start? At what level should I begin the selling process? Since getting to the Economic Buyer is so important, should I always try to start at the top?

Sure, if you can, and if you have credibility there. The place you should start any Complex Sale is the place where you have the greatest degree of credibility. This follows logically from our emphasis on leveraging from Strengths. If you're comfortable with the vice president, great: start there. But if you've never met that person and you have a strong sponsor in a User Buyer, start there. Your goal is to begin the selling process from as strong a foundation as possible, and to build on that foundation as you move higher. The last thing you want to do is to barge in on an Economic Buyer and start pitching your solution before you fully understand the organization's current problems, or the Economic Buyer's individual Wins. If you don't understand those things first—if you don't get solid Coaching to help you understand them—you might get in the door, but we'll guarantee this: Once you leave, it will never be opened to you again.

2. The One-Legged Stool. I've been dealing with the same person in my customer's organization for five years, and he just got fired. Help!

Developing a professional relationship with only one Buying Influence in an organization is an extremely common, and often deadly, scenario. It's what we refer to as the "one-legged stool" strategy because it's just about as stable as such a contraption. When you're negotiating the organizational labyrinth of the modern corporation, it's imperative that you develop as many relationships as possible, and to enhance them with a solid network of Coaches.

We've said many times that change is today's only constant. If you find yourself in the cold when a sole contact leaves, then you should probably take it both as a lesson and as an opening. You may or may not be able to rescue the Single Sales Objective that hinged on that one individual, but you can start developing a network for future opportunities. Starting from scratch isn't a very comfortable position, but at least it can't be confused with a false sense of confidence. Sometimes recognizing your ignorance is a very good starting point. It provides you the incentive that you need to build a stool that won't wobble.

3. Does She or Doesn't She? One of my Buying Influences says she has final approval authority, but I'm not sure. How can I tell if she really is the Economic Buyer?

If everybody who said he has final authority actually did have it, million-dollar deals would be approved daily by junior managers. The fact is, more often than not, the person who says "There's nobody above me" is trying to keep you from somebody who can veto his decisions. In cases like this, often the manner in which the Buying Influence describes his authority will give you a clue about whether it's real or illusory. When you're not sure, we recommend that you ask indirect questions to clarify the actual location of final authority. Rather than saying "Will you give final approval?" it's often better to ask "What's the decision process?" "Who has to OK the funding?" or "Is there anyone else whose approval we need to secure?

When you ask questions like these, you'll often discover a paradox. Generally, those who are most vociferous about proclaiming their power—"Don't you go around me or I'll cut you off at the knees"—are Technical Buyers who *don't* have the final say. Actual Economic Buyers are less full of themselves. Because they *have* the power, they don't need to batter you over the head with it. Remember that most Economic Buyers are comfortable with command. If the person with "final authority" looks nervous about losing it, the chances are good that she may not have it in the first place.

4. The "Not-a-Factor" Factor. If I've identified someone as having a Low Degree of Influence, why should I even bother talking to that person?

Two reasons. First, you may be misreading the situation. The person you've identified as having a Low level of influence may in fact have a greater Degree of Influence than you understand, and by treating him or her as irrelevant, you will at the very least be leaving a base uncovered. Recall our comment about the Economic Buyer with a Low Degree of Influence: He can increase that influence at will, if the need arises. The same is true, to an extent, of other Buying Influences. Jim might lack the authority or the interest to significantly impact your sale today, but a thousand factors could cause that to change tomorrow. So you need to be constantly alert to all the bases, and watch for decision-makers who might come "out of hiding."

Second, precisely because things change, minimizing the importance of a "Low"-impact decision-maker risks creating a potential enemy—a resentful antisponsor—not only on this sale but on future ones. Even if you're right about a person's current lack of authority or interest, treating him as if he doesn't matter could create a boomerang effect in a scenario where he *does* matter. In today's climate of musical office chairs, the person who is a low-level User Buyer on Monday morning could be a High-influence Economic Buyer by the end of the week. Remember the sobering reality of Buyer's Revenge. As Shakespeare might have put it (if he had ever met a payroll), "Hell hath no fury like a Buying Influence scorned."

5. Inside Customers. Some of my toughest "customers" are in my own company. When you have to sell a solution to your own production or support people, should you treat them like you do your Buying Influences?

Absolutely, because they *are* Buying Influences. Remember that we define a Buying Influence as *anyone* who can influence the outcome of your sale. Clearly, that includes an awful lot of people in your own organization—from production, design, research, marketing, follow-up—without whose help you cannot get quality sales. All of these people are individuals too, with their own needs and levels of receptivity and Win-Results. Even though in some ways dealing with them is different from dealing with your more obvious Buying Influences, one critical strategic requirement is the same: You have got to have their commitment, or your sale is in trouble.

Unfortunately, many salespeople make the mistake of assuming that this commitment exists, without even asking. "We're all on he same team here," they say to themselves, "so everybody here will want me to make this sale." That can turn out be a deadly mistake when you close the deal of the century and then find there's no support. Selling your own people on your solution can therefore be just as important as selling the customer. In our Large Account Management Process, where we address this fact, we recommend a corporate policy of "full organizational commitment." In working to secure that commitment, you've got to "sell your own."

6. Swimming the Channel. We sell indirectly to end users through distribution channels. Where should we be looking for Economic Buying Influences?

That depends on how much impact the end users have, or could have, on whatever it is that you deliver to the distributor. It's extremely common today for salespeople to sell through channels, whether they're identified as distributors, dealers, or value-added resellers (VARs). But no two of those channel situations are exactly alike, and therefore it's impractical—not to mention foolhardy—to generalize about decision-making as you "swim the channel." If you're selling an internal component for a consumer product—say, circuit boards for a personal computer—then Mr. Jones, who buys the PC at a retail outlet, may never see your product, and he may have no influence on its configuration, delivery, or price. Therefore, even though he's the end decision-maker for the PC, he's not a significant Buying Influence for the boards. On the other hand, if Mr. Jones runs a major national business that purchases hundreds of PCs, he may carry enough weight with the VAR or retailer to have a significant impact on specs, delivery schedules—even vendor choice. In that case, his decisions may directly affect your sale. He may even be your Economic Buying Influence.

The operative word here is "may." In any given sales opportunity, your task is to understand how a variety of individuals play one or more of the four Buying Influence roles for *that* sales opportunity. Doing that well means looking at each new situation individually, then asking questions to clarify the decision-making process. There's no universal pattern, so you can't assume. If you're not sure how involved an end user is in your VAR's buying decisions, *find out.* Otherwise you're in danger of drowning in the channel.

7. Who Needs a Coach? In fifteen years in sales, I've never needed a Coach before. Why should I worry about developing one now?

We used to hear this frequently in the early days of our business. We hear it less and less today, as major sales become increasingly complicated and salespeople recognize that strategizing without a Coach is like flying blind. Most of the people who still claim not to need Coaches fall into one of two categories. Some of them are staunch members of the old guard who have been adequate salespeople for fifteen, or thirty, years, but who have always fallen a little short of their full potential. Others have been using Coaches throughout their careers, but calling them by another name. Maybe they've been very skillful at getting guidance from inside salespeople or Economic Buyers, so that they've been profiting from Coaching without really acknowledging it as such.

We didn't invent the idea of Coaching. We simply identified the type of guidance that most successful salespeople were already getting on their Complex Sales, and isolated the three criteria that the best "guides" fulfilled. The Miller Heiman insistence on developing Coaches, far from being a novelty, is just common sense. And it's common sense that the best sales professionals have always utilized.

8. The "Double Agent" Coach. I think that the person Coaching me may also be providing information to my competitor. How can I tell and what should I do?

There is no such thing as a "double agent" Coach. By definition a Coach is a person who Wins when your solution is adopted: He or she wants *you* to make the sale. It's true that a Coach may provide information to more than one competitor.

It may simply be in the nature of his or her job to do so, and for that reason there *are* "double agent" information givers. But not all information is alike. If the person giving you information is truly a Coach, she'll provide you and only you with the uniquely useful information you need to make the sale—in other words, with *quality* information.

Of course, it's not always easy to tell the wheat from the chaff. That is why you need a network of Coaches, to test one person's information against that of others. And it's why you need to regularly ask yourself: Is this information helping me to understand the customer's decision-making process better? Is it improving my position with the Buying Influences? Is it making my management of this sale more predictable? If you can't answer yes to these questions, the person giving you information might not really be your Coach. Even worse, she might be Coaching your competition. If that's the case, you need to "fire" her and get Coaching elsewhere.

9. Beyond the Product. There's virtually no difference between our product and our competitor's, yet our price is higher. Is there any way that we can make this sale?

Not if you're convinced that there isn't any difference between you and them. Probably there is a difference, though. Maybe it's not in the product or service per se. Maybe what differentiates you from the competition is a better support system, or some specialized knowledge that you can bring your customer, or key people in your organization, or even the personal talents that you bring to the party. Look beyond the product or service to find what it is that makes your higher price worth it.

If there really is nothing different—on any level—between you and your competitors, then you're right. You're playing a commodity game, and low price will win. But as a sales professional, you have to go beyond price. You have to move beyond simply working up quotes and answering bids to determine the unique contributions that only you can make. Your interest and skill must be in understanding your individual customer's objectives, and in showing how your company, and yours alone, can best help to achieve them.

10. What, Me Worry? Our company is the undisputed leader in our industry. Why should we worry about competition?

Unless you have a crystal ball that tells you everything that's going to happen in your industry—and in your customers' industries—for the next century, you'd *better* think about the competition. At least you'd better think about it to the extent that you ask yourselves, constantly and honestly, how your solutions to your customers' problems are different from everything else that is out there. In other words, you should regularly review how you *became* the leader, so you can constantly reinforce the contributions that got you there. Selling is essentially the art of relieving problems. The biggest company in the world can lose its leadership overnight if it stops thinking about how it can do that best.

We don't mean you should obsess about what the other guy is doing. As we've stressed in the chapter on competition, one common, deadly strategy is to focus so intently on The Competition that you divert attention from your customers' concerns. But ignoring the competition can be deadly, too. No industry leader is so big that it can't be toppled. And when an upstart David takes Goliath down, it's usually because David has been listening more closely to the customers, while Goliath has been congratulating himself on his "undisputed" position.

11. Trapped in the Circus. My prospect doesn't want a conversation. All he wants is a fifty-minute dog and pony show. I can't even identify, much less understand, my Buying Influences under those constraints. What should I do?

When we're asked how to stage a dog and pony show, our first recommendation is to avoid them altogether because they're a clear indication that you are positioned badly, and that the prospect is forcing a comparison that obscures your uniqueness. If the show absolutely must go on, however, we recommend first that you try to position yourself with key players and aim for dialogues with them long *before* the scheduled shindig takes place. If you do not have established relationships and you come in cold on this kind of presentation, you are in a very weak position. We won't say absolutely that you won't get the business, but if you do, it will be one of those rare instances of seller's luck—not because you've really done your homework.

Another thing to consider—again, only if you can't avoid the situation—is not to make a unilateral presentation, but to create an interactive dialogue. Keep in mind that, in ten-ring circuses like these, the prospects are generally bored beyond recognition. If, instead of trying to dazzle them, you elicit opinions from them, you'll be in a better position than any of your competitors. Not only will a conversational, give-and-take "show" differentiate you from all the other speechmakers, but it will help you determine what's on the customer's mind, which is exactly what you need to know to highlight your contribution.

You can use all the lights and flip charts and transparencies you want. But avoid spending more than a couple of minutes at the outset laying out your agenda and view of things. Demand of yourself that you seek and get feedback in the first five minutes. That way, even though you're doing a "presentation," it will feel more like a conversation to your Buying Influences. Which is exactly what all good selling is ultimately about.

12. Beyond Features and Benefits. I like the idea of delivering Wins as well as Results, but isn't a Win-Results Statement basically the same thing as a features-and-benefits statement?

No. A features-and-benefits statement is generated internally, usually by your production or marketing departments. It describes what your people believe to be true about what you're trying to sell. Such a statement, by its very nature, is going to be general. However articulately or snazzily it is produced, it's still going to be basically a list of goodies that are inherent in the product or service itself. "This model will give you 34 miles per gallon in city driving," that sort of thing.

A Win-Results Statement, on the other hand, fuses the objective (Results) and the subjective (Wins), and in addition to that it's personalized for each Buying Influence. Such a statement is specific to a particular human being in a given situation at a certain point in time. If you reduce it to its general, objective aspects, you run the risk of "one size fits all" selling. That's a recipe for product cramming and eventually lost business.

13. Walking the Walk. One of my customers is nowhere near my Ideal Customer Profile, and I'd love to walk away. But what if I can't afford to lose his business?

Wouldn't it be great if we all had so many prospects that we could ignore every one but the Ideal Customer "perfect fits"? Unfortunately, that's a luxury most of us don't have. In the real world, salespeople are assigned accounts that they can't just walk away from, and they develop business that's just too lucrative to let go, no matter how many headaches it may involve. That's why, when we present the Ideal Customer key element, we say that it can help you in two ways: by concentrating on your most likely Win-Win customers, and by anticipating problems with the ones who don't measure up.

In anticipating those problems, you look for places where the fit between your two companies is imperfect, and you try as early as possible in every sale to address the discrepancies and adjust your strategy accordingly. You're constantly measuring potential aggravation against potential revenue, to determine the sacrifices you're willing to make to get the business. We say that's fine—as long as you know it's a calculated risk, and your eyes are open. In some cases you may not be able to eliminate all the Red Flags in a poor-fit sales opportunity. But at least the Ideal Customer Profile lets you know they're there.

14. The Surefire Close. When all is said and done, you still have to close. Do you have any reliable closing techniques for helping us to improve our hit ratio?

In a word: No. Sales managers have historically wanted "closers," that is, people with a consistently high "hit ratio." Most books on selling, in fact, include an obligatory chapter on "surefire closes," or "sixteen fail-safe ways to get his signature on the contract." We don't have such a chapter because we believe that the traditional emphasis on closing "techniques" is inappropriate. In our view, a close isn't something that you get as a reward for smooth talking, or that you should (or can) slam-dunk your customers into accepting. We don't believe that you succeed when you "take" somebody's order.

A close that you get by following Technique 14 is likely to be both artificial and ephemeral. Because it's built on trickery, it can never bring you the sustained business that every professional wants. A solid close, on the other hand, is the natural and inevitable outcome of a sales process that is built on incremental commitment and mutual understanding. If you have to "ask for the order," you probably haven't been following that process, because when you work with your customers toward mutually satisfying solutions, the close becomes, in the words of one of our clients, "almost automatic." Not entirely automatic, we admit: We're not in the business of offering magic bullets. But close enough for increased sales success. As another client puts it, "If I've done my job of fostering solid communication, it's often the customer who asks *me* where to sign."

15. The Secret of Success. We're often told that the salesperson's single most important quality is persistence. What do you think about this?

Persistence is an admirable quality, but it won't get you anywhere unless the people you're being persistent with believe in you and are absolutely convinced that they can trust you. The one quality that every great salesperson has got to have is not persistence but credibility. That's the open secret of success that every sales leader knows. When you and your company have credibility with a customer, it means you're reliable, you're trustworthy, you're deserving of his or her confidence and commitment. It means that the customer can depend on your word and feel certain that you're not trying to cram product down his or her throat. When that's the attitude that you elicit in your customers, you're miles ahead of the most persistent competitor.

The American songwriter Cole Porter once remarked about style that if you had it you really didn't need much else, and that if you didn't, there wasn't anything else that could save you. We'd go almost that far with regard to credibility. It's not quite true that it's all you need, because even if your customers believe in you, you still need product knowledge and analytical skills and, yes, persistence. But if you *don't* have credibility in their eyes, then nothing else matters. That's as good a note as any on which to end this book. The beginning of sales success is a sense of trust. And a Win-Win philosophy is the way to go about getting it.

INDEX

About Miller Heiman

Miller Heiman, Inc. is a global leader in building exceptional sales organizations. The company's team of world-class sales consultants helps organizations dramatically improve sales productivity through consistent, field-ready processes, benchmarking tools, development programs, and process consulting.

Best known for its time-tested *Strategic Selling*® program, Miller Heiman provides solutions for introducing a consistent sales process throughout an organization, identifying the strengths and weaknesses inherent in every sales force, and ensuring the cultural indoctrination of training programs.

With a prestigious client list including KLA-Tencor, BAX Global, Marriott Corporation, Dow Chemical, PricewaterhouseCoopers, and Wells Fargo, Miller Heiman understands the issues and challenges facing sales leaders in virtually every major industry, from manufacturing and consumer goods to technology and finance.

PREPARE YOUR ENTIRE ORGANIZATION

The Miller Heiman portfolio of sales training and development services addresses the most critical aspects of the selling cycle. From getting the right people doing the right things to uncovering new opportunities with your most established accounts, we prepare your entire sales organization to succeed.

Our consulting and training is supported worldwide through a global network of more than two hundred sales consultants in over twenty-five countries. Each is an independent sales professional with an average of eighteen years of real-world sales and sales management experience. Prior to working with Miller Heiman, our sales consultants were sales directors and vice presidents, so they truly understand your challenges and aspirations.

TRAINING SOLUTIONS

Our training solutions are proven to help establish and grow more productive customer relationships. These practical solutions include:

- *Conceptual Selling®*
- *Strategic Selling®*
- *Large Account Management Process (LAMP®)*
- *Negotiate Success℠*
- *Channel Partner Management℠*
- *Executive Impact℠*

BENCHMARKING TOOLS

Our benchmarking tools can help you quickly evaluate the strengths and weaknesses of your sales organization, analyze personnel data against position requirements, and make sure you have the right people in the right positions. We help you establish benchmarks to reach your sales goals. We bring clarity to what works and what doesn't. These powerful tools include:

- *Predictive Sales Performance℠*
- *StartPoint℠*
- *Conversion, Penetration, Retention (CPR℠)*

SALES WORKSHOPS

Throughout the world, we conduct hundreds of convenient and accessible sales workshops where your staff can learn the Miller Heiman sales process and apply it to real sales opportunities in their funnels. They'll learn to uncover why the customer is really buying, to identify a fit, and to develop and execute an action plan that's right for you and your customer.

For further information on LAMP or any of our other service offerings, call Miller Heiman today and we'll find you the right consulting partner who understands you, your company, and your market.

Miller Heiman Corporate Headquarters
10509 Professional Circle, Suite 100
Reno, Nevada 89521
1-877-552-1757
www.millerheiman.com

Miller Heiman International Headquarters
Nelson House, 1 Auckland Park
Milton Keynes, MK1 1BU England
+44 1908.211212
www.millerheiman.co.uk